Cambridge English

Grammar AND Vocabulary

FOR **FIRST** | AND

FIRST FOR SCHOOLS

with answers

BARBARA THOMAS

LOUISE HASHEMI

LAURA MATTHEWS

Cambridge University Press
www.cambridge.org/elt

Cambridge English Language Assessment
www.cambridgeenglish.org

Information on this title: www.cambridge.org/9781107481060

© Cambridge University Press 2015

First published 2015
20 19 18 17 16 15 14 13 12 11 10 9 8 7

Printed in Dubai by Oriental Press

A catalogue record for this publication is available from the British Library

ISBN 978-1-107-48106-0 Book with Answers and Audio

Additional resources for this publication available at www.cambridge.org/grammarvocabfirst

Acknowledgements

The authors would like to thank their editors, Neil Holloway and Meredith Levy, for their expertise, support, good humour and patience throughout the project.

The authors and publishers acknowledge the following sources of copyright material and are grateful for the permissions granted. While every effort has been made, it has not always been possible to identify the sources of all the material used, or to trace all copyright holders. If any omissions are brought to our notice, we will be happy to include the appropriate acknowledgements on reprinting.

Financial Times for the text on p. 30 adapted from 'Me and My Clothes' by Liz Gill, *The Financial Times, 12.02*. Copyright © The Financial Times Limited 2014. All Rights Reserved;

The Independent for the text on p. 176 adapted from 'A trip to Patagonia!' by Laura Holt, *The Independent*, 16.11.13. Copyright © The Independent;

Text on p. 183 adapted from 'The Importance of Music Education' by Patricia Guth, www.more4kids.info;

Life Coach Directory for text on p. 205 adapted from 'The Benefits of Having a Hobby.' Reproduced with permission of Katherine Nicholls;

Doubleday for the text on p. 217 extracted from *A Painted House* by John Grisham, Copyright © 2000, 2001 by Belfry Holdings, Inc. Used by permission of Doubleday, an imprint of the Knopf Doubleday Publishing Group, a division of Random House LLC. All rights reserved;

Text on p. 218 from 'How to Make Your House a Home' by Kara O'Reilly, *Psychologies*, 11.06.12. Copyright © KELSEY Publishing Group;

Text on p. 228 adapted from 'Understanding Teenagers' Sleeping Habits' by Kristin Jenkins;

Text on p. 232 extracted from 'A School with a Difference' by M.J. Prabhu, *The Hindu*, 14.07.13;

Guardian News & Media for the text on p. 234 from 'How to Write Fiction: Andrew Millier on Creating Characters' by Andrew Miller, *The Guardian*, 16.10.11. Copyright © Guardian News & Media Ltd 2014;

Guardian News & Media for text on p. 238 from 'Students: Bring your own technology to Uni,' by Mirren Gidda, *The Guardian*, 11.04.14. Copyright © Guardian News & Media Ltd 2014.

Corpus

Development of this publication has made use of the Cambridge English Corpus (CEC). The CEC is a computer database of contemporary spoken and written English, which currently stands at over one billion words. It includes British English, American English and other varieties of English. It also includes the Cambridge Learner Corpus, developed in collaboration with Cambridge English Language Assessment. Cambridge University Press has built up the CEC to provide evidence about language use that helps to produce better language teaching materials.

Cambridge Dictionaries

Cambridge dictionaries are the world's most widely used dictionaries for learners of English. The dictionaries are available in print and online at dictionary.cambridge.org. Copyright © Cambridge University Press, reproduced with permission.

Photo Acknowledgements

The authors and publishers acknowledge the following sources of copyright material and are grateful for the permissions granted. While every effort has been made, it has not always been possible to identify the sources of all the material used, or to trace all copyright holders. If any omissions are brought to our notice, we will be happy to include the appropriate acknowledgements on reprinting.

The publisher has used its best endeavours to ensure that the URLs for external websites referred to in this book are correct and active at the time of going to press. However, the publisher has no responsibility for the websites and can make no guarantee that a site will remain live or that the content is or will remain appropriate.

Photo acknowledgements:

p. 4: Visions of America, LLC / Alamy; p. 6 (L): Adrian Sherratt/Alamy; p. 6 (R): THE FARM: THE STORY OF ONE FAMILY AND THE ENGLISH COUNTRYSIDE by Richard Benson (Hamish Hamilton 2005, 2006). Cover reproduced with permission from Penguin Ltd. p. 8: Cultura/Rex Features; p. 9 (T): Artmin/Shutterstock; p. 9 (B): SnowWhiteimages/Shutterstock; p. 14: Flaming June, c.1895 (oil on canvas) by Leighton, Frederic (1830–96) Museo de Arte, Ponce, Puerto Rico, West Indies/ © The Maas Gallery, London, UK/ The Bridgeman Art Library; p. 18: kjorgen/iStock/Thinkstock; p. 19 (L): Wavebreakmedia Ltd/Thinkstock; p. 19 (R): Werner Dietrich/Alamy; p. 21: Blend Images/Alamy; p. 23 (L): Cultura/Rex Features; p. 23 (R): Patti McConville/Getty Images; p. 24: Royal Geographical Society/Alamy; p. 27: Jeff Gilbert/Rex Features; p. 28: Jelle-vd-Wolf/Shutterstock; p. 29: The Thirteenth Tale by Diane Setterfield, The Orion Publishing Group Ltd. p. 31: Tim Sloan/AFP/Getty Images; p. 32: maurice joseph/Alamy; p. 33: sturti/Getty Images; p. 34: Michael Kemp/Alamy; p. 35: Ragnarock/Shutterstock; p. 36: Lorenzo Fanchi; p. 38: Bettina Strenske/Alamy; p. 39: www.railimages.co.uk; p. 41: Niamh Baldock/Alamy; p. 43: marc macdonald/Alamy; p. 44: RA/Lebrecht Music & Arts Library; p. 46: Courtesy of the Air Force Flight Test Center History Office p. 48: Suzi Eszterhas/Minden Pictures/FLPA; p. 50: H. Mark Weidman Photography/Alamy; p. 51: Courtesy of Boston College, MA, USA p. 52: Andreas Rodriguez/Thinkstock; p. 53: UPPA/Photoshot; p. 54: turtix/iStock/Thinkstock; p. 57: Mahler Attar/Sygma/Corbis p. 58: Bettmann/Corbis; p. 60: dirkr/Getty Images; p. 62: Ray Roberts/Alamy; p. 63: Purestock/Punchstock/Getty Images; p. 64 (BL): Alex Segre/Alamy; p. 64 (TR): VCL/Tim Barnett/Getty Images; p. 64 (BR): Digital Vision/Punchstock/Getty Images; p. 68: Jupiterimages/Thinkstock; p. 70: Janine Wiedel/Rex Features; p. 72 (T): Roger-Viollet/Rex Features; p. 72 (B): Robert Harding Picture Library/Superstock; p. 73: iStockphoto.com/Remus Eserblom.

Cover image: Aleksandr Markin/Shutterstock (front, back).

Picture research: Kevin Brown

Text design and make up: Blooberry Design

Illustrations: Clive Goodyer

Contents

Introduction

This book is for students who want to study and practise English grammar and vocabulary, especially if they are preparing for the *Cambridge English: First* or *Cambridge English: First for Schools* examination. It offers practice for all the tasks in the Reading and Use of English, Listening and Writing papers.

It can be used by students working alone or with a teacher.

What is in this book?

This book is updated for the new *Cambridge English: First* examinations introduced in 2015 and contains two main sections: **Grammar** (Units 1–24) and **Vocabulary** (Units 25–44).

The book also contains the following:

- **Map of the book:** This shows the topics that are covered and the exam tasks that are practised in each unit.
- **Exam summary:** This explains the aims and organisation of *Cambridge English: First* and *Cambridge English: First for Schools*.
- **Learning and revising vocabulary:** These pages give useful ideas to make your study more effective.
- **Answer key:** This gives the answers for all exercises and for all exam tasks except the Writing ones (for Writing answers, see *Model answers* below).

What material can I find online?

The following resources for use with this book can be found online at [address?]

- **Audio recordings** for all listening exercises and for exam practice Listening tasks.
- **Audio scripts:** These are the full recording scripts for all listening tasks.
- **Model answers:** A sample answer is provided for each of the Writing tasks in the Exam practice sections of the Vocabulary units.
- **Wordlists** for Vocabulary units: These contain key words that you need to learn and also their pronunciation in IPA (International Phonetic Alphabet).
- **Irregular verbs list:** This gives the forms of important irregular verbs for *Cambridge First*.
- **Phrasal verbs list:** This gives the most important phrasal verbs that you need to know for *Cambridge First*.
- **Phrasal verb exercises:** These give extra practice of many of the important phrasal verbs for *Cambridge First*.

- **Word-building exercises:** These give extra practice of related nouns, verbs and adjectives, which is especially useful for *Cambridge First* Reading and Use of English Part 3 tasks.
- **Spelling:** This page helps you to avoid spelling errors commonly made by *Cambridge First* candidates.
- **Grammar glossary:** This explains the words we use to describe grammar.

How do I use the book?

You can work through the units in any order, but we advise you to study every unit if you want to prepare thoroughly for the exam.

If you are studying alone, you may like to do alternate Grammar and Vocabulary units – this will give you more variety and give you time to absorb each topic.

How are the Grammar units organised?

Each of the 24 Grammar units has four sections. You should work through Sections A, B and C in order. You can do the Exam practice section immediately after these, or you can come back to it later for revision.

A Context listening: This section introduces the grammar of the unit in a short recording. You can listen to the recording, answer the questions and check your answers in the Answer key. This will help you to understand the grammar more easily when you study Section B. It also gives you useful listening practice.

B Grammar: This section explains the grammar points and gives examples. You should read it before doing the exercises in Section C and you can also refer to it while you are doing the exercises.

C Grammar exercises: The exercises cover the grammar in Section B. Check your answers in the Answer key. This gives the answers and also tells you which parts of Section B each exercise refers to.

You will see this symbol 👁 in some of the exercises in Section C. It indicates that the sentences are ones in which candidates made errors as identified in the Cambridge Learner Corpus, a database made up of many thousands of exam scripts written by students taking Cambridge English exams in countries around the world.

Exam practice: There is one exam task, either Listening or Reading and Use of English, for each Grammar unit. These will prepare you for the types of tasks you will face in the exam.
Note: Some of the Use of English tasks test mainly the grammar taught in the unit, to give extra practice. However, in the real exam each question tests a different grammar point.

How are the Vocabulary units organised?

Each of the 20 Vocabulary units has three pages based on a general topic.

On the first two pages, key vocabulary is introduced and practised in a range of different exercises. Some of these are listening exercises. To get the most out of the Vocabulary exercises, you will need access to a good dictionary. Use the *Cambridge Advanced Learner's Dictionary* (either online or as a book) or another suitable monolingual dictionary. You should try to do each vocabulary exercise without any assistance first, and then use your dictionary to help you with any answers you didn't know. Use the Answer key as a final check.

The third page is an **Exam practice** section with two exam tasks. The first is either a Listening or a Reading and Use of English task, and this is always followed by a Writing task. These tasks give you an opportunity to use the vocabulary from the unit.

There is a **Wordlist** for each Vocabulary unit on the website. When you finish the first two pages of each unit, go through the wordlist and check that you know the meaning of all the words and expressions. Note any words you don't remember and go back through the unit to revise them. You may want to note translations for some words or write them on a mind map, table or word tree (see **Learning and revising vocabulary** on pages 172–173).

How should I use the Exam practice tasks?

You may want to do the exam tasks immediately after finishing the exercises in each unit, or you may choose to come back to them later for revision. In the Grammar section, if you do the exam task immediately, you can use the Grammar focus exercise(s) for revision later on if you wish.

To check how much you have learnt, it is a good idea to do the exam tasks without referring back to the unit, and then check the answers. Always answer all the questions in an exam task, even if you are not sure, before you check your answers. This is good exam practice, as you may get a mark for a good guess, but you can't get a mark for an empty answer space! Answers for the Reading and Use of English and the Listening tasks are in the Answer key. For the Writing tasks you will find model answers on the website – these show you the kind of answer you could produce, although the content of yours will of course be different.

Recordings for the Listening tasks follow the format of the exam, with the examiner's instructions included. For Part 1 tasks, the eight short recordings are repeated as in the exam, but for Parts 2–4 you will need to replay the whole recording yourself after you have listened to it the first time.

Note on contractions

This book generally uses contractions, for example *I'm* for *I am*, *wasn't* for *was not*, because these are always used in speech and are common in written English. The full forms are used in formal written English.

Note to teachers

This book can be used alongside a coursebook, in class or for private study. The flexible organisation of the book makes it particularly suitable for revision for students who are taking *Cambridge First* or for those who are re-taking the exam and also for classes where not all students are preparing for the exam. The Vocabulary units can be chosen to supplement topics in the order in which they arise in your coursebook. The Context listening (Section A) in the Grammar units can be used in class as an introduction, with students working in pairs or groups as preferred. Sections B and C and the Exam practice can be used in class or for private study as conditions allow.

The Exam practice tasks in this book have been informed by the English Vocabulary Profile, which is an online resource with detailed and up-to-date information about the words, phrases, phrasal verbs and idioms that learners of English should know at each of the six levels of the Common European Framework.

Map of the book

GRAMMAR SECTION

Unit	Title	Topics	Exam practice
1	Present tenses	Present simple; present continuous; state verbs; the verb *to be*	Listening Part 4
2	Past tenses	Past simple; past continuous; *used to* + verb and *would* + verb; *be/get used to* + *-ing* or noun	Reading and Use of English Part 1
3	Present perfect and past simple	Present perfect and past simple; present perfect simple and continuous	Reading and Use of English Part 7
4	Past perfect	Past perfect simple and continuous	Reading and Use of English Part 5
5	Future (1)	Present tenses for future; *will*; future continuous	Listening Part 2
6	Future (2)	*going to*; future in the past; present tenses after time conjunctions; future perfect; *to be about to*	Reading and Use of English Part 7
7	Adjectives	Comparative and superlative adjectives; position; order; adjectives ending in *-ing* and *-ed*	Reading and Use of English Part 1
8	Adverbs	Adverb forms; adverbs and adjectives easily confused; comparative and superlative adverbs; modifiers; adverb position	Reading and Use of English Part 3
9	Questions	*Yes/no* questions; short answers; question words; question tags; agreeing	Listening Part 1
10	Countable and uncountable nouns; articles	Countable and uncountable nouns; *(a)n, the* and no article; special uses of articles	Reading and Use of English Part 4
11	Modals (1)	Use of modals; rules and obligation; necessity	Reading and Use of English Part 6
12	Pronouns and determiners	Possessives; reflexive pronouns and *own*; *each other* and *one another*; *there* and *it*; *someone*, etc.; *all, most, some, no* and *none*; *each* and *every*; *both, neither* and *either*	Reading and Use of English Part 2
13	Modals (2)	Permission; requests; offers; suggestions; orders; advice	Listening Part 3
14	Modals (3)	Ability; deduction: certainty and possibility; expectations	Reading and Use of English Part 3
15	Reported speech	Tense changes in reported speech; reporting in the same tense; verbs for reporting; verbs for reporting with *to* infinitive; reporting questions; references to time, place, etc.	Reading and Use of English Part 4
16	The passive	The passive; *to have/get something done*; *it is said that ...*	Reading and Use of English Part 4
17	Conditionals (1)	Zero, first, second and third conditionals; mixed conditionals	Reading and Use of English Part 6

18	The *to* infinitive and *-ing*	Verb + *to* infinitive; verb + infinitive without *to*; verb + *-ing*; verb + *that* clause; adjective + *to* infinitive	Reading and Use of English Part 1
19	Conditionals (2)	*unless*; *in case*; *provided/providing that* and *as/so long as*; *I wish* and *if only*; *it's time*; *would rather (not)*; *otherwise* and *or else*	Reading and Use of English Part 4
20	Prepositions (1)	Prepositions of place and time	Reading and Use of English Part 2
21	Prepositions (2)	Prepositions which follow verbs and adjectives; prepositions to express *who*, *how* and *why*; expressions with prepositions	Reading and Use of English Part 3
22	Relative clauses	Defining and non-defining relative clauses; relative pronouns and prepositions	Reading and Use of English Part 4
23	Linking words (1)	*because*, *as* and *since*; *so* and *therefore*; *in order to*, *to* + infinitive and *so (that)*; *so* and *such*; *enough* and *too*	Reading and Use of English Part 1
24	Linking words (2)	*in spite of* and *despite*; *but*, *although* and *though*; *even though* and *even if*; participle clauses; *before* and *after* + *-ing*; *when*, *while* and *since* + *-ing*	Reading and Use of English Part 2

VOCABULARY SECTION

Unit	Title	Topics	Exam practice
25	Earth, sea and sky	Geography, climate and weather	Reading and Use of English Part 6 Writing Part 2 (email)
26	Living a healthy life	Health and fitness	Reading and Use of English Part 2 Writing Part 1 (essay)
27	Sound waves	Music, sounds	Reading and Use of English Part 2 Writing Part 1 (essay)
28	Highs and lows	Feelings	Listening Part 1 Writing Part 2 (article)
29	Looking back	The past, time	Reading and Use of English Part 1 Writing Part 2 (review)
30	Everyone's different	Personality	Reading and Use of English Part 5 Writing Part 2 (article)
31	Get active	Sport	Reading and Use of English Part 4 Writing Part 2 (email)
32	My world	Friends, family and relationships	Listening Part 3 Writing Part 1 (essay)
33	Moving around	Travel	Reading and Use of English Part 4 Writing Part 2 (article)
34	Time off	Leisure time, hobbies and games	Reading and Use of English Part 3 Writing Part 2 (email)
35	Where you live	Cities and towns	Reading and Use of English Part 1 Writing Part 2 (article)

36	Shared tastes	Food and art	Listening Part 2 Writing Part 1 (essay)
37	Entertain me	Television, cinema and theatre	Reading and Use of English Part 7 Writing Part 2 (review)
38	Home territory	Houses and homes	Reading and Use of English Part 3 Writing Part 1 (essay)
39	Green planet	Science, the environment	Listening Part 4 Writing Part 2 (letter)
40	Read all about it	Books and writing	Reading and Use of English Part 5 Writing Part 2 (review)
41	Teenage style	Clothes, rooms	Reading and Use of English Part 6 Writing Part 2 (story)
42	School days	School and education	Reading and Use of English Part 2 Writing Part 2 (story)
43	The world of work	Jobs and personal qualities	Reading and Use of English Part 3 Writing Part 2 (letter of application)
44	University life	University courses, expressing opinions	Reading and Use of English Part 7 Writing Part 2 (report)

Exam summary

The *Cambridge English: First* and *Cambridge English: First for Schools* exams are for students who are at a B2 level in the CEFR. The *for Schools* version is for younger students who want to take the exam. Both exams have four papers with the *for Schools* version having topics that are more suitable for younger candidates.

Reading and Use of English   1 hour 15 minutes

Parts 1 and 3 of the exam are designed to test vocabulary, Part 2 tests mainly grammar and Part 4 tests both grammar and vocabulary.

Parts 5, 6 and 7 are reading tasks based on texts of about 550–650 words. The texts can come from fiction or non-fiction sources such as newspapers and magazines, or informational sources like brochures, guides and websites.

You must write your answers on a separate sheet.

Part	Task information
1	8 multiple choice questions. You choose words from A–D to complete a gap in a text.
2	8 open gap-fill questions. You think of one word to complete each gap.
3	8 word formation questions. You complete the gaps with the correct form of the given word.
4	6 key word transformation questions. You complete a sentence with a given word to make a sentence with the same meaning as another one.
5	6 multiple choice questions. You read a text and then choose the correct answer from options A–D.
6	6 gapped text questions. You read a text which has had 6 sentences removed and you must decide where the sentences go in the text. There is one extra sentence which doesn't belong to the text.
7	10 multiple matching questions. You read a text or group of short texts and match the information in each question to the correct part of the text(s).

Writing   1 hour 20 minutes

You must do Part 1 and choose one of the Part 2 tasks. You must write your answers in the booklet.

Part	Task information
1	You write an essay giving your opinion on the topic. You use your own ideas and the ideas given.
2	You may be asked to write an email, a letter, an article, a review, or a report (*First* only) or story (*First for Schools* only), based on a specific situation. The topic, purpose and reader will be explained to you. In the *for Schools* exam you can also choose from a set text.

Listening about 40 minutes

You hear and see the instructions for the exam. You hear each part of the exam twice.
Recordings are taken from a wide variety of sources. When one person is speaking
you may hear news, instructions, a lecture, a report, a speech, a talk or an
advertisement. If two people are speaking you may hear a discussion, a conversation,
an interview or a radio programme.

You must write your answers on a separate sheet.

Part	Task information
1	8 multiple choice questions . You hear one or two people talking in eight different situations of about 30 seconds. You choose the answers from options A–C.
2	10 sentence completion questions. You hear one person talking and you complete sentences by writing a word or short phrase. The speech lasts for about 3 minutes.
3	5 multiple matching questions. You hear five short extracts that are linked by a common theme. Each extract is about 30 seconds. For each extract you choose from a list of eight possible answers.
4	7 multiple choice questions – You hear an interview or conversation between two people lasting for about three minutes. For each question you choose the answers from options A–C.

Speaking 14 minutes

You usually do the Speaking part of the exam with another candidate.
Sometimes you might be asked to do it in a group of three. There are
two examiners in the room, but only one of them will ask you questions.

Each part of the exam lasts for 3 to 4 minutes.

Part	Task information
1	The examiner asks you some questions about yourself.
2	You talk for one minute about two pictures and then comment on the other candidate's pictures.
3	You discuss some prompts with the other candidate.
4	You have a conversation with the other candidate and the examiner about things connected to the topic in Part 3.

(Note that there are no Speaking tasks in the Exam practice sections of this book.)

Present tenses

Present simple; present continuous; state verbs; the verb *to be*

A Context listening

1 You are going to hear Millie talking on her phone to her friend Lisa. It's Saturday morning. Before you listen, answer these questions.

1 Where is Lisa? _____   2 Where is Millie? _____

3 Why do you think Millie is phoning Lisa? _____

Lisa   Millie

2 ▶02 Listen and check if you were right.

3 ▶02 Listen again and answer these questions. Write complete sentences.

1 What's Millie doing this morning? _____*She's looking round the shops.*_____

2 What does she do nearly every Saturday? _____

3 What's she looking for? _____

4 What's Lisa wearing? _____

5 What's she doing this morning? _____

6 What does she do whenever she goes to town? _____

7 What's Millie looking at right now? _____

8 What does Lisa want Millie to do now? _____

4 Look at your answers to Exercise 3 and answer these questions.

1 Look at answers 2 and 6. What tense are they? _____

2 Look at answers 1, 3, 4, 5 and 7. What tense are they? _____

3 Which sentences are about regular actions? _____

4 Which sentences are about actions at or around the time of speaking? _____

5 Look at answer 8. Does it fit the pattern? _____

B Grammar

1 Present simple

+	verb / verb + -s	She **works** in London.
–	do/does not + verb	He **doesn't work** in London.
?	do/does ... + verb?	Where **do** you **work**?

We use the present simple:

- to say when things happen if they take place regularly:
  They **eat** lunch **at two o'clock**.
- to talk about permanent situations:
  I **work** in London.
- to state general truths:
  Those bags **sell** really fast.
  The moon **goes** round the earth.
- to talk about habits and how often they happen:
  You **buy** new clothes **every Saturday**.
- to describe the plots of books and films:
  The story **begins** and **ends** in Spain. The year **is** 1937.

2 Present continuous

+	am/is/are + verb + -ing	He**'s working** in London this week.
–	am/is/are not + verb + -ing	I**'m not working** in London this week.
?	am/is/are ... + verb + -ing?	**Are** you **working** in London this week?

We use the present continuous:

- to talk about the present moment:
  I**'m wearing** a pair of old jeans.
  I**'m looking** at a blue bag right now.
- to suggest that an action is temporary, often with words like now, at the moment, at present or just:
  They**'re eating** lunch at the moment.
  I**'m working** in London this week. (= I don't usually work in London)
- for an action around the time of speaking, which has begun but is not finished:
  I**'m cleaning** my room.
  I**'m looking** round the shops. (Millie isn't looking round at this moment – she has stopped to talk to Lisa – but she plans to continue looking round later.)
- for changing or developing situations:
  Navy blue bags **are getting** really fashionable.
  The Earth's temperature **is rising**.
- with a word like always or continually if we want to criticise or complain:
  You**'re always buying** new clothes! (= you buy too many)
  He**'s always complaining** about things.
- with always when something unexpected happens several times:
  I**'m always meeting** my neighbour John near the station. I guess he works somewhere near there.

3 State verbs

These verbs are nearly always used in a simple rather than a continuous tense. They are mostly about thoughts, feelings, belonging and the senses:

... that leather bag you want to get (**not** *~~you are wanting to~~*)
You don't deserve to hear it. (**not** *~~you aren't deserving to~~*)

The following are some important state verbs:

- thoughts: *believe, know, mean, realise, recognise, remember, suppose, understand, feel* (= believe),
think (= believe):
I **think** *you're wrong.*
We **feel** *this decision is right.*
- feelings: *adore, dislike, despise, hate, like, love, want, wish, prefer*:
They **despise** *me because of the way I'm living.*
- belonging: *belong, have* (= possess), *own, possess*:
It **belongs** *to my father.*
The manager **has** *the biggest company car.*
- senses: *smell, taste, hear, see*:
This sauce **tastes** *great.*
I **hear** *what you're saying to me, but I don't agree.*
Do *you* **see** *anything you want to buy here?*
We use *can* with these verbs to show we are talking about this moment:
I **can see** *you're tired.*
I **can hear** *someone in the next room.*
- other state verbs: *need, contain, deserve, fit, seem, look* (= seem), *look like, matter, weigh*:
This medicine **contains** *aspirin.*
Mark **weighs** *70 kilos.*

⚠ *Think* is not a state verb when it refers to what someone is doing, not what they believe:
I'm **thinking** *about my holiday.*

⚠ *Have* can be continuous when it does not mean 'possess':
Steve **is having** *a difficult time at college this term.*
Can I phone you back later? We're **having** *lunch right now.*

⚠ *Taste* and *smell* can be continuous when they refer to what someone is doing:
I'm **tasting** *the sauce.*

⚠ *Listen to, watch* and *look at* are not state verbs and can be continuous:
We're **listening** *to music and Diane* **is watching** *a DVD upstairs.*

⚠ *See* can be continuous when it means 'meet with':
Lara's at the medical centre. She's **seeing** *a doctor about her sore throat.*

⚠ *Weigh* can be continuous when it refers to what someone is doing:
The shop assistant **is weighing** *the cheese.*

4 The verb *to be*

The verb *to be* is nearly always used in a simple rather than a continuous tense. When it is continuous it emphasises that a situation is temporary. It often describes a person's behaviour:
You're **being** *so impatient!* (Millie doesn't believe that Lisa is normally an impatient person.)
My brother **is being** *very nice to me this week. I wonder what he wants!*
Francis is filling in a form online, so we're all **being** *quiet as we don't want him to make any mistakes.*

C Grammar exercises

1 Choose the correct sentence from each pair.

1 a My brother lives with us until he can find a flat of his own.

 b My brother is living with us until he can find a flat of his own. ✓

2 a Megan goes to Hong Kong every January.

 b Megan's going to Hong Kong every January.

3 a I don't have enough money for a long holiday this year.

 b I'm not having enough money for a long holiday this year.

4 a Everyone needs a break from work sometimes.

 b Everyone is needing a break from work sometimes.

5 a What period of history do you study this term?

 b What period of history are you studying this term?

6 a The team manager looks bad-tempered in public, but he's always being very kind to young players.

 b The team manager looks bad-tempered in public, but he's always very kind to young players.

2 Complete these sentences with the present simple or present continuous form of the verbs.

1 My father _____knows_____ (know) all about mending cars, but nothing about bicycles.

2 This pie _____ (smell) a bit odd. What's in it?

3 I _____ (like) the jacket of this suit, but unfortunately the trousers _____
(not fit) me any more.

4 You're very quiet this evening. What _____ (you / think) about?

5 Who _____ (be) that man? Why _____ (your sister / be) so rude to him?
She _____ (have) such beautiful manners normally.

3 Fill in the gaps with the present simple or present continuous form of the verbs.

1 **Alex:** Why _are you wearing_ (you / wear) my coat?

 Ben: Oh, I'm sorry. It _____ (look) like mine in this light.

2 **Carl:** I _____ (have) no idea what this sentence _____ (mean).
Can you translate it?

 Donna: No, sorry. I _____ (not understand) it either.

3 **Eddie:** _____ (you / see) those men near the door? They _____ (look)
at us very strangely.

 Fergus: Yes. You're right. _____ (you / recognise) them from anywhere?

 Eddie: No, but they certainly _____ (seem) to know us. They _____ (come)
across to speak to us.

4 **Gina:** What _____ (you / do) in the kitchen? Our guests _____ (wait) for
their dessert, and you _____ (get) in my way!

 Hamid: I just _____ (want) to be somewhere quiet for a while. Everyone _____ (be)
so noisy this evening! I _____ (not know) why – it's very unusual.

4 Complete the email using the present simple or present continuous form of these verbs.

behave   come   cost   eat   enjoy   feel   ~~go~~   have   like   love   pay   realise   say
seem   serve   show   smile   stay   take   visit

Dear Stephanie,

How are you? We're fine. Our trip round the States **(1)** ___*is going*___ well and we
(2) _____ ourselves a lot. One good surprise is that things **(3)** _____
less here than back home. For example, this weekend we **(4)** _____ in a motel beside
a lake and we **(5)** _____ only $65 per night for a room with a beautiful view.

The only thing we **(6)** _____ (*not*) much is the food. Restaurants **(7)** _____
dinner rather early. We **(8)** _____ (*never*) at six o'clock at home so we
(9) _____ (*not*) hungry then and American portions **(10)** _____ very big to
us. Apart from that, we **(11)** _____ a wonderful time. We **(12)** _____ lots of
interesting little towns and we absolutely **(13)** _____ the scenery.

People here **(14)** _____ in a very friendly manner towards strangers. All the shop
assistants **(15)** _____ at us, and everyone **(16)** _____ 'Have a nice day!'
At home, the TV **(17)** _____ (*always*) us bad news stories about the States, but in fact,
when you **(18)** _____
here, you **(19)** _____
it's a really great place.
We **(20)** _____ lots
of photos to show you.

Much love,

Mick and Mary

---

5 👁 Cambridge First candidates made mistakes in the following sentences. Choose the correct verb forms.

1   I *want* / *am wanting* to help out at the camp this summer.

2   Most Spanish companies *belong* / *are belonging* to multinationals nowadays.

3   I *think* / *am thinking* about interviewing my grandfather's friend, who collects vintage cars.

4   My father went to that university, so he *knows* / *is knowing* all about it.

5   Ned *has* / *is having* a lot of problems with his teacher at the moment.

6   Every town *needs* / *is needing* a library, even though everyone has the internet nowadays.

Exam practice

Listening Part 4

▶ 03 You will hear an interview with a man called Martin Holloway who is a sound engineer. For questions **1–7**, choose the best answer (**A**, **B** or **C**).

1 The mistake people make about sound engineers is to think that
   A they spend most of their time working indoors.
   B their job is the same as that of a disc jockey.
   C they are responsible for the quality of the music.

2 What does Martin say helped him to begin earning money?
   A the course he did
   B some of the bands he played in
   C some people he met

3 Martin first gets involved in a project
   A as soon as the band is booked.
   B when he visits the venue.
   C while the band is rehearsing.

4 What does Martin often find during a show?
   A There are problems with the equipment.
   B Very little goes wrong for him.
   C The performers don't communicate with him.

5 What change in equipment has Martin appreciated the most over the years?
   A It is more portable.
   B The sound quality is better.
   C It is less expensive.

6 According to Martin, what is the most important quality in a sound engineer?
   A some musical ability
   B good communication skills
   C practical technical knowledge

7 What does Martin find most difficult about his job?
   A working in difficult environments
   B being away for periods of time
   C waiting for things to happen

 Exam tip

The question helps you find your place in the recording. If you miss an answer, listen for the next one and go back later.

Grammar focus task

▶ 03 Here are some extracts from the interview. Choose the present tense that the speaker uses. Listen again to check.

1 I *usually set up* / *am usually setting up* the equipment before the show.
2 What you *hear* / *are hearing* is out of tune.
3 People sometimes *call* / *are calling* me a disc jockey.
4 This weekend, I *work* / *am working* at a music festival.
5 I mostly *work* / *am working* out of doors.
6 Some people *think* / *are thinking* we just turn up on the day.
7 Everything *gets* / *is getting* smaller all the time.
8 But I *always tell* / *I'm always telling* people and they never listen.
9 They just *don't realise* / *aren't realising* that what's crucial is being able to get on with people.
10 An interest in music *means* / *is meaning* it is more enjoyable.

Past tenses

Past simple; past continuous; *used to* and *would*; *be/get* used to + *-ing* or noun

A Context listening

1 You are going to hear Jack talking to his grandmother about something he did last week. Before you listen, look at questions 1–5. Guess which things Jack, his mother and his grandmother did. Write J, M or G.

1 go to London   _____J_____
2 see a famous footballer   _____
3 go up to town alone   _____
4 worry about school work   _____
5 go to a club   _____

2 ▶04 Listen and check if you were right.

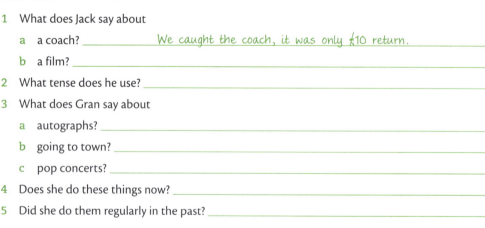

3 ▶04 Listen again and answer these questions.

1 What does Jack say about
   a a coach? _____ We caught the coach, it was only £10 return. _____
   b a film? _____
2 What tense does he use? _____
3 What does Gran say about
   a autographs? _____
   b going to town? _____
   c pop concerts? _____
4 Does she do these things now? _____
5 Did she do them regularly in the past? _____

4 ▶04 Listen again and complete these sentences with the words that the speakers use.

1 We did some revision for our exams while we _____ .
2 When we _____ for the cinema, we saw a really famous footballer.
3 He _____ a burger and all the crowds _____ past but nobody noticed him except me.

5 Which tense is in the gaps in Exercise 4? _____

B Grammar

1 Past simple

+	verb + -ed*	*I **wanted** it.*
–	*did not* + verb	*I **didn't want** it.*
?	*did ... + verb?*	*What **did** you **want**?*

*Regular verbs add *-ed* or *-d* to the verb:
want → *wanted*   *hope* → *hoped*

Many common verbs are irregular (➢ See Web page: Irregular verbs):
think → *thought*   *make* → *made*

To be is irregular:
am/is (not) → *was (not);*   *are (not)* → *were (not)*

We use the past simple:
- for completed actions and events in the past:
  *We **had** an exam on Thursday.*
  *We **caught** the coach.*
- for a sequence of actions or events:
  *I **went** round the shops, then I **went** to the cinema.*
- for permanent or long-term situations in the past:
  *I really **enjoyed** myself when I **was** a teenager.*
- for repeated events:
  *Jack's grandmother **went** to lots of concerts.*
  *She always **asked** for an autograph when she **met** someone famous.*

➢ See also Unit 3 for further uses of the past simple.

2 Past continuous

+	*was/were* + verb + -ing	*They **were waiting**.*
–	*was/were not* + verb + -ing	*She **wasn't waiting**.*
?	*was/were ... + verb + -ing?*	***Were** you **waiting**?*

We use the past continuous:
- for an activity beginning before a past action and continuing until or after it. The action is usually in the past simple:
  *We did some revision while we **were travelling**.*
  *When we **were queuing** for the cinema, we saw a famous footballer.*
- for two things happening at the same time:
  *He **was buying** a burger and all the crowds **were walking** past.*
- for repeated events, with a word like *always* or *continually*, especially if the speaker is criticising the activity:
  *She **was always worrying** about her homework.* (= Jack's grandmother thinks she worried too much.)
- for unfulfilled plans, with verbs like *hope, plan*, etc.:
  *I **was hoping** to find a new jacket.* (= but I didn't find one)

we were travelling

we did some revision

we were queuing

we saw a famous footballer

he was buying a burger
the crowds were walking past

⚠ State verbs are nearly always used in the past simple, not the past continuous (➢ see Unit 1, B3):
I didn't know him. (**not** ~~I wasn't knowing him~~)

3 *used to* + verb and *would* + verb

+	*used to* + verb	*He **used to read** comics.*
–	*did not use to* + verb	*We **didn't use to read** comics.*
?	*did ... use to* + verb?	***Did** you **use to read** comics?*

+	*would* + verb	*He **would read** comics.*
–	*would not* + verb	*We **wouldn't read** comics.*
?	*would ... + verb?*	***Would** you **read** comics?*

We use *used to* and *would* to talk about past habits when we are emphasising that they are no longer true:
*I **used to collect** all the autographs of film stars when I was a teenager.* (= she doesn't do this now)
*I **would go** up to town on my own.* (= she doesn't do this now)

Used to can describe actions and states, but *would* can only describe actions:
*All the teenagers **used to / would scream** at pop concerts.*
*They **used to be** crazy about the Beatles.* (**not** ~~would be crazy~~)

⚠ Notice the position of frequency adverbs (➤ see Unit 8) with *used to*:
*I **often used to study** on my own.* (**not** ~~I used to often study~~)

⚠ *Used to* is much more common than *would*.

4 *be/get used to* + *-ing* or noun

Be used to means 'be accustomed to'. It can be past, present or future, unlike *used to*, which is a past tense.
*I**'m used to working** at weekends.* (= I often work at weekends, it's normal for me now)

The question form is:
***Are** you **used to working** at weekends?*

Get used to means 'gradually become accustomed to'. It can be past, present or future, unlike *used to*, which is a past tense.
*My new school starts at 7.30. I'm not used to starting classes so early but I guess I**'ll** soon **get used to doing** it.*
(= My previous school started later, but I'll soon become accustomed to the change and it won't bother me.)

Be/get used to can be followed by *-ing* or by a noun/pronoun:
*He **wasn't used to criticism** and found it hard to accept.*
(= People hadn't criticised him before so he didn't like it.)
*My parents **are getting used to** a quiet **house**, now the children have all left home.*
(= When the children first left, my parents found the house strangely quiet, but it's gradually becoming normal for them.)

C Grammar exercises

1 Complete the text with the past simple form of these verbs.

be ~~begin~~ come drink eat explain feed find get give go have know learn
meet read seem speak spread write

◀ ▶ C ⌂ [_____]   ⊖ ⊜ ⊗

The mystery of Kaspar Hauser

The mystery of Kaspar Hauser **(1)** _____began_____ in Nuremberg,
Germany, about 200 years ago. One morning, the people of the
town **(2)** _____ a young man standing alone in the square.
He was holding a piece of paper in his hand. The paper
(3) _____ only that he **(4)** _____ the son of a soldier.
Kaspar **(5)** _____ how to say a few words and when given
a paper and pencil he **(6)** _____ his name, but he
(7) _____ completely ignorant about everyday life. At first
he **(8)** _____ only bread and **(9)** _____ only water,
but he gradually **(10)** _____ used to ordinary meals. He also
(11) _____ to talk properly.

The real truth about his birth remains a mystery, but it is probable that his father kept him
in one small room for the whole of his early life. He **(12)** _____ him on bread and
(13) _____ him water to drink. Kaspar never **(14)** _____ out, he never
(15) _____ to anyone or **(16)** _____ other children. In spite of this extraordinary
childhood, Kaspar was not stupid. He **(17)** _____ books and **(18)** _____ discussions
with teachers and philosophers. News about Kaspar **(19)** _____ through Europe and
visitors **(20)** _____ from abroad to meet him.

2 Fill in the gaps with the past simple or past continuous form of the verbs.

1 My parents _____got_____ (get) to know each other when they ___were studying___ (study) at university.

2 Doctor Fisher _____ (travel) widely as a young man and _____ (always keep)
a diary.

3 I _____ (see) my brother and his friend when I _____ (wait) for the bus, but
they _____ (not see) me.

4 Lily _____ (fill) in the application form and _____ (give) it to the
receptionist.

5 While I _____ (work) in Rome, I _____ (meet) a girl who
_____ (look) just like your sister.

6 Simon _____ (buy) a new laptop because his old one _____ (always crash).

7 I _____ (miss) your text because my phone _____ (charge) in another room.

8 Anna's feeling depressed because she _____ (hope) for a pay rise last week, but she
_____ (not get) one.

3 **Choose the correct form of the verbs in this text.**

My granny is 93 and she's come to live with us at our house. We're all pleased because we love
having her near us. She's a very independent person and until this year, she **(1)** _refused_ / _was
refusing_ to move to the flat on our ground floor. But last month she suddenly **(2)** _changed_ / _was
changing_ her mind and I **(3)** _asked_ / _would ask_ her why. She explained that for years, nobody in
her village **(4)** _would lock_ / _was locking_ their front doors and the place **(5)** _used to feel_ / _would
feel_ safe, but last month **(6)** she _met_ / _was meeting_ a neighbour in the street when she
(7) _was walking_ / _would walk_ home from the shops and **(8)** _heard_ / _was hearing_ some bad news.
Thieves **(9)** _were breaking_ / _got used to breaking_ into people's houses while they **(10)** _were
sitting_ / _would sit_ in their back gardens.

She **(11)** _realised_ / _was realising_ that she **(12)** _wasn't wanting_ / _didn't want_ to live alone any
more. She **(13)** _isn't used_ / _didn't use_ to being in the town yet, but it's not as difficult as she
(14) _was thinking_ / _thought_ it might be, and she loves seeing us more often.

4 **Fill in the gaps with a suitable form of _be/get used_ to.**

1   Rita's very tired this morning. She ___isn't used to___ (not) going to bed late.

2   Don't worry about the children: they _____ going to school by bus.

3   My new boss _____ giving orders, not receiving them.

4   She _____ (not) drinking very strong coffee and it made her ill.

5   _____ (you) our climate or do you still miss the sunshine?

6   I had never stayed in such an expensive hotel before, but I soon _____ it.

5 ◉ **Complete these sentences by Cambridge First candidates with the past simple or past
continuous form of the verbs.**

1   Don't ask me about the concert! I ___was working___ (work) in the stadium café when the band
    ___was playing___ (play).

2   I _____ (look) round the palace when a man _____ (stop) me to ask for directions.

3   The lights _____ (go) out while she _____ (have) a party in her house.

4   She _____ (go) quietly out of her bedroom and _____ (stand) behind the door so
    she could hear what they were saying.

5   I _____ (hope) my colleagues would say 'happy birthday' when I got to work, but nobody
    _____ (say) anything.

6 ◉ **Correct the mistakes with _used to_ in these sentences by Cambridge First candidates.**

1   When I was a child I ~~am used~~ to go camping.   ___used___

2   My parents used to often take me to the zoo.   _____

3   They didn't used to help their parents with housework, but now they do.   _____

4   We use to go to the beach every day last summer.   _____

5   Helen is a teacher at a primary school, so she used to teach children.   _____

6   I would like to be a sports instructor because I was used to train tennis
    players before I came to England.   _____

Exam practice

Reading and Use of English Part 1

For questions **1–8**, read the text below and decide which answer (**A**, **B**, **C** or **D**) best fits each gap. There is an example at the beginning **(0)**.

A musician is discovered

When Jimmy Yates was a small boy, his family **(0)** __A__ their holidays on his grandfather's farm.
This was in a valley **(1)** _____ by mountains. It was during one of these visits that Jimmy's **(2)** _____ to remember a tune led to the suggestion that the boy should **(3)** _____ a musical instrument. One evening a discussion **(4)** _____ among the adults about the differences between two hit songs. His father tried to prove the **(5)** _____ of the two tunes by playing them, not very well, on his guitar. No one thought that Jimmy, who was only five, was listening, but suddenly he made his **(6)** _____ to the ancient piano which stood in the corner and played first one of the tunes and then the other. The family was amazed **(7)** _____ no one had heard him play any music before. In this way, Jimmy's musical **(8)** _____ began.

0	**(A)**	spent	**B**	made	**C**	took	**D**	went
1	**A**	surrounded	**B**	closed	**C**	held	**D**	circled
2	**A**	talent	**B**	gift	**C**	ability	**D**	skill
3	**A**	take up	**B**	start up	**C**	pick up	**D**	join up
4	**A**	happened	**B**	came	**C**	entered	**D**	arose
5	**A**	comparison	**B**	closeness	**C**	likeness	**D**	similarity
6	**A**	path	**B**	way	**C**	route	**D**	line
7	**A**	so	**B**	although	**C**	when	**D**	as
8	**A**	work	**B**	living	**C**	career	**D**	study

> **Exam tip**
>
> If you are unsure, try to work out which answers are wrong. See what is left, and if you are still unsure, make a guess!

Grammar focus task

In the exam task there are some irregular past simple verbs. Without looking back at the text, write the past simple form of these verbs.

1	arise	_arose_	5	hear	_____	9	spend	_____
2	begin	_____	6	hold	_____	10	stand	_____
3	come	_____	7	lead	_____	11	take	_____
4	go	_____	8	make	_____	12	think	_____

Present perfect and past simple

Present perfect simple and past simple; present perfect simple and continuous

A Context listening

1 You are going to hear two people called Mike and Lucy talking to each other. Before you listen, look at the picture.

1   How do Mike and Lucy know each other? _____

2   What is Lucy's problem? _____

2 ▶05 Listen and check if you were right.

3 ▶05 Listen again and write Mike and Lucy's exact words. Stop the recording when you need to.

1   What does Mike say about finishing work? He says: '_____ *I finished at lunchtime today.* _____'

2   What does he say about this afternoon? He says: '_____'

3   What does Lucy say about finishing her essay? She says: '_____'

4   When does she say she started it? She says: '_____'

5   What does Mike say about studying history? He says: '_____'

6   How long has Lucy lived next door? She says: '_____'

7   How long has Mike lived there? He says: '_____'

8   Why is Mike surprised? He says: '_____'

4 Look at your answers to Exercise 3 and answer these questions.

1   Look at answers 1, 4 and 5. What tense are they? _____

2   Look at answers 2, 3, 6, 7 and 8. What tense are they? _____

3   Which sentences are about a time period which continues up to the moment of speaking? _____

4   Which sentences are about a period of time which is finished? _____

B Grammar

1 Present perfect simple or past simple?

Present perfect simple

+	has/have + past participle	*I've written it.*
–	has/have not + past participle	*She hasn't written it.*
?	has/have ... + past participle?	*Have you written it?*

Some verbs are irregular: *break → broken; go → gone* (➤ See Web page: Irregular verbs.)
➤ For past simple forms, see Unit 2, B1.

We use the present perfect simple:

- with *since* or *for*, about a period of time which continues up to the present moment:
I've lived there for four years. (= and I still live there)

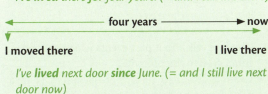

four years ——————→ now

I moved there   I live there

I've lived next door since June. (= and I still live next door now)

- with questions asking *how long*:
***How long have** you **lived** here?* (= I know you still live here)
Sometimes we can also use the present perfect continuous. ➤ See B2

- in the negative, for unfinished actions and events, often with *still* or *yet*:
*I **still haven't sent** the email.*
*I **haven't sent** the email **yet**.*
Still and *yet* are always used with a negative in the present perfect. *Still* goes before the verb; *yet* goes after it.

- for events repeated over a period of time until the present (they may continue):
*You've **played** the saxophone every night. (= until now, and you will probably continue to play every night)*

- for events which happened in the past at a time which is unknown and/or irrelevant:
*I've **started** my essay. (= we don't know when)*
*I've **lost** my new camera. (= it's not important when or where)*

We use the past simple:

- with *for*, about a period of time which is finished:
*I **lived** there **for** four years. (= but I don't live there now)*

four years ——→   now

I moved there   I moved out   I don't live there

- with questions asking *when*:
*When **did** you **move** here? (= the move is in the past)*

- for completed actions and events in the past, often with *ago*:
*I **sent** the email half an hour **ago**.*

- for events repeated over a period of time in the past (they are now finished):
*You **played** the saxophone every night. (= but you don't any more)*

3 Present perfect and past simple

We use the present perfect simple:

- for events that happened in the recent past (often with *just*):
  *Flight 206 **has landed**.* (= in the last few minutes)
  *She's **just gone** to the cinema.* (= she's on her way or she's already there now)

- when the time stated is not finished:
  *I've **spent** this morning writing an essay.* (= it's still morning)

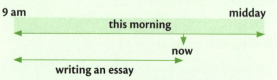

  *The builders **have started** working on the kitchen this week.* (= it's still this week)

- when we talk about a period of time up to the present:
  *I've **been** to Los Angeles but not to New York.* (= in my life up to now)
  *The team **has won** several matches.* (= and may win more)

- when we talk about how many times something has happened up to now:
  *Alex **has phoned** Ella three times.* (= and he might phone her again)

- with adverbs like *already*, *before*, *ever* and *never*:
  *Nobody's **ever complained** before.* (= until now)
  *I've **never tried** Japanese food.* (= but I might one day)
  *She's **already gone** to the airport.*
  *I've **met** her **before** somewhere.*
  Never, *ever* and *already* go between the auxiliary and the main verb. *Before* goes after the verb.

- after a superlative (➤ see Unit 7):
  *It's the best cup of coffee I've **had** here.*
  *This is the most exciting place we've **been** to.*

We use the past simple:

- for events that happened at a particular time in the past:
  *Flight 206 **landed** at one o'clock.*
  or within a period of time in the past:
  *She **was** at the cinema between midday and two o'clock.* (= but she's not there now)

- when the time stated is finished:
  *I **spent** this morning writing an essay.* (= it's now afternoon so 'this morning' is in the past)

  I started my essay last week. (= 'last week' is definitely in the past)
  *I **lost** my new camera in London.* (= the place fixes it at a time in the past)

- when we talk about past events which are not connected to the present:
  *I **went** to Los Angeles but not to New York.* (= on a particular trip which is in the past)
  *The Chinese **invented** printing.*

- when we talk about how many times something happened in the past:
  *Alex **phoned** Ella three times yesterday.*

2   **Present perfect simple or continuous?**

Present perfect continuous

+	has/have been + verb + -ing	*I've been working hard.*
–	has/have not been + verb + -ing	*She hasn't been working hard.*
?	has/have … + been + verb + -ing?	*Have you been working hard?*

The present perfect and the present perfect continuous are both used to describe events or activities which started in the past and have continued up to the present, or activities which stopped recently. Some verbs can be used in either the present perfect simple or continuous with little difference in meaning. These are verbs which describe activities which normally happen over a period of time, e.g. *live, study, wait, work*:
*Martin **has lived** / **has been living** in Japan for five years.*

We use the present perfect continuous:

- to talk about how long something has been happening:
  I've been driving since five o'clock this morning.
  The children have been playing happily all morning.
  We've been worrying about her all week.
  How long have you been watching TV?

- to focus on the activity or event itself (whether it is complete or not is unimportant):
  He's been reading that book since he got up.
  (= we're interested in how he passed the time)
  I've been mending the car. (= that's why I'm dirty)

We use the present perfect simple:

- to talk about how often or how many times something has happened:
  I've driven there several times before.
  The children have played four games of tennis this morning.
  I've worried about her every day since she set off.
  I've watched three programmes.

- to focus on the present result of an activity or event which is complete:
  I've read the newspapers. (= I've finished reading them)
  I've mended the car. (= I've finished so we can go out in it now)

⚠ We never use the present tense to talk about how long we have been doing something:
I've been learning the piano for a long time. (**not** ~~I'm learning the piano for a long time~~)
He's been playing in a band for two years. (**not** ~~He's playing in a band for two years~~)

⚠ State verbs are not usually used in the present perfect continuous (➤ see Unit 1, B3):
I've known her since she was four years old. (**not** ~~I've been knowing her~~)
I've always hated cold weather. (**not** ~~I've always been hating cold weather~~)

C Grammar exercises

1 **Match the beginnings and endings of these sentences.**

1	He's talked to her on the phone		A	for years.
2	This summer the pool was only open		B	on my way home from school yesterday.
3	The whole team felt exhausted		C	since nine o'clock this morning.
4	The rent of my flat has gone up		D	when the match finished.
5	She's had nothing to eat		E	ever since she was very young.
6	I got very wet		F	by 20 per cent this year.
7	I spent a month in Brazil		G	a few minutes ago.
8	She's always enjoyed painting		H	from April till September.
9	I haven't had such a good time		I	in 2002.
10	This text arrived		J	every night this week.

2 **Fill in the gaps with the present perfect or past simple form of the verbs.**

1 This is only the second time I ___'ve ever flown___ (*ever fly*) in an aeroplane.

2 The child _____ (*sleep*) from seven till seven without waking once.

3 Gabriella _____ (*grow*) five centimetres since last month.

4 I _____ (*send*) Ed three emails last week but he _____ (*not reply*) to any of them yet.

5 _____ (*you / learn*) to play chess when you were a child?

6 I _____ (*buy*) this bicycle five years ago and I _____ (*use*) it every day since then.

7 How long _____ (*you / have*) that bad cough?

8 The train _____ (*just arrive*), so hurry and you might catch it.

9 I _____ (*never see*) such a beautiful rainbow before.

10 I _____ (*dream*) about a beautiful desert island last night.

11 On Sunday we _____ (*meet*) outside the cinema as usual.

12 When _____ (*you / get*) that jacket? I _____ (*not notice*) it before.

3 ◉ **Choose the correct verb forms in these sentences by Cambridge First candidates.**

1 I think that my friend Andrew *has worked / has been working* too hard recently and needs a rest.

2 I *have been working / worked* with children when I was at university.

3 How many times *have you eaten / have you been eating* Japanese food?

4 Since I left school in the summer I *have been doing / have done* a holiday job.

5 Two years ago I *did / have done* a course in coaching basketball.

6 I am so happy to receive your invitation. I *have waited / have been waiting* for it for ages!

4 Fill in the gaps with suitable verbs in the present perfect or the past simple.

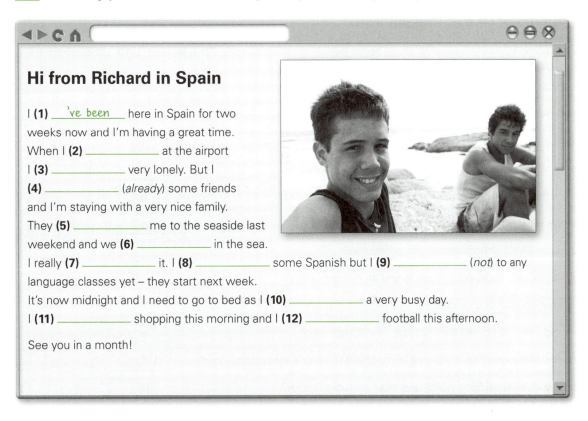

Hi from Richard in Spain

I **(1)** ___'ve been___ here in Spain for two
weeks now and I'm having a great time.
When I **(2)** _____ at the airport
I **(3)** _____ very lonely. But I
(4) _____ (*already*) some friends
and I'm staying with a very nice family.
They **(5)** _____ me to the seaside last
weekend and we **(6)** _____ in the sea.
I really **(7)** _____ it. I **(8)** _____ some Spanish but I **(9)** _____ (*not*) to any
language classes yet – they start next week.
It's now midnight and I need to go to bed as I **(10)** _____ a very busy day.
I **(11)** _____ shopping this morning and I **(12)** _____ football this afternoon.

See you in a month!

5 Read this conversation between two people in a sports club. Choose the correct verb forms.

Anna: Excuse me. **(1)** *We've waited* / <u>*We've been waiting*</u> to play tennis since 10.30. It must be our turn now.

Tim: I don't think so.

Anna: **(2)** *We've stood* / *We've been standing* here patiently watching you and it's time for you to stop.
How long **(3)** *have you played* / *have you been playing*?

Tim: Since about 9.30. **(4)** *We've played* / *We've been playing* two matches so far this morning and
(5) *we haven't finished* / *we haven't been finishing* the third yet. You'll have to wait or do
something else.

Anna: But **(6)** *you've played* / *you've been playing* for more than two hours and it's our turn now.

Tim: I said you'll have to wait.

Anna: We're tired of waiting and we haven't got anything to do. **(7)** *We've read* / *We've been reading* the
magazines we brought with us.

Tim: Why don't you do something else? **(8)** *Have you tried* / *Have you been trying* the swimming pool?

Anna: We don't want to swim, we want to play tennis.

Tim: Well, I always play on a Saturday morning. Anyway, **(9)** *we've already started* / *we've already been
starting* the third match.

Anna: Oh well, it looks like we've got no choice, but **(10)** *we've booked* / *we've been booking* for next
Saturday so you'll be unlucky then.

Reading and Use of English Part 7

You are going to read a magazine article about people who like clothes. For questions **1–10**, choose from the people (**A–D**). The people may be chosen more than once.

Which person

thinks people don't give enough importance to one kind of clothing?	1
learned something after an experience with some clothing?	2
made a decision to buy something they had always wanted?	3
is happy with the social requirements of their job?	4
admits not giving importance to self-promotion?	5
chooses clothes so as not to draw attention to themselves?	6
did something out of character?	7
never expected to go into their present line of business?	8
mentions circumstances in which it is important to keep a sense of humour?	9
no longer does something which they now consider foolish?	10

Me and my clothes

A   Paula, a clothes designer

When you're young you can get away with cheap clothes, though I think I had expensive tastes even then. In fact I've always spent a lot on clothes and I've always loved what they can do for you but I never anticipated making money from them. At one point when I didn't have a job my husband said, 'Surely you must be able to make something'. That was the kick I needed to get me started.

I'm mad about swimsuits. Because I make my own clothes, I'm always thinking about changing a collar on something or changing a fabric, but because I don't make swimsuits they're free from all that. I have several. People take one on holiday and think that's enough, yet they wouldn't dream of wearing the same trousers day after day. I don't understand that.

B   Len, a businessman

I've enjoyed motorbikes since I was 16. But for a long time I didn't own one; I rode my brother's instead. Then about two years ago I bought one. I thought: if I don't get one now, I never will. I always walked to work every morning until I got the motorbike, but now I ride there most days. I bought a leather jacket as a solution to the problem of needing to wear a suit to work and wanting to come in by bike. It would be impossible to be changing all the time. When I was younger I rode a bike several times without a helmet. That was in parts of the United States where it wasn't compulsory, but it's madness. There's enough risk on a bike without adding more.

Exam practice

C Marion, a singer

When I was in a musical I wore wonderful skirts made by a designer but they were incredibly heavy, and during the first performance I fell over twice on stage dancing in them. That hasn't happened to me again because I know now that you need much lighter clothes to dance in. A little while after that, I was singing at a friend's wedding so I asked the same designer to make a really stunning dress for me. I've worn it just a few times since then – to awards ceremonies – but I feel great in it. My career's never been structured. Perhaps it should have been but I'm hopeless at pushing myself. I went to the United States when a film I was in, *Enchanted April*, was really big but I never dreamed of hiring a publicist or anything. I suppose one measure of success was when I did my first TV advert and I went into the sort of shop I'd always been scared to go into before and bought something without looking at the price. That just wasn't like me.

D Tom, chief executive of a charity

I worked as a lawyer until I was in my forties but I've been director of a charity for ten years now. I'm out two or three nights a week at dinners to raise money. It goes with a job like this and it's fun too. I wear a suit and tie to most events. They're a kind of uniform, which is helpful because I'm not naturally a stylish dresser. I like to feel comfortable and fit in, and this way I'm not conscious of my appearance. If I was, I'd probably be horrendously shy. One of my big mistakes in my early days was to make a speech that was too serious. People said afterwards that it was very powerful but that wasn't what I'd intended. If you're too serious in my kind of business it puts people off.

> **Exam tip**
>
> There will be at least one answer for each text, so check again if you have one text with no answers in it.

Grammar focus task

Without looking back at the text, complete these extracts with the present perfect simple or the past simple form of the verbs in the box.

anticipate be be buy enjoy fall get happen own ~~spend~~ walk wear work

1   I <u>'ve always spent</u> (*always*) a lot on clothes but I never _____ making money from them.

2   I _____ motorbikes since I was 16. But for a long time I _____ (*not*) one. Then about two years ago I _____ one.

3   I always _____ to work every morning until I _____ the motorbike, but now I ride there most days.

4   During the first performance, I _____ over twice on stage dancing in them. That _____ (*not*) to me again.

5   I _____ it just a few times since then.

6   I _____ as a lawyer until I _____ in my forties but I _____ director of a charity for ten years now.

Past perfect

Past perfect simple and continuous

A Context listening

1 You are going to hear a teenage boy called Richard talking to his mother. Before you listen, look at the picture and answer these questions.

1 How has Richard spent the weekend? _____

2 How does his mother feel? Why? _____

2 ▶06 Listen and check if you were right.

3 ▶06 Listen again and fill in the gaps. Stop the recording when you need to.

Richard: I (1) *'d done* the ceiling, and I (2) _____ one wall, when I
(3) _____ paint.

Richard: And yesterday afternoon I (4) _____ bored. I (5) _____ to town for
a few hours – you know, round the centre. I (6) _____ the shopping – everything on
your list – and I (7) _____ all my homework.

Mother: I (8) _____ for only an hour when the car (9) _____ .

4 Look at your answers to Exercise 3 and answer these questions.

1 Look at answers 1, 2 and 3. Did 3 happen before or after 1 and 2? _____

What tenses does Richard use? _____

2 Look at answers 4, 5, 6 and 7. Did 4 happen before or after 5, 6 and 7? _____

What tenses does Richard use? _____

3 Look at answers 8 and 9. Which happened first? _____

What tenses does Richard's mother use? _____

B Grammar

1 Past perfect simple

Present perfect simple

+	*had* + past participle	He**'d painted** the ceiling.
–	*had not* + past participle	He **hadn't painted** the ceiling.
?	*had ...* + past participle?	**Had** he **painted** the ceiling?

We use the past perfect simple:
- when we are already talking about the past and want to make it clear that we are referring back to an even
earlier time:
  *Yesterday afternoon I was bored. I**'d been** to town, I**'d done** the shopping and I**'d finished** all my homework so I decided to paint my room.*

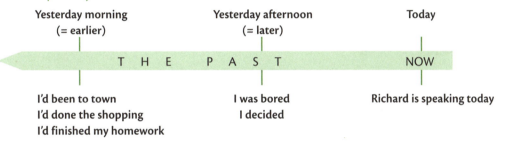

Yesterday morning (= earlier)	Yesterday afternoon (= later)	Today
T H E P A S T		NOW
I'd been to town I'd done the shopping I'd finished my homework	I was bored I decided	Richard is speaking today

- in some sentences with time expressions (*when, after, by the time, as soon as*) when one event happened before the other:
  *I**'d painted** one wall when I **ran** out of paint.*
  ***By the time** Richard's mother **got** home, he**'d finished** painting the room.*
- with the adverbs *just, already, ever* and *never*. They go between the auxiliary and the main verb
  (➤ see also Unit 8):
  *He**'d just finished** painting when his mother came in.*
  *When she got home he**'d already finished** painting the room.*
  *Until last weekend he**'d never painted** a room.*
  ***Had** he **ever done** any painting before?*

We don't use the past perfect:
- if one action happened at the same time as another:
  *When Richard's mother **saw** the room, she **was** horrified.* (**not** ~~When Richard's mother had seen~~ ...)
- if one action happened immediately after the other and was connected to it. In sentences like these, the first action is often the cause of the second:
  *When Jill **heard** the baby cry, she **ran** to pick him up.* (**not** ~~When Jill had heard~~ ...)

⚠️ Notice the difference in meaning between these two sentences:

*When Richard's mother came into the room, he **stopped** painting.* (= she came in, so he stopped)

Richard's mother came into the room.
|
Richard stopped painting.

*When Richard's mother came into the room, he**'d stopped** painting.* (= he stopped some time before she came in)

Richard's mother came into the room.
|
Richard stopped painting.

2 Past perfect continuous

+	had been + verb + -ing	I'**d been working** hard.
–	had not been + verb + -ing	She **hadn't been working** hard.
?	had ... been + verb + -ing?	**Had** you **been working** hard?

We use the past perfect continuous:

- to emphasise a continuous activity or how long it continued:
  *He had a headache because he'**d been playing** computer games for hours.*

• •

- when we talk about how long something happened up to a point in the past:
  *How long **had** you **been driving** when the car broke down?*
  *By the time she arrived I'**d been waiting** for two hours.*

We use the past perfect simple:

- when we do not need to emphasise a continuous activity or the period of time:
  *He'**d played** all of the computer games and wanted to do something different.*

• •

- when we talk about how many or how often up to a point in the past:
  *I'**d driven** six kilometres when the car broke down.*
  *By the time I was 18 I'**d visited** Canada six times.*

⚠️ State verbs (➤ see Unit 1, B3) are not usually used in the past perfect continuous:
*I'**d known** her since she was four years old.* (**not** ~~I'd been knowing her~~ ...)

C Grammar exercises

1 Complete the sentences with the correct form of the past perfect simple.

1 The new school building _had only been_ (only / be) open for a month before it was destroyed in a fire.

2 I sent back the trainers that I _____ (order) online because they were too small.

3 We _____ (plan) to arrive early, but we overslept as usual.

4 As soon as I tasted the curry, I realised I _____ (leave) the garlic out.

5 How many questions _____ (you / answer) when the bell rang?

6 Luckily, the band _____ (not start) playing when we reached our seats.

7 _____ (you / already / book) tickets when you heard the match was cancelled?

8 It was only after I _____ (post) the parcel that I realised I _____ (forget) to put my address on the back of it.

9 _____ (anyone / not tell) Andy that the bus times _____ (change)?

10 Because the team _____ (never do) very well before, they were delighted to reach the final.

2 Complete the sentences with the correct form of the past perfect continuous.

1 I _'d been hoping_ (hope) no one would notice I wasn't at the meeting.

2 What _____ (you / eat) that made you so ill?

3 The students _____ (not expect) a test that day.

4 We couldn't understand where the cat _____ (live) for the past twelve months.

5 Alexi gave the wrong answer because he _____ (not pay) attention.

6 Where _____ (Anya's family / live) before they moved to this street?

7 Nobody _____ (watch) the television for some time so I turned it off.

8 Why was Jeff in such bad temper? _____ (the other boys / tease) him again?

9 We were so disappointed when the hotel closed. We _____ (go) there for holidays since I was a small child.

10 It wasn't until I got home that I noticed that I _____ (wear) odd socks all day.

3 **Fill in the gaps with suitable verbs in the past perfect continuous.**

1 The phone ___had been ringing___ for several minutes before I heard it.

2 Katya _____ (*not*) German with Mr Fauser for very long when he retired.

3 Liz didn't know about the surprise party which her parents _____ for weeks.

4 I was very pleased when the bus finally arrived because I _____ that I would be late for work.

5 When the doctor eventually called my name I _____ for 40 minutes.

6 My brother lost his job because he _____ jokes to everyone in the office by email.

7 The band _____ (*not*) for long when the lights went out.

8 We _____ our money to buy a car but we decided to go to Brazil instead.

9 I finally got through to Ellie but we _____ (*only*) for a few minutes when we got cut off.

10 How long _____ (*they*) for the car keys when Peta found them in her pocket?

4 **Each of these sentences has a verb in the past perfect simple. Is it possible to replace it with the past perfect continuous?**

1 I'd worked for the engineering company for three months before I realised my neighbour also worked there.
    ___Yes – I'd been working___

2 As soon as George had finished the race, he drank three glasses of water.
    _____

3 Everything was white because it had snowed heavily during the night.
    _____

4 My parents were delighted when I qualified because they had always wanted me to be a doctor.
    _____

5 She was exhausted when she got out of the pool because she'd swum three kilometres.
    _____

6 We'd only just sat down at our table when the waitress came to take our order.
    _____

7 I could tell immediately from their faces that they had argued about something.
    _____

8 Our dinner wasn't cooked because I'd forgotten to switch the oven on.
    _____

9 The tourist guide hadn't spoken loudly enough for all the group to hear what he was saying.
    _____

10 When I got to the café, my friends had already left, so I had to run to catch up with them.
    _____

5 Fill in the gaps with the past simple, past perfect or past perfect continuous form of the verbs.

1 I _____'d never ridden_____ (never ride) a bike until I _____went_____ (go) to live in Amsterdam.

2 When Martin _____ (come) into the room, his mother nearly _____ (faint) because she _____ (not see) him for nearly 20 years.

3 We were held up in a traffic jam so the concert _____ (begin) by the time we _____ (arrive).

4 How long _____ (you / apply) for jobs when you _____ (get) this one?

5 I _____ (not see) Lisa when I went round last night because she _____ (go) to stay with her grandmother.

6 I _____ (drive) for about four hours when I _____ (realise) that I was completely lost.

7 When I _____ (go) into the room, everyone _____ (stop) talking and _____ (look) at me.

8 After he _____ (wash) his clothes, he _____ (hang) them outside to dry.

9 The manager was shocked when he _____ (discover) that Jane was a thief. Up until then, he _____ (believe) that she was completely honest.

10 (you / ever do) _____ any carpentry before you _____ (build) that cupboard?

6 Fill in the gaps with the past simple, past perfect or past perfect continuous form of these verbs.

agree answer arrange arrive bang come forget have hear move phone play

The band played on …

I had a rather embarrassing experience last year. At that time I played in a band with some friends of mine and, rather nervously, we **(1)** _____'d agreed_____ to provide the music at a friend's wedding. We **(2)** _____ together for about three months and it was the first booking we **(3)** _____ (ever) so we'd been practising really hard. The wedding was on a Saturday.

The day before the wedding I had moved to a new flat so I **(4)** _____ furniture all day and gone to bed exhausted. At nine o'clock on the Saturday morning the rest of the band met, as we **(5)** _____ , to practise. They kept phoning me but I **(6)** _____ (not). So in the end one of them **(7)** _____ round and **(8)** _____ on my door for fifteen minutes until I woke up.

He told me that they **(9)** _____ me all morning. I **(10)** _____ (not) anything and I nearly missed the wedding. Then, when I finally **(11)** _____ at the wedding, I realised that I **(12)** _____ my guitar.

Exam practice

Reading and Use of English Part 5

You are going to read an extract from a novel. For questions **1–6**, choose the answer (**A**, **B**, **C** or **D**) which you think fits best according to the text.

Falicon Park was a typical English suburban road, some fifty years old. The individuality of the properties had increased over the years as successive owners had remodelled and added to their homes. Garages had been converted into kitchen extensions and lawns had become parking spaces while adventurous gardeners had experimented with rocks and olive trees or palm trees. About halfway along the southern side of the road was number 18. It was a detached house, double-fronted. The paintwork was in good order although it was not fresh. The concrete driveway was scarred with cracks and oil stains, and the space for parking had been extended with gravel. A yew hedge straggled across in front of the gravelled area. The curtains were firmly closed and the windows too. The place had an unloved air, unlike the majority of its neighbours.

It was a quiet morning. About eleven o'clock, a car drew up outside number 18. It was a grey saloon, not very new, not very clean. There were two men in it. They had an air of determination about them, with a hint of aggression. They could have been debt-collectors. The driver got out and walked to the front door. He rang the bell. It echoed and re-echoed inside the house. No one opened the door. The air was still and the house seemed deserted. The man took out his phone and called a number. He listened, then turned away from the house, went back to the car and drove away.

Around midday the sky clouded over and a nippy little wind started. The children who had been playing a fairly unenthusiastic game of football around various parked cars therefore decided at that point to take themselves off to see if the weekend sport had begun on television.

The street was almost empty when a large dark green van parked outside number 18 and three men in matching fleeces got out. The tallest of them approached a woman working in the garden of number 20 and asked her if she had a water meter.

'We've had a report that there may be a leak round here,' he explained.

The woman at number 20 was no doubt mindful of a crime prevention circular she had received very recently and said that she would expect them to know whether she had a water meter if they were genuine employees of the water company. The tall man from the van showed a card to the
line 26 sceptical woman, which seemed to satisfy her. She went into her house and left them to it. The three men busied themselves in the driveway of number 18. They raised a manhole cover, then one man got a toolbox from the van, went round the side of the house and into the back garden. After a few minutes the front door opened and he appeared at it, signalling to his colleagues. The tall man closed the manhole cover, took another toolbox from the van and went to the doorstep. He glanced around, then he also entered the house, leaving the front door ajar. The third man reversed the van into the driveway.

line 33 Suddenly, the two men came running out of the house and scrambled into the van as it accelerated out of the drive and disappeared up the road, narrowly missing a teenager who was sauntering across it. Ten minutes later, a police car turned sharply into Falicon Park and drew to a halt outside number 18. Two uniformed officers got out and entered the house. Someone had forced the door on a locked cupboard in the study and the police found the contents scattered on the floor and in the kitchen at the end of the hall the frosted glass in the back door had been neatly removed and placed under a bush.

Exam practice

1 Most of the houses in Falicon Park

   A were almost identical.

   B had large gardens.

   C were well looked after.

   D belonged to large families.

2 The writer suggests that the driver of the grey car

   A had visited number 18 before.

   B might threaten the residents in some way.

   C had been invited to call by the owner.

   D was upset when no one answered the door.

3 The children decided to go indoors because

   A there was a change in the weather.

   B there were too many cars in the road.

   C they had finished their game of football.

   D they were missing the sport on television.

> ### Exam tip
> The questions follow the text but there may be more than one question on a paragraph.

4 What made the woman at number 20 suspicious?

   A She had heard a news report about thieves.

   B She didn't like the way the tall man spoke to her.

   C She was surprised to be asked about her water meter.

   D She knew nothing about a leak in the area.

5 What does 'it' in line 26 refer to?

   A the tall man's card

   B the driveway of number 18

   C the house next door

   D the work they had to do

6 The word 'scrambled' is used in line 33 to emphasise the fact that the men were

   A trying not to make a noise.

   B in a great hurry.

   C out of condition.

   D being chased by somebody.

Grammar focus task

1 Without looking back at the text, complete these sentences with the verbs in the box. Use the correct tense – past simple, past perfect or past perfect continuous. Then check your answers in the text.

> be   become   decide   experiment   find   force   ~~increase~~   play   receive   remodel

   1 The individuality of the properties _had increased_ over the years as sucessive owners _____ their homes.

   2 Lawns _____ parking spaces while adventurous gardeners _____ with rocks and olive trees or palm trees.

   3 The children who _____ a fairly unenthusiastic game of football therefore _____ to take themselves off.

   4 The woman at number 20 _____ no doubt mindful of a crime prevention circular she _____ very recently.

   5 Someone _____ the door on a locked cupboard in the study and the police _____ the contents scattered on the floor.

2 Why do you think the men came running out of the house? What had happened?

Future (1)

Present tenses for future; *will*; future continuous

A Context listening

1 You are going to hear a man called Tom having four conversations. Before you listen, look at the pictures. What do you think Tom's job is?

2 ▶07 Listen and check if you were right. As you listen, match the conversations with the pictures.

1 _____ 2 _____ 3 _____ 4 _____

3 ▶07 Listen again and write the verbs.

Conversation 1

1 Tom's plane ___leaves___ at 11.05.

2 It _____ at Amsterdam airport at 13.40.

3 The conference _____ on Wednesday at 9.30.

Conversation 2

4 I _____ badminton in a few minutes with Paul.

5 I _____ to a conference in Amsterdam tomorrow morning.

6 I _____ my eyes tested on Saturday afternoon.

Conversation 3

7 I probably _____ back in time.

8 I think I _____ a meal in town.

9 I _____ breakfast in my room.

Conversation 4

10 In a hundred years' time, the world _____ a very different place.

11 There _____ much oil available for energy.

12 People _____ much longer.

4 Look at your answers to Exercise 3 and answer these questions.

1 Which sentences are about events fixed by a timetable? _____

What tense is used? _____

2 Which sentences are about actions being decided or still not certain? _____

What tense is used? _____

3 Which sentences are about arrangements people have made? _____

What tense is used? _____

4 Which sentences are about general predictions about the future? _____

What tense is used? _____

B Grammar

In English, several different tenses are used to talk about the future: the present simple (➤ see Unit 1), the present continuous (➤ see Unit 1), *will/shall*, the future continuous and *going to* (➤ see Unit 6 for *going to*).

1 Present simple

We use the present simple for scheduled events with a future meaning:

*   for timetables (planes, buses, etc. leaving and arriving):
    *My plane **arrives** at Amsterdam airport at 13.40.*
    *The London train **leaves** in half an hour from platform 2.*
*   for programmes (when a conference, a course, a football match, a film, etc. begins and ends):
    *The conference **starts** on Wednesday at 9.30.*
    *The match **ends** at about five o'clock.*
*   for people if their plans are fixed by a timetable:
    *The students **have** their written English exam on Monday and the oral on Tuesday.*
    *Jo **starts** her drama course in two weeks' time.*

2 Present continuous

We use the present continuous:

*   for plans which have already been arranged:
    *People **are travelling** from all over the world.*
    *What **are** you **doing** tomorrow evening?*
    *I'm **flying** to a conference in Amsterdam. (= already arranged)*
    *I'm **having** my eyes tested on Saturday afternoon. (= I have an appointment)*

3 *will* future

+	*will* + verb	*They'**ll arrive** soon.*
–	*will not* + verb	*They **won't arrive** today.*
?	*will ...* + verb?	***Will** they **arrive** soon?*

In formal English, *shall* is occasionally used with *I/we* instead of *will*. (➤ For the use of *shall* with offers and suggestions, see Unit 13, B3–4.)

We use *will*:

*   for decisions made at the moment of speaking:
    *No, actually, I'**ll have** breakfast in my room. (he changes his mind)*
    *Thanks for telling me. I'**ll ring** the office now.*
    *These plates aren't clean. I'**ll put** them in the dishwasher.*

*   for anything which is uncertain, especially with *probably, maybe, I think, I expect* and *I hope*:
    *I **probably won't be** back in time.*
    *I **think I'll get** a meal in town.*
    *I **expect you'll be** tired after the match.*
    *We **hope you'll visit** us again soon.*

- for situations that we predict will happen but which are not definitely decided or arranged:
  *In 100 years the world **will be** a very different place. There **will be** millions more people but there **won't be** much oil available for energy.* (= nobody knows definitely what the world will be like in 100 years)

  ⚠ Compare:
  *I**'m taking** my History exam again tomorrow.* (= arranged)
  *I**'ll get** higher marks this time.* (= not something which is arranged or decided in advance – a hopeful prediction)

- for something in the future which doesn't depend on personal judgment:
  *I**'ll be** 23 on my next birthday.* (= I can't change this, it will just happen)
  *There**'ll be** a full moon tomorrow.*

4 Future continuous

+	will be + verb + -ing	She**'ll be working** at 7.30.
–	will not be + verb + -ing	She **won't be working** at 7.30.
?	will ... be + verb + -ing?	**Will** she **be working** at 7.30?

We use the future continuous for an event which is going on at a particular time or over a period of time in the future:
*I**'ll be working** at seven o'clock.* (= I will start before seven and I will continue after seven)

7 pm

I'll be working

*By the time you read this postcard, I**'ll be walking** in the mountains.*

⚠ Compare:
*I**'ll be interviewing** him at 6.30.* (= the interview begins before 6.30 and continues afterwards)

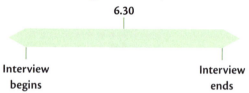

6.30

Interview begins   Interview ends

*I**'m interviewing** him at 6.30.* (= the interview is arranged to begin at 6.30)

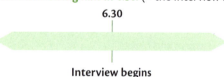

6.30

Interview begins

C Grammar exercises

1 Choose the most suitable form of the verbs.

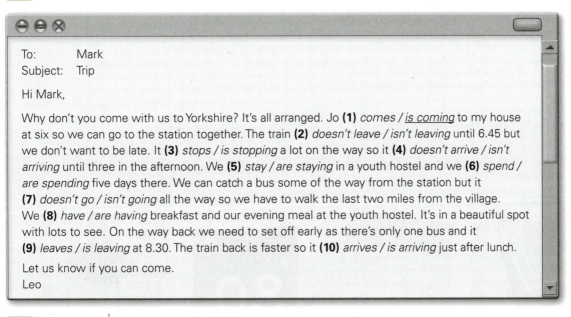

To: Mark
Subject: Trip

Hi Mark,

Why don't you come with us to Yorkshire? It's all arranged. Jo **(1)** *comes / is coming* to my house at six so we can go to the station together. The train **(2)** *doesn't leave / isn't leaving* until 6.45 but we don't want to be late. It **(3)** *stops / is stopping* a lot on the way so it **(4)** *doesn't arrive / isn't arriving* until three in the afternoon. We **(5)** *stay / are staying* in a youth hostel and we **(6)** *spend / are spending* five days there. We can catch a bus some of the way from the station but it **(7)** *doesn't go / isn't going* all the way so we have to walk the last two miles from the village. We **(8)** *have / are having* breakfast and our evening meal at the youth hostel. It's in a beautiful spot with lots to see. On the way back we need to set off early as there's only one bus and it **(9)** *leaves / is leaving* at 8.30. The train back is faster so it **(10)** *arrives / is arriving* just after lunch.

Let us know if you can come.
Leo

2 Complete these dialogues. Use the present continuous or the *will* future form of the verbs.

1 **Tim:**   Where are you going?
  Julie: To the cinema.
  Tim: Wait for me. I think I 'll come _____ (come) with you.

2 From next week all enquiries should be sent to Mary because Frances _____ (leave) on Friday.

3 **Rachel:** I _____ (give) Sophie a CD for her birthday. What _____ (you / give) her?

  Fiona: I _____ (probably get) her a new purse. She keeps losing money from her old one.

4 **John:**   I need to finish packing today because we _____ (move) tomorrow and there's still lots to do.

  Peter: Don't worry. I _____ (come) round tonight and help you.

5 **James:**   Never walk under a ladder or you _____ (have) ten years' bad luck.
  Kay: Rubbish!

6 Details of the president's visit are now confirmed. He _____ (stay) at the Castle Hotel for two days.

7 **Assistant:** We have milk chocolate, plain chocolate, with nuts, with fruit.
  Man: Er … what a lot of choice! I _____ (have) a bar of milk chocolate, please.

8 **Sarah:**   _____ (you / do) anything special next Saturday?

  Lee: Yes, I am. My cousin _____ (arrive) from Italy so I _____ (drive) to the airport in the afternoon to meet him.

9 **Carol:**   Have you finished that book I lent you?
  Sam: Oh, sorry. I forgot all about it. I _____ (get) it now.

3 👁 **Complete the following sentences by Cambridge First candidates. Use the present simple, present continuous, *will* future or future continuous form of the verbs.**

1   There's a special bus to the conference centre, which _____leaves_____ (leave) the hotel at 8 am.

2   We're going to Miami! This time tomorrow we _____ (sit) on a boat fishing.

3   I think I _____ (apply) for a job when I have finished university.

4   I'm worried about the meeting because we _____ (speak) English for the whole two hours.

5   My friends _____ (have) dinner at my house tonight and I haven't started cooking yet!

6   You should meet me at 7 o'clock, the concert _____ (start) at 7:30.

7   I can't meet you on Saturday because a cousin of mine _____ (come) from Bologna.

8   I have just bought a new bicycle, so maybe I _____ (lose) some weight.

4   **Look at the pictures and fill in the gaps with suitable verbs in the present continuous, *will* future or future continuous.**

1   I expect my parents _____will give_____ me books again for my birthday.

2   Sam _____ the doctor tomorrow morning at ten o'clock so he can't meet us then.

3   My grandfather _____ eighty on his next birthday.

4   I think I _____ a teacher when I grow up.

5   At midday tomorrow I _____ over the Atlantic.

6   This time next week we _____ in Austria.

7   We _____ to Ireland by ferry this summer.

8   Maybe my father _____ me the money I need.

Exam practice

Listening Part 2

▶08 You will hear a tutor talking to a group of students about a geography trip to New Zealand. For questions **1–10**, complete the sentences with a word or short phrase.

GEOGRAPHY FIELD TRIP

New Zealand was chosen because of the range of **(1)** _____ which can be seen.

The first week concentrates on changes in **(2)** _____ over the last thirty years.

The second week is spent studying the **(3)** _____ on the west coast.

There is a limited chance of seeing a particular kind of **(4)** _____ on the boat trip.

People are often not prepared for the **(5)** _____ on the west coast.

Students should try to take a photograph of the **(6)** _____ if possible.

Students need to write a **(7)** _____ before they leave for New Zealand.

Most students choose to go **(8)** _____ on their free weekend.

Everyone needs to bring at least one **(9)** _____ with them.

Accommodation will be in **(10)** _____ for most of the trip.

> ### Exam tip
> Listen for words in the recording which mean the same as the words around the gap.

Grammar focus task

▶08 Complete these extracts from the Listening task with the correct form of the verbs in brackets. Then listen again to check.

1   Our flight _____ departs _____ (*depart*) at 10.30.

2   During our first week we _____ (*stay*) in a very rural area.

3   We _____ (*go*) on a couple of boat trips.

4   I expect we _____ (*have*) some rain.

5   They _____ (*wait*) for us.

6   We _____ (*work*) all day.

7   I hope you _____ (*get*) some good shots.

8   Maybe we _____ (*see*) some of the fishing boats too.

9   We probably _____ (*not get*) a chance to buy much.

10 We _____ (*hire*) everything we need.

Future (2)

going to; future in the past; present tenses after time conjunctions; future perfect; *to be about to*

A Context listening

1 You are going to hear a man called Simon Trite talking to a group of people on the remote and uninhabited island of Wildrock in the North Atlantic. They went there as an experiment in survival. Simon has just come to the island.

Before you listen, look at the picture and answer these questions.

1   Why do you think Simon has come to the island?
_____

2   What do you think it is like to live on this island?
_____

2 ▶09 Listen and check if you were right.

3 ▶09 Listen again and answer these questions. Stop the recording when you need to.

1   How long were they going to stay on Wildrock? _____ *for at least a year* _____
2   Why are the people going to leave Wildrock? _____
3   When are they going to leave? _____
4   By the end of this week, what will they have achieved? _____
5   By the end of this week, how long will they have been living on Wildrock? _____
6   When are they going to eat a big hot meal? _____
7   Who is going to stay on the island? Why? _____

4 Look at Exercise 3 and answer these questions.

1   Which questions refer only to the future?   _____
2   Which question is about old plans which have been changed?   _____
3   Which questions are about actions which are incomplete now but will be complete at some future time?   _____

B Grammar

1 *going to*

+	am/is/are going to + verb	*I'm going to leave.*
−	am/is/are not going to + verb	*They're not going to leave.*
?	am/is/are ... going to + verb?	*Are you going to leave?*

It is often possible to use *going to* to express the future instead of the present continuous or *will* (▷ see Unit 5). *Going to* is used extremely often in everyday speech. In formal and written English, *will* and the present tenses are generally used more often than *going to*.

We use *going to*:

- for future actions which we have already decided about.

  Compare:
  We're going to pack up our stuff, we're going to send a message to the mainland and we're going to leave. (= the speaker says they already have a clear plan)
  Oh dear! We can't get everything in the boat. We'll leave this stuff behind. (= the speaker decides at that moment) (▷ see Unit 5)
  I'm going to buy a new phone at the weekend because I lost my old one last week and nobody's found it. (= the speaker has decided to replace his phone because he doesn't expect it to be found)
  Look at this phone – it's really cheap. I think I'll buy it. (= the speaker has just seen this phone and is making the decision as he speaks)

- to predict something, when we already see evidence for our prediction:
  It's going to rain soon. (= the speaker knows it's going to rain because he can see the clouds)
  I'm going to enjoy this meal. (= the speaker can see some delicious food on her plate)
  There are many situations when either *going to* or *will* can be used for predictions with no real difference in meaning.

Pronunciation note: *going to* is often pronounced *gonna*. You may see it spelt this way in comic books and pop songs.

2 Future in the past (*was/were going to*)

We use *was/were going to*:

- to talk about something which was planned but did not or will not happen:
  You were going to stay here for at least a year. (= but now you have changed your mind)

- to show that we don't mind changing our plans:
  Ben: Are you busy this evening?
  Jim: Well, I was going to watch a film. (= Jim may forget about the film if Ben suggests a more exciting idea)

3 Present tenses after time conjunctions

In clauses referring to future time and beginning with *when, until, before, after* and *as soon as* we use:

- a present tense (for actions at the same time as the other verb or following the other verb):
  Everyone's going to be very surprised when you arrive.
  Will you phone me before you go on holiday?

- the present perfect (for actions completed before the other verb):
  *And we're not going to talk to any reporters **until** we**'ve had** a long sleep.*
  *I'm going to have a shower **after** I**'ve answered** these emails.*

Sometimes we can use either a present or present perfect tense with the same meaning:
*We're going to eat a big hot meal as soon as we **find** a restaurant.*
*We're going to eat a big hot meal as soon as we**'ve found** a restaurant.*

4　Future perfect simple and future perfect continuous

+	*will have* + past participle	*I**'ll have finished** by six o'clock.*
–	*will not have* + past participle	*He **won't have finished** by six o'clock.*
?	*will … have* + past participle?	*Will you **have finished** by six o'clock?*

We use the future perfect simple to say that an action will be complete before a point of time in the future. It is usual to mention the point in time:
*By the end of this week we**'ll have survived** longer than anyone else.*
*I**'ll have cycled** twelve kilometres by lunchtime.*
*This time next year, she**'ll have finished** university.*
*You**'ll** soon **have earned** enough to replace your phone.*

+	*will have been* + verb + *-ing*	*By one o'clock, I**'ll have been waiting** for three hours.*
–	*will not have been* + verb + *-ing*	*She **won't have been waiting** for long.*
?	*will … have been* + verb + *-ing?*	*Will they **have been waiting** for a long time?*

We use the future perfect continuous to emphasise how long an action will have lasted at a point in the future. It is usually necessary to mention the point of time and the length of time:
*By the end of this week, we**'ll have been living** here for six months.*
*I**'ll have been cycling** for three hours by lunchtime.*

State verbs (➤ see Unit 1, B3) are not used in the future perfect continuous.

5　*to be about to*

+	*am/is/are about to* + verb	*I**'m about to go** out.*
–	*am/is/are not about to* + verb	*He **isn't about to go** out.*
?	*am/is/are … about to* + verb?	*Are you **about to go** out?*

We use *to be about to* to talk about something which is going to happen almost immediately and for which we are already prepared:
*Actually, we**'re about to leave**.*
*I need to talk to you but if you**'re about to start** dinner, I can phone again later.*

In informal language, the negative often means 'do not intend to' do something:
*We **aren't about to change** the rules just because you don't like them.* (= we refuse to change the rules just because you don't like them)
*Barbara wants me to go sky-diving with her, but **I'm not about to do** that!*

C Grammar exercises

1 Look at these pictures and predict what is going to happen. Complete the first sentence using *going to* and the second using *about to*.

1 She *'s going to fall asleep* .   2 They _____ .   3 He _____ .

   She *'s about to fall asleep* .   They _____ .   He _____ .

 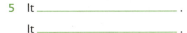 

4 It _____ .   5 It _____ .   6 She _____ .

  It _____ .   It _____ .   She _____ .

2 These are a researcher's notes, with predictions about how the world will have changed by the year 2100. Use the notes to write sentences in the future perfect simple.

> **By the year 2100**
>
> 1 human beings / travel / to Mars
>
> 2 robots / replace / most manual workers
>
> 3 we / use / all the oil resources on Earth
>
> 4 doctors / discover / a cure for the common cold
>
> 5 scientists / invent / new sources of energy
>
> 6 sea temperatures / rise / by several degrees

1 *Human beings will have travelled to Mars.*

2 _____

3 _____

4 _____

5 _____

6 _____

3 Choose the correct sentence from each pair.

1 a I'm not going to pay you until you have cleaned up all this mess! ✓

 b I'm not going to pay you until you'll have cleaned up all this mess!

2 a Paul will probably arrive after all the others will have started work.

 b Paul will probably arrive after all the others have started work.

3 a When you'll see David, will you ask him if he wants to come to the cinema?

 b When you see David, will you ask him if he wants to come to the cinema?

4 a I'll collect your things from the cleaners when I go to the shops tomorrow.

 b I'll collect your things from the cleaners when I'll go to the shops tomorrow.

5 a Margaret's going to phone as soon as she'll have found out what the tickets will cost.

 b Margaret's going to phone as soon as she's found out what the tickets will cost.

4 These people work in a hotel. It's now 12 o'clock. At 2 o'clock, how long will they have been working? Write a sentence about each person, using the future perfect continuous.

1 chef / cook meals (started work at eight o'clock)

 The chef will have been cooking meals for six hours.

2 gardener / cut hedges (started work at ten o'clock)

3 manager / interview new staff (started work at eight thirty)

4 waitress / serve customers in the dining room (started work at eleven o'clock)

5 cleaner / vacuum floors (started work at seven o'clock)

5 Fill in the gaps with the correct form of the verbs. Use *going to*, future in the past, the present simple, *about to* or the future perfect.

A **John:** What are your plans for the weekend?

  Sue: Well, we've just changed our plans, actually. We **(1)** _were going to have_ (*have*) a barbecue on Sunday. But the weather forecast says it **(2)** _____ (*be*) cold and windy, so we **(3)** _____ (*stay*) indoors and watch a film.

B **Beth:** Is it all right for you to use the boss's office while he's on holiday?

  Nick: I don't think he'll mind when he **(4)** _____ (*find out*) how many cars I've sold this week.

C **Terry:** Are you very busy this afternoon?

  Eddy: Well, that depends on why you're asking. I **(5)** _____ (*wash*) the car. Do you have a better idea?

  Terry: Yes. I **(6)** _____ (*look round*) the new sports club. Do you want to come? You can wash the car tomorrow.

  Eddy: Sure. Let's go.

D **Ben:** Hurry up! We **(7)** _____ (*miss*) the beginning of the concert.

  Mary: Don't be silly. We've got plenty of time.

  Ben: But it starts at nine. I want to arrive before the hall **(8)** _____ (*get*) full, otherwise other people **(9)** _____ (*take*) all the good seats by the time we get there.

E **Chloe:** Next month I **(10)** _____ (*work*) in this office for three years. Nobody has ever thanked me for anything I've done, so I **(11)** _____ (*start*) looking for another job!

6 ◉ Correct the mistakes in the following sentences by Cambridge First candidates.

1 Do you remember I ~~am~~ going to buy a computer with the money I earned in the holidays? Well, I changed my mind and I've bought a bike! _____was_____

2 I'll tell you all about it as soon as I will see you. _____

3 Some scientists say by the year 3000 women will take over the world. _____

4 When he will come to my house I will ask him to fix my TV. _____

5 She is retiring next month, so this time next year she will have been leaving the company. _____

6 When you are going to finish the job, the invoice will be paid. _____

7 I need the money today because I will buy a present for my sister after college. _____

Reading and Use of English Part 7

You are going to read an article about young people who have started their own businesses. For questions **1–10**, choose from the people (**A–D**). The people may be chosen more than once.

Which person

advises not giving up at an early stage?	1
is doing something in a way they didn't expect?	2
mentions an advantage they sometimes have over other people in their business?	3
went through a period when they felt unable to cope?	4
realises that their own ways of doing things might not always be the best?	5
realises that their fascination with their present business may not last?	6
says their success has not followed a steady path?	7
mentions how determined they are when they decide to do something?	8
received positive encouragement to start their own business?	9
became aware of how much knowledge they already had in a particular area?	10

I STARTED MY OWN BUSINESS

We talked to four young people who started successful businesses when they were teenagers

A   Santiago has a business designing websites

I was going to do a course in graphic design when I left school but I started doing websites for some of my dad's friends when I was about 17 and realised I had acquired a lot of expertise from doing the school website. Since then I've hardly been without work. I once had a client who didn't find out my age until after they had hired me and they mentioned that they might not have hired me if they had known my age. But I've also often had clients who have done so because of my age so it can work in my favour. When I asked them why, they said it was because they wanted a 'fresh, younger approach' to business.

B   Lucas started a magazine about skateboarding

I wanted to do something that nobody else around me was doing and I love writing so I started my own magazine. I'm like my dad – if he says he's going to do something, nothing will get in the way of that. I started the magazine when I was 13, so by the end of this year I'll have produced 24 editions in four years. At one point recently, I wondered if it was putting too much strain on me with homework and everything. I thought I might have to stop, despite the fact that the magazine was doing well, but I got through that by asking for help from my family and I bounced back. I'll move on to something else if I get bored with it – maybe a blog or something related – but for the moment I still find it inspiring.

C   Yana has a business making videos of musicians

Young and *inexperienced* go together in a lot of people's minds but that's not the way I see it. It's a kind of prejudice. I've certainly come up against it and most young people will face some prejudice before anyone recognises their talent and expertise. When I left school I told my parents I didn't want to go to college. I wanted to be creative and make videos. They told me to give it a go and if it didn't work out after a year, I could reconsider my options. They thought I would always regret it otherwise. I'm not sure I would have gone ahead without them behind me. Some people say, 'This isn't a success and I've been trying for a week' but you have to give it more of a chance. Next month I will have been making videos for a year and they're now getting thousands of hits a day online.

D   Annie has a photography business

You won't know until you try whether a business will work. It's like riding a roller coaster at the funfair. At every turn you take there is another twist to throw you off track. The lows for me have been low, but the highs can be really high and I'm now where I want to be. There will be times, though, when you need to accept advice. If you're still in or just through those teen years and you think you know everything, it's difficult to say to somebody 'You're right about that. How can I improve the way I'm doing this?' It's not something I'm really comfortable with but I've figured out that it is really important if I want to succeed. I always knew I wanted to do something I felt passionate about – and that's photography. I really wasn't interested in business but I ended up starting my own just so I could spend my time doing what I enjoy.

Grammar focus task

Without looking back at the text above, complete these extracts with the correct form of the verbs.

1   I _____*was going to do*_____ (*do*) a course in graphic design but I started doing websites.

2   If he says he _____ (*do*) something, nothing will get in the way of that.

3   By the end of this year I _____ (*produce*) 24 editions in four years.

4   I'll move on to something else when I _____ (*get*) bored with it.

5   Most young people will face some prejudice before anyone _____ (*recognise*) their talent and expertise.

6   Next month I _____ (*make*) videos for a year.

7   You won't know until you _____ (*try*) whether a business will work.

8   There will be times, though, when you _____ (*need*) to accept advice.

Adjectives

Comparative and superlative adjectives; position; order; adjectives ending in -ing and -ed

A Context listening

1   You are going to hear some advertisements. Before you listen, look at the photos and guess what will be advertised.

1 _____   2 _____   3 _____   4 _____

2   ▶10   Listen and check if you were right.

3   ▶10   Listen to the advertisements again and write the words which describe these people and things. Stop the recording when you need to.

1   The sort of person you can become: _____

2   The lions and monkeys: _____

3   The way you feel before phoning The Sparklers: _____

4   The variety of games: _____

4   ▶10   Listen again and fill in the gaps with the words that describe these people and things. Stop the recording when you need to.

1   _professional_ advisers   _____ route   _____ welcome   _____ facilities

2   _____ day out   _____ wildlife park   _____ brochure
    _____ offers

3   _____ carpets   _____ sinks and surfaces   _____ finger marks
    _____ prices

4   _____ savings   _____ road races and fantasy lands   _____ graphics
    _____ battles

B Grammar

1 Comparative and superlative adjectives

Adjectives are words which describe nouns (things and people). ➤ Compare with adverbs in Unit 8.

Adjective	Comparative	Superlative
one syllable *strong* *great*	add *-er* *stronger*	add *-est* *the strongest*
	*You can become **stronger** at Transformers Fitness Centre.* *We've got **the greatest** variety of games ever!*	
two syllables, ending in *-y* *tidy* *funny*	drop *-y* and add *-ier* *tidier*	drop *-y* and add *-iest* *the tidiest*
	*Their flat is **tidier** than ours.* *They're **the funniest** monkeys you've ever seen.*	
two/three/four syllables *famous* *beautiful* *self-confident*	*more* + adjective *more self-confident*	*the most* + adjective *the most self-confident*
	*You can become a **more self-confident** person.* *He is **the most famous** actor in the film.*	

A few two-syllable adjectives (e.g. *quiet, pleasant, common, polite*) sometimes also use *-er* or *-est*:
*It's **quieter** than any garden I've visited before.*

Two-syllable adjectives ending in *-ow* and *-er* can usually add *-er* or *-est*:
clever ➝ *cleverer*   *narrow* ➝ *the narrowest*

Two-syllable adjectives ending in *-le* usually add *-r* or *-st*:
simple ➝ *simpler* ➝ *the simplest*

Most one-syllable adjectives ending in one vowel + *-b, -d, -g, -n, -p* or *-t* double the last letter before adding *-er* or *-est*:
big ➝ *bi**gg**er*   *sad* ➝ *the sa**dd**est*

A few adjectives have irregular comparative and superlative forms:
good ➝ *better* ➝ *best*   *bad* ➝ *worse* ➝ *worst*   *far* ➝ *farther/further* ➝ *farthest/furthest*

2 Comparative structures

We can use comparative structures to say that:

● things are more:
*Our prices are **better than** those of our rivals.*
*We have a **more exciting** range of games **than** you'll see anywhere else.*

● things are less:
*Pre-owned games usually aren't **as/so expensive as** new ones.*
*The games in the sale are much **less expensive than** usual.*

● or things are equal:
*Fantasy games are **as popular as** football games with our customers.*

3 Adjectives ending in *-ing* and *-ed*

Some common adjectives are formed from verbs and have both *-ing* and *-ed* forms.

We use the *-ed* form to describe our feelings:
*I'm **tired**.* (= a description of how I feel: I've used up all my energy so I need a rest)

We use the *-ing* form to describe the things which make us feel like this:
*This work is **tiring**.* (= a description of the work: it takes a lot of energy to do it)

Compare these sentences:

I'm tired.

It's tiring.

*It's a **boring** film.* (= there's no action in it)	*The visitors are **bored**.* (= they have nothing to do)
*We had a **relaxing** holiday.* (= the atmosphere was restful)	*Good driving instructors always have a **relaxed** manner.* (= they don't seem nervous)
*That was a very **satisfying** meal.* (= there was plenty to eat)	*The airline has many **satisfied** customers.* (= the customers feel happy)

4 Adjective position

Adjectives in English usually go in front of the word they describe:
*We visited an **old** house. We saw some **beautiful** paintings and some **elegant** furniture.*

Adjectives can also follow verbs such as *be, get, become, look, seem, appear, sound, taste, smell* and *feel*:
*Everything seemed **pleasant** when we started. The flowers smelt **beautiful** and the gardens looked **wonderful**. But the weather got very **hot** and we all felt **exhausted** by the end of the day.*

There are many nouns in English which are used as adjectives:
*a **diamond** ring   a **library** book   a **seaside** hotel   **folk** music   **strawberry** jam*

5 Adjective order

When we use more than one adjective, we usually put them in a certain order. We say:
a strange old wooden chair (**not** *a wooden old strange chair*)

We usually begin with adjectives which give an opinion or general impression:
*a **dangerous** old car   a **delicate** oval tray   a **valuable** silver spoon*

Adjectives giving factual information usually follow the opinion/impression adjective and go in this order:

	Size	Age	Shape	Colour	Origin	Material	Purpose	
an	enormous	old		red				car
a	small		oval		French			mirror
an		antique				silver	soup	spoon

Two colour adjectives are separated by *and*:
*a **black and white** photograph*

When we put more than one adjective after a verb, we use *and* before the last one:
*The day was **hot and tiring**.*
*Lord Byron was described as **mad**, **bad and dangerous** to know.*

C Grammar exercises

1 Complete this email with the comparative or superlative form of the adjectives and any other words (e.g. *the, as, so, than*) that are needed.

Hi Lily

Well, we've moved at last! When we first got here, the house seemed **(1)** _____larger_____ (*large*) than we remembered, because it was empty, but now it's got our furniture in it, it doesn't feel **(2)** _____ (*spacious*) before. We've got to do some decorating, and that will be **(3)** _____ (*expensive*) we expected because the walls are in a **(4)** _____ (*bad*) condition than we thought. But we'll manage somehow, and soon we'll have **(5)** _____ (*smart*) house in the town. And if your Uncle Bob has his way, we'll have **(6)** _____ (*lovely*) garden as well. We'll also be **(7)** _____ (*poor*) and **(8)** _____ (*exhausted*) householders in the country, but never mind. We still think moving here is **(9)** _____ (*good*) thing we've done for years. We can't imagine now why we didn't do it when we were **(10)** _____ (*young*).

Come and see us soon. Catch a train if you can, because it's almost **(11)** _____ (*cheap*) the bus, and the railway station is **(12)** _____ (*near*) our end of town.

Love, Auntie Rosie

2 Choose the correct adjectives.

1 James told us some *fascinating* / *fascinated* stories about the music business.

2 Why are you looking so *depressing* / *depressed*? What's wrong?

3 Sarah's got an *amazing* / *amazed* collection of computer games.

4 Felix has this really *annoying* / *annoyed* habit of reading my emails.

5 The *boring* / *bored* students started causing trouble in class.

6 I watched the show for a while, but it wasn't really *interesting* / *interested*, so I left.

7 The food in this canteen is absolutely *disgusting* / *disgusted*.

8 The astronaut gave a *relaxing* / *relaxed* wave and entered the space capsule.

3 👁 Correct the mistake in each of the following sentences by Cambridge First candidates.

1 I would like to join the club as I have been ~~interesting~~ in local history for a long time.   ___interested___

2 Young people find it bored to visit art galleries at the weekend.   _____

3 The hotel is situated in a place that is as beautiful than any other place in the country.   _____

4 It is easyer for me to do my studies now that I have bought a computer.   _____

5 It's more quicker to learn a language if you study in that country.   _____

6 I think that animals are more safe in zoos than in other places.   _____

7 If we plant more trees, the city will be greener and pleasanter.   _____

8 She feels even more worse now that everybody knows about her bad news.   _____

4   **Choose the correct sentence from each pair.**

1   a   That was the worse film I've ever seen!

     b   That was the worst film I've ever seen! ✔

2   a   Michael's got a fantastic new leather jacket.

     b   Michael's got a leather new fantastic jacket.

3   a   I didn't eat any bread because I thought it looked as stale.

     b   I didn't eat any bread because I thought it looked stale.

4   a   Our last holiday wasn't so enjoyable than this one.

     b   Our last holiday wasn't so enjoyable as this one.

5   a   The frightening teenagers locked the door and called the police.

     b   The frightened teenagers locked the door and called the police.

6   a   Lucia should catch an earlier train if she wants to get to London by five.

     b   Lucia should catch a more earlier train if she wants to get to London by five.

7   a   Our hockey team plays in blue white striped shirts.

     b   Our hockey team plays in blue and white striped shirts.

8   a   I think your new dress looks beautiful.

     b   I think your new dress looks beautifully.

5   **Look at this designer's sketch of a costume for a film and complete the notes. Fill in the gaps with adjectives for each part of the costume.**

1   an _____ enormous round blue _____ hat

2   a _____ shirt

3   a _____ ring

4   a pair of _____ boots

5   a pair of _____ trousers

Exam practice

Reading and Use of English Part 1

For questions **1–8**, read the text below and decide which answer (**A**, **B**, **C** or **D**) best fits each gap.
There is an example at the beginning (**0**).

Welcome guests?

My wife Penny and I usually love to (**0**) ___A___ our friends but we will never invite my old friend Fred
and his wife Kate again! We are currently (**1**) _____ from the weekend they spent with us. We've known
them both since our school (**2**) _____ . So, although we rarely see them, you'd think we'd have a fairly
(**3**) _____ idea of what sort of people they were. However, we discovered that our lives have
(**4**) _____ very different directions.

We have good jobs but they are very (**5**) _____ and we work long hours. At weekends we try to
snatch a few moments of (**6**) _____ in between catching up with the housework. Kate and Fred are
postgraduate students and they live with his parents. His mother cooks their (**7**) _____ meals for them
and does all their washing. So they (**8**) _____ weekends as leisure time and never think of offering to
help with daily chores.

By the time they left, we were both cross and worn out!

0	**A** entertain	**B** visit	**C** receive	**D** host
1	**A** repairing	**B** recovering	**C** revising	**D** retiring
2	**A** terms	**B** days	**C** times	**D** ages
3	**A** fine	**B** strong	**C** good	**D** right
4	**A** taken	**B** left	**C** chosen	**D** gone
5	**A** exhausted	**B** tired	**C** demanding	**D** caring
6	**A** extension	**B** relaxation	**C** expression	**D** reflection
7	**A** major	**B** essential	**C** key	**D** main
8	**A** regard	**B** believe	**C** think	**D** expect

Grammar focus task

1 The words in the box are from the exam text. Which of them are adjectives and which of them are nouns
that can be used as adjectives?

daily	different	good	leisure	long	main	old	school	postgraduate

2 Without looking back to the text, match each word from the box with the noun it describes in the text.

1 ___daily___ chores   4 _____ idea   7 _____ students
2 _____ friend   5 _____ directions   8 _____ meals
3 _____ days   6 _____ hours   9 _____ time

8 Adverbs

Adverb forms; adverbs and adjectives easily confused;
comparative and superlative adverbs; modifiers; adverb position

A Context listening

1 You are going to hear the beginning of a radio commentary on a football match. Before you listen, think about what you can see and hear at a match. Tick the words you think you might hear.

- ☐ ball ☐ chair ☐ goal ☐ ground ☐ helmet ☐ loudly ☐ peacefully
- ☐ quickly ☐ racket ☐ scored ☐ shyly ☐ stadium ☐ spectators ☐ whistle

2 ▶11 Listen and check if you were right. Number the words in the order you hear them and cross out the ones you don't hear.

3 ▶11 Listen again and fill in the gaps. Stop the recording when you need to.

1 And _____*finally*_____ the players are coming onto the pitch.

2 There were such terrible traffic jams _____ that the match is starting _____ .

3 Most of the spectators have been waiting _____ since two o'clock.

4 As the players come out they're cheering _____ .

5 Rossi has the ball and is running _____ down the pitch.

6 He's fallen _____ .

7 He's so experienced in these kinds of conditions that he _____ falls.

8 Parker is playing incredibly _____ .

9 _____ he scored the winning goal.

10 It's _____ Parker who scores that important goal.

4 All the words you have filled in for Exercise 3 are adverbs or adverbial phrases. They tell us about when, where, how or how often something happened. Write them in the correct place in the table below.

When?	Where?	How?	How often?
finally	*in the city*	*patiently*	*rarely*

There are four adverbs in Exercise 1. Which column do they go in?

B Grammar

1 Adverb forms

Adjectives (*happy*) tell us about a noun. Adverbs (*happily*) tell us about a verb, an adjective or another adverb.

Adverbs can give us information about time (when?), place (where?), manner (how?) and frequency (how often?).

Sometimes we use a phrase instead of one word:
__This morning__ I feel happy because the weather is __pleasantly__ warm. Some children are playing __happily in the__
__street__ and a blackbird is singing very __beautifully__.

Most adverbs are formed by adding *-ly* to an adjective:
sad → *sadly*   *safe* → *safely*   *hopeful* → *hopefully*

There is a spelling change in adjectives ending *-y* or *-able/-ible* when they become adverbs:
angry → *angrily*   *miserable* → *miserably*

An adjective ending in *-ly* (*friendly, likely, lively, lonely, lovely, silly, ugly*) cannot be made into an adverb. We have to use an adverbial phrase instead:
She started the interview __in a friendly manner__.
He laughed __in a silly way__.

2 Adverbs and adjectives easily confused

Some adjectives and adverbs have the same form. Some common ones are *fast, early, hard, late, daily*:

He caught the __early__ train. (adjective)	*He always arrives __early__.* (adverb)
She's a __hard__ worker. (adjective)	*She works __hard__.* (adverb)
The bus is always __late__. (adjective)	*I got home __late__.* (adverb)
My __daily__ coffee costs £2.50. (adjective)	*I swim __daily__.* (adverb)

⚠ *Hard* and *hardly* are both adverbs but they have different meanings. *Hardly* means 'almost not' and it is often used with *ever* and *any*. It can go in various positions in the sentence:
She __hardly__ noticed when he came into the room. (= she almost didn't notice)
I had __hardly__ finished my breakfast when they arrived. (= only just)
Rachel is __hardly ever__ absent. (= almost never)
There was __hardly anyone__ in the cinema. (= almost nobody)
__Hardly any__ of the children could read. (= almost none of them)

⚠ *Late* and *lately* are both adverbs but they have different meanings. *Lately* means 'recently':
I haven't read any good books __lately__.

⚠ The adverb for *good* is *well*, but *well* can also be an adjective which means the opposite of *ill*:
It was a good concert. The musicians played __well__. (= adverb)
I had a bad headache yesterday but I'm __well__ today. (= adjective)

Some verbs are followed by adjectives, not adverbs (➤ see Unit 7, B4).

3 Comparative and superlative adverbs

Most adverbs use *more* or *less* to make comparatives and *the most* or *the least* to make superlatives:
My brother speaks Italian __more fluently__ than me.
I speak Italian __less fluently__ than my brother does.
Of all the students, Maria speaks English __the most fluently__.

Adverbs without -ly make comparatives and superlatives in the same way as short adjectives (➤ see Unit 7, B1):

hard → harder → hardest   high → higher → highest   late → later → latest
I work hard, my sister works **harder** than I do but Alex works **the hardest**.

⚠ Note also: early → earlier → earliest (**not** ~~more early~~ / ~~the most early~~)

Some comparative and superlative adverbs are irregular:

well → better → best   badly → worse → worst   far → farther/further → farthest/furthest

Adverbs use the same comparative structures as adjectives:
I can't add up **as quickly as** you can.
They arrived **later than** us.

4   Modifying adverbs and adjectives

Some adverbs are used to change the strength of adjectives or other adverbs.

| incredibly | extremely | really | very | rather | fairly | quite | slightly |

← **stronger**   **weaker** →

He dances **extremely** well.   The weather was **very** hot.
He spoke to her **rather** fiercely.   The house was **quite** old.

Some adjectives (e.g. perfect, impossible, excellent) can only be strengthened with adverbs like completely, absolutely, totally, entirely:
This crossword puzzle is **completely** impossible. (not ~~very impossible~~)

5   Adverb position

The most common position for most adverbs is after the verb, or after the object of the verb if there is one. However, they may also go before the verb or at the beginning of a sentence for emphasis:
He packed his suitcase **carefully**. (end-position)
He **carefully** packed his suitcase. (mid-position)
Carefully, he packed his **suitcase**. (front-position)

⚠ An adverb does not usually go between a verb and its object:
(**not** ~~He packed carefully his suitcase.~~)

If there are several adverbs and/or adverbial phrases in the end-position, we usually put them in this order:

                how?   where?   when?
The meeting took place   **unexpectedly**   **in the Town Hall**   **last Tuesday**.

Frequency adverbs (which tell us how often) are usually in the mid-position before a single word verb:
I **usually travel** by train.

but after am/is/are/was/were:
I **am often** late.

If the verb has two or more parts, the frequency adverb usually goes after the first part:
I **have never been** to this part of town before.

Adverbs can sometimes go in the front-position to give special emphasis to how, when or how often:
Angrily, she stormed out of the room.
Sometimes we shop at a supermarket, but **usually** we go to the market.

Opinion adverbs, which tell us about the speaker's attitude to the situation, usually go in the front-position, often followed by a comma:
Luckily, we found the money which I thought I'd lost.
Actually, I don't agree with what you said.
In fact, the weather was better than we'd expected.

C Grammar exercises

1 Fill in the gaps using the adverb form of the adjectives in brackets.

1 Franca picked up the sleeping baby ____gently____ (*gentle*).

2 When she handed him his lost wallet, he smiled at her _____ (*grateful*).

3 Irma couldn't see her son anywhere and called his name _____ (*anxious*).

4 They followed the directions to the hotel _____ (*easy*).

5 Tomo admitted his mistake and apologised _____ (*sincere*).

6 I can't text as _____ as my sister. (*fast*)

7 You have to press the button _____ to make the machine start. (*hard*)

8 The taxi driver was _____ rude to the man with the big suitcase. (*terrible*)

2 Choose the correct words.

1 Eleni stepped *confident / confidently* onto the stage to begin her talk.

2 The meeting at lunchtime was a *complete / completely* waste of time.

3 Marushka did *good / well* in the exam and she won a prize.

4 Mark tried *hard / hardly* to make the hotel receptionist understand him, but his Spanish wasn't *fluent / fluently* enough.

5 After looking at the computer screen all day, I had an *awful / awfully* headache.

6 Even though Deborah did the job *efficient / efficiently*, they sacked her after two months.

7 The doctor couldn't understand why Carol felt so hot because her temperature was *normal / normally*.

8 The boy behaved *bad / badly* on a school trip so the school refused to take him on any more.

9 The hotel was *far / further* from the station than we'd expected.

3 Rewrite these sentences with the adverbs and adverbial phrases in suitable positions.

1 Pavel plays the guitar well for his age. (*incredibly*)
Pavel plays the guitar incredibly well for his age.

2 They eat steak because it is so expensive. (*rarely, nowadays*)
_____

3 My grandfather used to take us swimming. (*in the summer holidays, in the lake*)
_____

4 There is a good film on TV. (*usually, on Sunday evenings*)
_____

5 My mother insisted that good manners are important. (*terribly, always*)
_____

6 The party had started when the sound system broke, which meant we couldn't dance. (*hardly, all evening*)
_____

4 **Complete the text below with these adverbs.**

| always   earlier   hardly   now   rather   ~~silently~~   skilfully   stiffly   very   warmly |

She shut the door (1) ___silently___ after her. Her father wasn't expecting her – she had arrived
(2) _____ than she had said. He was sitting where he (3) _____ sat, in his favourite
armchair by the window. It was (4) _____ old but had been repaired (5) _____ so that
he could continue using it. The room had been redecorated since her last visit and was looking
(6) _____ elegant. On the shelves were all the books which her father (7) _____ ever
looked at any more.

She called his name. He stood up and she noticed that he moved very (8) _____ . He smiled
and held out his arms to her. She hadn't been in touch with him for five years but (9) _____ he
welcomed her as (10) _____ as he always had.

5 **Choose the correct sentence from each pair.**

1 a The child spread the jam thickly on the piece of bread. ✓

   b The child spread thickly the jam on the piece of bread.

2 a My grandmother drives more careful since she got older.

   b My grandmother drives more carefully since she got older.

3 a I never have bought anything from that expensive shop over there.

   b I have never bought anything from that expensive shop over there.

4 a Unfortunately, we can't come to the party after all.

   b We can't unfortunately come to the party after all.

5 a My uncle speaks Spanish very well because he lived in Peru for a while.

   b My uncle speaks very well Spanish because he lived in Peru for a while.

6 a My sister doesn't make friends as easily than I do.

   b My sister doesn't make friends as easily as I do.

6 👁 **Correct the mistake in each of the following sentences by Cambridge First candidates.**

1 The new trains will help them to get back to their homes ~~quicklier~~.   ___more quickly___

2 The new computer system means that you can find what you are looking for more easy. _____

3 The teacher was happy with our work because we had worked hardly all day. _____

4 I like shoes really much because they say so much about a person. _____

5 We had a party on the beach and it was very fun. _____

6 You have to pay attention very well carefully to your health and eat properly. _____

7 If you go and live in Paris for a year, you will be able to speak French fluent. _____

8 You need to dress good for the interview, so they think you are professional. _____

Exam practice

Reading and Use of English Part 3

For questions **1–8**, read the text below. Use the word given in capitals at the end of some of the lines to form a word that fits in the gap in **the same line**. There is an example at the beginning **(0)**.

ASTRONAUTS

There are two types of astronaut. Some people are **(0)** _commanders_ and
they fly the spacecraft. Others are carefully trained specialists who conduct
(1) _____ experiments of various kinds and also carry out spacewalks
to repair damaged **(2)** _____ .

COMMAND

SCIENCE
EQUIP

Astronauts must pass a lot of medical tests and be qualified in a relevant subject.
They have to be willing to live in an **(3)** _____ small space and work well
with other people. It is possible for experiments to go **(4)** _____ wrong,
threatening the **(5)** _____ of the astronauts. They have to be able
to react calmly in a difficult situation and they must also be prepared to work hard.

EXTREME
DANGER
SAFE

The first British astronaut was, **(6)** _____ , a woman – most astronauts
are male. Helen Sharman got the job after hearing an announcement on the radio.
There were 18,000 applicants and, **(7)** _____ for Helen, she was chosen.
She said that the most **(8)** _____ thing for her was seeing the Earth from
120 miles into space.

USUAL

LUCK
AMAZE

> 💡 **Exam tip**
>
> You will need to make more than one change to some words.

Grammar focus task

Find eight adverbs in the completed text above. Write the adverb and the adjective which it comes from.

1   _carefully_   _careful_
2   _____   _____
3   _____   _____
4   _____   _____
5   _____   _____
6   _____   _____
7   _____   _____
8   _____   _____

9 Questions

yes /no questions; short answers; question words; question tags; agreeing

A Context listening

1 You are going to hear a telephone conversation between Mina and her father. Before you listen, look at the picture. Why do you think her father is phoning?

2 ▶12 Listen and check if you were right.

3 ▶12 Listen again and answer these questions.

1 What did Mina forget to do? _____ *charge her phone* _____
2 How many times did her father text Mina and get no answer? _____
3 What had Mina promised to do? _____
4 How do Mina's parents feel when she's away at college? _____
5 What's happening at the weekend? _____
6 Where will they meet? _____
7 What are Mina and her father looking forward to? _____

4 ▶12 Listen again and write down the question for each of these replies. Then circle the verbs in the questions and the replies.

1 (Have) you (charged) your phone at last?   Yes, I (have).
2 _____   No, I haven't.
3 _____   Yes, I did.
4 _____   Yes, of course I do.
5 _____   Don't worry, I will.
6 _____   Yes, I can.
7 _____   Yes, it does.
8 _____   No, she doesn't.
9 _____   Oh yes, let's.

B Grammar

1 Making *yes/no* questions

To make questions which can be answered with *yes* or *no*:

- we put the auxiliary verb before its subject:
  You're going on holiday soon. ➝ *Are you going* on holiday soon?
  He's packed his case. ➝ *Has he packed* his case?

- in the present simple or past simple (➢ see Units 1 and 2), we use the auxiliary verb *do/does* or *did* to make the question:
  I like Italy. ➝ *Do you like* Italy?
  She prefers Greece. ➝ *Does she prefer* Greece? (not ~~*Does she prefers*~~)
  They went to Corsica. ➝ *Did they go* to Corsica?

- with the verb *to be*, we put *to be* before the subject:
  They're in Madrid today. ➝ *Are they* in Madrid today?

- with modal verbs, we put the modal verb before the subject:
  We can stay here. ➝ *Can we stay* here?

Negative questions often express surprise:
Don't they like big cities? (= I thought they liked big cities. Am I wrong?)
Can't she stay here? (= I thought she could stay here. Is that impossible?)

2 Short answers for *yes/no* questions

We answer a *yes/no* question using the same auxiliary or modal verb as in the question:

Is she staying in Spain?	Yes, she **is**. / No, she **isn't**.
Have you been to New York?	Yes, I **have** / No, I **haven't**.
Are you going to Greece?	Yes, I **am**. / No, I'm **not**.
Did they like the hotel?	Yes, they **did**. / No, they **didn't**.
Can we book our flight online?	Yes, we **can**. / No, we **can't**.
Should I contact the police?	Yes, you **should**. / No, you **shouldn't**.

3 Making questions with question words

When we use *What*, *Which* or *Who* to make questions about the **subject** of the verb, we do not change the word order (unlike *yes/no* questions):
The pool looks too small. ➝ *What* looks too small? (Answer: The pool.)
This hotel offers the best view. ➝ *Which hotel* offers the best view? (Answer: This hotel.)

In a subject question, *who* is always followed by a singular verb:
Who is coming to your party? (**not** ~~Who are coming?~~)
unless two or more people are actually mentioned in the question:
Who are your favourite **singers**?

When we use *What*, *Which* or *Who* to make questions about the **object** of the verb, we change the word order (as in *yes/no* questions).
This hotel offers **the best view**. ➝*What does* this hotel **offer**? (Answer: The best view.)

Compare these subject and object questions:
Molly's visiting Shirin ➝ *Who's visiting Shirin?* **Molly**. (*Who* = subject)
Molly's visiting **Shirin**. ➝ *Who's Molly visiting?* **Shirin**. (*Who* = object)

When we use other question words (*When*, *Why*, *How*, etc.) we change the word order in the same way as in *yes/no* questions:

They'll be in Madrid tomorrow. → *When **will they be** in Madrid?* (Answer: Tomorrow.)
We can't stay here because it's full. → *Why **can't we stay** here?* (Answer: Because it's full.)
She prefers to travel by train. → *How **does she prefer** to travel?* (Answer: By train.)

⚠ Remember the difference between these questions with *like*:

*What **does** Molly **like**?* (= what does she enjoy?)	*She likes dancing.*
*What **does** Molly **look like**?* (= tell me about her appearance)	*She's pretty.*
*What **is** Molly **like**?* (= tell me about her character and/or appearance)	*She's intelligent and pretty.*

4 Question tags

We often make a statement into a question by adding a question tag at the end. The verb in the tag must match the form of the auxiliary verb in the statement.
If the statement is positive, the tag is negative:

    +   –

*They**'re** going to Greece, **aren't they**?* (the speaker expects the answer *yes*)

If the statement is negative, the tag is positive:

    –   +

*You **aren't** going to Greece, **are you**?* (the speaker expects the answer *no*)

We make question tags:
- with *do/does* or *did* for all verbs in the present simple or past simple except *to be*:

*You **like** the seaside, **don't you**?*	*You **don't like** the seaside, **do you**?*
*Molly **prefers** Greece, **doesn't she**?*	*Molly **doesn't prefer** Greece, **does she**?*
*Your **friends are** in Madrid, **aren't they**?*	*Your **friends aren't** in Madrid now, **are they**?*

- with the same auxiliary or modal as in the statement for verbs in other tenses:

  *They **haven't** arrived yet, **have they**?*
  *We **can** stay here, **can't we**?*

The question tag for *I am* is *aren't I?*:
*I'm doing the right exercise, **aren't I**?*

The question tag for *I'm not* is *am I?*:
*I'm **not** in the right place, **am I**?*

The question tag for *let's* is *shall we?*:
*Let's go to France, **shall we?***

We use question tags:
- to check that what we have just said is true – our voice does not rise at the end:

  *They're going to Greece, **aren't they?*** (= I'm almost certain they're going there, but will you confirm this?)

- to ask for information – our voice rises at the end:

  *They're going to Greece, **aren't they?*** (= I'm not sure if that's where they're going – will you tell me?)

5 Agreeing with statements

To agree with statements we use *so* for positive statements and *neither* or *nor* for negative statements, and we put the verb before its subject. We can do this

- with the verb *to be* or with a modal:
  He was really angry. **So was I.**
  He can't speak French. **Nor can we.**

- with an auxiliary verb:
  I went to Spain last year. **So did they.**
  I don't want to have a fight about it. **Neither do I.**

C Grammar exercises

1   **Choose the correct verb forms in these sentences.**

1   Who *did make / made* the cake for the wedding?

2   We haven't got to do the washing-up, *do we / have we*?

3   Does your sister live with your parents or *she has got / has she got* a flat of her own?

4   Why *can't you walk / you can't walk* faster?

5   You went to school in Paris, *didn't you / haven't you*?

6   What *does / is* Julie's brother look like?

7   **A:** Can Sylvia come to the barbecue?   **B:** No, she *doesn't / can't*.

8   Which shoes *do you prefer / prefer you* – the flat ones or the ones with high heels?

9   **A:** Are they going to record a new album?   **B:** Yes, they *do / are*.

10   **A:** Who *did you invite / invited you* to the party ?   **B:** Robbie. He called me last week.

2   👁   **Correct the mistake in each of the following sentences by Cambridge First candidates.**

1   Why ~~he doesn't~~ call me directly if he is having problems?   *doesn't he*

2   How much costs it to study English in London?   _____

3   What you are bringing on the trip with you?   _____

4   What does annoy you most about your job?   _____

5   Where was you going when you saw James?   _____

6   Who did paint the picture you have on the wall?   _____

7   Why you don't come to visit me next weekend?   _____

8   How long it lasts the cookery course?   _____

3   **Add the correct question tags to these questions.**

1   The teachers didn't see me, _____ *did they* _____ ?

2   He always forgets his homework, _____ ?

3   You would like to come with us, _____ ?

4   I've got plenty of time, _____ ?

5   Let's have another coffee, _____ ?

6   It couldn't possibly rain, _____ ?

7   Those men played really well, _____ ?

8   Molly will have to tell the truth, _____ ?

9   We can't stop here, _____ ?

10   You promise not to tell anyone, _____ ?

4 Read this article and write questions to match the answers given below.

LAST NIGHT BRIAN BAINES was celebrating his appointment as manager of Farley City Football Club. He says he is particularly happy to be going back to Farley, where he was born in 1978, after playing for a number of European teams.

Baines telephoned his wife Shirley as soon as he had signed the contract. He said that she is really pleased that their three children will be able to settle at schools in the city. Their many old friends are looking forward to welcoming them back to Farley.

1 *What was Brian Baines celebrating last night?*

His appointment as manager of Farley City Football Club.

2 _____

In Farley.

3 _____

His wife Shirley.

4 _____

As soon as he had signed the contract.

5 _____

Three.

6 _____

Because their children will be able to settle at schools in Farley.

7 _____

Their many old friends.

5 Match the statements with the short answers.

1	I started learning English when I was ten.	A	So am I.
2	I didn't find it very easy.	B	Neither will I.
3	I was always trying to sing English songs.	C	Nor did I.
4	But I couldn't understand the words at first.	D	So did I.
5	I'm quite good at English now.	E	So must I.
6	I've read a couple of novels in English.	F	So have I.
7	I won't have many problems in England, I guess.	G	Neither could I.
8	I must do my homework now.	H	So was I.

Exam practice

Listening Part 1

▶13 You will hear people talking in eight different situations. For questions **1–8**, choose the best answer (**A**, **B** or **C**).

1 You overhear a girl leaving a voicemail message. Why is she calling?

   A to issue an invitation

   B to ask for some advice

   C to change an arrangement

2 You hear two friends talking about the weekend. What is Martin annoyed about?

   A The adventure camp wasn't what he expected.

   B He didn't have any friends with him.

   C His brother hadn't explained his plans fully.

3 You hear two students talking about a school project. What do they decide about their projects?

   A They will do the project together.

   B They will do projects in the same field.

   C They need more time to plan their projects.

4 You hear two people talking about a gym. What do they agree about?

   A It should provide a wider range of classes.

   B It should have better equipment.

   C It should have longer opening hours.

5 You hear a girl talking about a website. What pleased her about it?

   A how easy it is to use

   B how detailed the information is

   C how up to date it is

6 You hear a man talking about his job. What does he dislike about it?

   A working at night

   B getting no exercise

   C dealing with customers

7 You hear a teacher talking to a group of students. What will the weather be like tomorrow?

   A It will get warmer during the day.

   B There will be some rain in the morning.

   C There might be thunderstorms later.

8 You hear two people talking about someone they met. What do they agree about?

   A He talked too much.

   B He had interesting things to say.

   C He was amusing.

 Exam tip

The question tells you who the people are and exactly what to listen for.

Grammar focus task

These sentences are from the recording. Complete the missing question tags.

1 You know what I mean, _____*don't you*_____ ?

2 That wasn't why we went, _____ ?

3 We can help each other out, _____ ?

4 They'd get more people using the gym then, _____ ?

5 You've looked at the websites Mrs Wilson recommended, _____ ?

6 You're not working today, _____ ?

7 You won't forget them, _____ ?

8 You didn't really think his jokes were funny, _____ ?

Countable and uncountable nouns; articles

Countable and uncountable nouns; *a(n)*, *the* and no article; special uses of articles

A Context listening

1 You are going to hear four people talk about their jobs. Look at the pictures and guess what jobs they do.

1 _____   2 _____
3 _____   4 _____

2 ▶14 Listen and check if you were right.

3 ▶14 Listen again and answer these questions.

1 What does Angela's company make? _____ *furniture* _____
2 What important part of her work does she mention? _____
3 What does she care about? _____
4 Which drivers really annoy Ken? _____
5 What does he say motorists should have? _____
6 Why does Charlie deliver pizzas? _____
7 What subject is he studying? _____
8 What is terrible, according to Hazel? _____
9 Why does she say she mustn't grumble? _____

4 ▶14 Listen again and answer these questions.

1 What does Angela avoid eating? _____
2 Where does Ken work? _____
3 What does Charlie deliver? _____
4 What does Charlie usually avoid? _____
5 What sort of job does he want when he graduates? _____
6 What does Hazel say about her family? _____

5 Look at the nouns in your answers to Exercise 3 and compare them with the nouns in your answers to Exercise 4. Can you say how they are different?

_____

B Grammar

1 Countable and uncountable nouns

Countable nouns:

- can be singular:
  a company, a job, a biscuit
- or plural:
  many companies, few jobs, some biscuits

Uncountable nouns:

- cannot be plural:
  health, advice, luggage, scenery (**not** *healths, advices, luggages, sceneries*)
- take a singular verb:
  Petrol *is expensive.*   **Exercise** *is good for you.*
- use expressions like *a piece of* to refer to quantity:
  a piece of furniture, a piece of advice, a sum of money, a litre of petrol (**not** *a furniture, an advice, a money, a petrol*)

⚠ *News* is uncountable and takes a singular verb, even though it looks plural. We say:
an item / a piece of news (not *a news*)

Many nouns can be countable and uncountable, but with different meanings:

These grammar **exercises** *are easy!* (= tasks for practising grammar)
Exercise *is good for you.* (= taking exercise in general)

The gallery was showing **works** *by several artists.* (= paintings, sculptures, etc.)
I don't enjoy hard **work**. (= the activity of working)

The French produce some wonderful **cheeses**. (= different types of cheese)
Do we have any **cheese** *in the fridge?* (= cheese in general)

2 *a(n)*, *the* and no article

	Means:	Introduces:	Use it with:
a(n)	• one of many • anyone/anything like this	• a person/thing we haven't identified before • an unspecific person/thing • a general type of person/thing	singular countable nouns
the	• the particular one(s) • the only one(s)	• a person/people/thing(s) we have mentioned before • someone/something that is unique • someone/something that the speaker and listener already know about	singular countable nouns plural countable nouns uncountable nouns
no article	• all of these • the quantity is uncertain or unimportant	• things/people in general • a general type of substance, quality, etc.	plural countable nouns uncountable nouns

Compare the use of articles in these sentences:

*There's **a supermarket** in most towns nowadays.* (= one of many that exist)
*We buy most of our food from **the local supermarket**.* (= one particular supermarket near our house)

*Have you got **a pen**?* (= one of many that exist)
***The pen** is on **the table**.* (= the only pen here; the only table here)

*I don't like **the music** my brother plays.* (= that particular music)
***Music** helps me to concentrate when I'm working.* (= any music)

*We planted **the trees** in our garden five years ago.* (= the particular trees in our garden)
***Trees** are easily damaged by **pollution**.* (= all trees; any pollution)
***Trees** are good for **the environment**.* (= all trees; the only environment we have)

***The cheese** is in **the fridge**.* (= the cheese you need; the only fridge here)
*I like **cheese**.* (= all kinds of cheese)

***People** used to believe **the moon** was **a goddess**.* (= people in general; the moon that goes round this planet; one of many goddesses)

3 Special uses of articles

Look out for special uses of articles. Here are some common examples.

Places

We use *the* with the names of:
- oceans, seas and rivers:
  the Pacific, the Black Sea, the Danube
- regions:
  the Far East, the Midlands
- groups of islands:
  the Philippines
- countries that include a word such as *Republic, Kingdom, States* or *Emirates*:
  the United States, the People's Republic of China, the United Arab Emirates
- deserts and mountain ranges:
  the Kalahari, the Alps

We say: *the sea, the coast, the seaside, the country(side), the mountains, the hills*:
*My parents spend their holidays on **the coast**, but I prefer walking in **the mountains**.*

We do not use *the* with the names of:
- lakes:
  Lake Garda
- continents, most countries, states, cities, towns and villages:
  Europe, France, Florida, Rome

  ⚠ but we say *the Netherlands, The Hague*
- most buildings and places such as schools, universities, stations and airports that use the name of their town in the name:
  Manchester Airport, Cardiff station, Edinburgh Castle, Durham University, Chelmsford High School, Wembley Stadium

  ⚠ but when the name includes *of* we use *the*:
  the University of Rome, the Museum of London

Fixed expressions
Some fixed expressions use *the* and some have no article:
*We travel **by train/bus**.* (**not** *by the train/bus*)
*We **have lunch/dinner**.* but if there is an adjective, we use *a*: *I had a **big breakfast** today.*
*We listen to **the radio**.* but *We watch **television**.*
*We play **the guitar**.* (= a musical instrument) but *We **play tennis**.* (= a sport).
*We go to **the cinema** or **the theatre**.*
*We say: My mother is **at work**.* but *My mother is **at the office**.* (= the office where she works)

⚠ We use *the* or no article before some places, with a difference in meaning:
*The children are **at school** now.* (= they are students there)
*My father is **at the school** now.* (= he is visiting it)

*Peter spent a lot of time **in hospital** as a child.*
(= he was a patient)

*Dr Dibble has an office **in the hospital** and*
another at home. (= she works there)

This also applies to *at church, in prison, at college* and *at university*, but we always say **the** *mosque,* **the** *temple.*

Jobs

We use *a(n)* when we talk about someone's occupation:
*I'm **a doctor**.* (**not** ~~I'm doctor~~)
*She's **a website designer**.*
*I'm **a student**.*

Publications and organisations

We use *the* for most newspapers:
The *Australian,* **The** *Guardian,* **The** *Dartmouth Chronicle*

and many organisations, in words or initials:
the *UN / United Nations,* **the** *BBC / British Broadcasting Corporation,* **the** *WHO / World Health Organisation*

but not for most magazines:
Vogue, Wired, Sports Illustrated

or companies:
Volkswagen, Apple, Microsoft, Gucci

Online

We say **the internet** and **the web** but *Wikipedia, Facebook, Twitter.*

Definitions

We use *a(n)* to give a definition of something:
***A department store** is a shop which sells a wide range of goods.* (**not** ~~Department store is~~ ...)

Exclamations

We use *a(n)* with a singular noun in exclamations:
*What **an exciting film**!* (**not** ~~What exciting film!~~)
*What **a gorgeous dress**!*

but no article if the noun is uncountable or plural:
*What **fun**!* (**not** ~~What a fun!~~)
*What **lovely flowers**!*

C Grammar exercises

1 Match the phrases on the left with the uncountable nouns on the right. Some of the phrases match more than one noun.

1	a tube of	A	glass
2	a sheet of	B	meat
3	a drop of	C	paper
4	a bar of	D	news
5	an item of	E	rice
6	a grain of	F	oil
7	a slice of	G	toothpaste
		H	chocolate
		I	bread

2 Complete the diagram with the words that belong in each group.

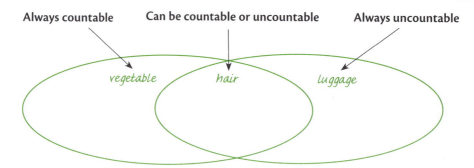

accommodation advice cheese coffee experience experiment glass ~~hair~~ hobby homework information journey leisure luck ~~luggage~~ meat scenery time traffic ~~vegetable~~

Always countable   Can be countable or uncountable   Always uncountable

vegetable   *hair*   *luggage*

3 Complete the recipe with *a, an, the* or – (for no article).

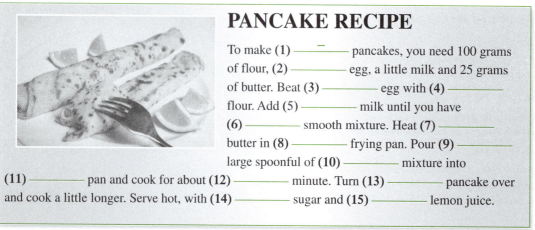

PANCAKE RECIPE

To make **(1)** ――― pancakes, you need 100 grams of flour, **(2)** ――― egg, a little milk and 25 grams of butter. Beat **(3)** ――― egg with **(4)** ――― flour. Add **(5)** ――― milk until you have **(6)** ――― smooth mixture. Heat **(7)** ――― butter in **(8)** ――― frying pan. Pour **(9)** ――― large spoonful of **(10)** ――― mixture into **(11)** ――― pan and cook for about **(12)** ――― minute. Turn **(13)** ――― pancake over and cook a little longer. Serve hot, with **(14)** ――― sugar and **(15)** ――― lemon juice.

4 Fill in the gaps with the words in brackets, adding *a* or *the* where necessary.

1 We've got some important visitors flying in from _____the West Indies_____ next week. Can you meet them at _____ ? (*West Indies, Birmingham Airport*)

2 How long does it take to sail across _____ from _____ to _____ ? (*Mediterranean, Naples, Corsica*)

3 My brother's idea of a holiday is trekking across _____ or exploring _____ . Personally, I'd rather explore _____ and do some shopping! (*Sahara, Andes, Paris*)

4 Have you met Cora's new boyfriend? He's _____ from _____ . (*ski instructor, Switzerland*)

5 What _____ ! Our train broke down and there was no wifi so I couldn't even use _____ . Luckily, another passenger lent me a magazine called _____ . It had an article about some new software that _____ has developed. (*terrible journey, internet, Computer User, Microsoft*)

5 Correct the mistakes in this email.

Hi Monique

We had $\overset{a}{\wedge}$ great trip to the France last weekend. We went to little hotel that you recommended and it was very pleasant. Foods at the hotel weren't so good, as you warned us, but we strolled down to city centre on Saturday evening and had lovely meal there. In fact, we ate so much for the dinner that we didn't want a breakfast on Sunday! Thanks again for the advice. The Wikipedia gave us some good informations about the town, but your local knowledge really helped. Now I must unpack and do the washings. Here is photo of the hotel to remind you.

xx Freda

6 👁 Choose the correct words (or – for no article) in these sentences by Cambridge First students.

1 I thought that he would eat all the food because <u>it</u> / *they* looked really nice.

2 If I have to give you *an* / – advice, I think you should give up sport for now.

3 Yesterday I finished work early and did some *shopping* / *shoppings*.

4 I would like to have some *information* / *informations* about the courses that you are offering.

5 I think I will sell the bedroom *furniture* / *furnitures* when I move house.

6 We should feel – / *a* respect for the man who invented this machine.

Exam practice

Reading and Use of English Part 4

For questions **1–6**, complete the second sentence so that it has a similar meaning to the first sentence, using the word given. **Do not change the word given.** You must use between **two** and **five** words, including the word given. There is an example at the beginning **(0)**.

0   The hotel staff had permission to use the tennis courts on Mondays.

   ALLOWED

   The hotel staff _____ *were allowed to play* _____ tennis on Mondays.

1   Alison loves to buy presents for her grandchildren.

   PLEASURE

   Alison _____ presents for her grandchildren.

2   My boss advised me which computer I should buy.

   GAVE

   My boss _____ choosing a computer.

3   We've been queuing for an hour and we still have another hour to wait.

   WAITING

   By the time we get to the front of the queue we _____ two hours.

4   Although Toby keeps his room tidy he seldom cleans it.

   EVER

   Toby keeps his room tidy _____ cleans it.

5   Can you tell me precisely how much money was stolen?

   EXACT

   Can you tell me _____ that was stolen?

6   The announcer began the news with a story about the prince's visit.

   ITEM

   The first _____ a story about the prince's visit.

> **Exam tip**
>
> Contracted words like *they've* count as two words so make sure you don't write more than five words.

Grammar focus task

Which of these nouns from the exam task are countable (C), which are uncountable (U) and which can be both (B)? Use your dictionary if you need to.

1   permission   *U*

2   pleasure   _____

3   advice   _____

4   queue   _____

5   room   _____

6   money   _____

7   item   _____

8   news   _____

Modals (1)

Use of modals; rules and obligation; necessity

A Context listening

1   You are going to hear a conversation between a man called Krish and a boy called Ahmed. Look at the picture of Krish. What can you guess about his daily routine?

_____

_____

2 ▶15 Listen and check if you were right.

3 ▶15 Listen again and answer these questions.

1   Why isn't Ahmed at school? _____ *Because he's left school.* _____

2   How many rich and famous people does Krish meet? _____

3   Why isn't Krish at work today? _____

4   How is this job different from Krish's last job? _____

5   What does Krish offer to do? _____

4 ▶15 Listen again and match the beginnings and endings of these sentences. Stop the recording when you need to.

1	You need	A	think about the hotel kitchen today.
2	Chefs have	B	to work every day except Monday.
3	I needn't	C	to spend their time in the kitchen.
4	You don't have	D	come to the hotel one day.
5	I need	E	to talk to me if you want to know what the job is like.
6	I have	F	to work longer hours.
7	I had	G	to work all day.
8	I'll have	H	go now.
9	I must	I	to get up early.
10	You must	J	to stay until all the food is cooked and served.

5   Look at your answers to Exercise 4. Which verbs in 1–10 are not followed by *to*?

_____

B Grammar

1 Use of modals

The modal verbs *can, could, may, might, must, ought to, shall, should, will* and *would*:

- are always used before another verb:
  *He **can** swim.*

- never change – they do not add *-s* or *-ed* or *-ing*.

- are followed by a verb in its infinitive form without *to*:
  *You **should** get up earlier.* (**not** ~~You should to get up~~)

  except for *ought* which must be followed by *to*:
  *You **ought to** get up earlier.*

- are immediately followed by *not* in the negative:
  *You **should not / shouldn't** be late for college.*
  *You **ought not to** be late for college.*

- go immediately before the subject in a question:
  ***Could you** wake me up?*

2 Rules and obligation

must and *have to*

+	*must* + verb	We **must leave** now.
?	*must ... + verb?*	**Must** we **leave** now?
+	*have to / has to* + verb	He **has to leave** now.
?	*do / does ... + have to* + verb?	**Do** we **have to leave** now?

For obligation, we can often use either *must* or *have to*:
*I **must** go now or I'll miss the bus.* or *I **have to** go now or I'll miss the bus.*

We use *must* to give orders, for written notices or for strong advice, including to ourselves:
*You **must** tell me everything.* (= I feel strongly about this)
*Lucia **must** be home by midnight.* (= these are my instructions)
*You **must** come to the hotel one day.* (= I strongly advise you to)
*I **must** go now.* (= I have decided to do this, or it's important for me to do this)

When the obligation does not come from the speaker, *must* is possible but *have to* is more usual:
*You **have to** pay to park your car here.* (= the local council has made this rule)
*I **have to** stay until the food is cooked.* (= this is part of my job)

We usually use *have to* for habits:
*I **have to** get up early to cook breakfast.*
*Franco **has to** practise the piano for twenty minutes a day.*

We only use *must* in one form and it refers only to the present or future. For other verb forms, we use *have to*:
*I **had to** work every day.* (past simple)
*I'll (**will**) **have to** work longer hours.* (future)
*I avoided **having to** speak to him by crossing the street.* (verb + *-ing*)
*If I got the job, I'd (**would**) **have to** buy a car.* (conditional)

mustn't and *don't have to*

must not + verb	We **mustn't be** late.
do/does not have to + verb	We **don't have to be** early.

⚠ Although *must* and *have to* both express obligation, *mustn't* and *don't have to* have different meanings. *Mustn't* means 'don't do it' and *don't have to* means 'it's not necessary to do it':
*We **mustn't** make a lot of noise.* (= it is wrong to do this, it isn't allowed)
*You **don't have to** stay at school until you're 18.* (= you are not obliged to but you can if you want)

have/has got to

In speech and informal writing, we often use *have/has got to* instead of *have/has to*. *Have/has got to* normally refers to a particular action rather than a general situation. We can say:
*We **have to** work very hard this afternoon.* or *We**'ve got to** work very hard this afternoon.*
***Don't** you **have to** finish that essay today?* or ***Haven't** you **got to** finish that essay today?*
*Teachers **have to** work very long hours in my country.* (**not** ~~Teachers have got to work~~ very long hours)

⚠ When we refer to the past we use *had to*.
*I **had to** get up early when I was your age.* (**not** ~~I'd got to get up~~)

should

When we are talking about the right thing to do, we use *should*:
*Adam **should** take more care when he's cycling.* (= it's the right thing to do but he doesn't do it)
*I **shouldn't** spend so much time watching TV.* (= it's the wrong thing to do but I still do it)

To talk about the past, we use *should have* + past participle:
*I **should have told** the truth.* (= this was the right thing to do but I didn't do it)
*We **shouldn't have lent** her that money.* (= this wasn't the right thing to do but we did it)

It is also possible to use *ought to* or *ought to have* in these sentences, but it is less common.
(➤ See Unit 13, B5 for more on the modal verbs in this section.)

3 Necessity

We can use *need* (+ *to* infinitive) as a normal main verb in all the tenses, but it also has a modal form in the negative. We can say:
*She **doesn't need to** come.* or *She **needn't** come.* (= she doesn't have to come – it's not necessary)

In positive statements, we say:
*She **needs to** come.* (**not** ~~She need come~~)

To talk about the past, we say:
*Oliver **needed to** buy a computer.* (= it was necessary because he didn't have one)
*Oliver **didn't need to** buy a computer.* (= it wasn't necessary because he already had one)

Needn't have has a different meaning:
*Oliver **needn't have bought** a computer.* (= he bought a computer but his parents gave him one so now he has two!)

C Grammar exercises

1 Fill in the gaps with the correct form of *have to* or *must*. Where can you use *have got to*?

1 Most students in Britain _____*have to*_____ pay to go to university.

2 Joe _____ get up early on Fridays as he has no lectures in the morning.

3 You _____ talk during the film because other people will get annoyed.

4 My library books are overdue so I _____ pay a fine when I return them.

5 Luke _____ drive to work these days because the buses don't start early enough any more.

6 Because Sue could play the guitar, she _____ practise much when she took up the ukulele.

7 You _____ borrow this film – you'll enjoy watching it.

8 _____ (*you*) work every Saturday in your new job?

9 Non-swimmers _____ go into the deep end of the pool.

10 You _____ come to the rehearsal with me tomorrow if you want to be in the play.

11 When I was a child, I _____ keep changing schools because my parents moved house a lot.

12 We've moved into a smaller flat and I _____ share a room with my sister.

13 I _____ stop eating so much chocolate or none of my clothes will fit.

14 They provide towels at the pool so I _____ take one.

2 Match the beginnings and endings of these sentences.

1 I shouldn't   A wear a helmet when he's cycling on a busy road.

2 Do I need to   B to take any money for the funfair or is it free?

3 We don't need   C to ask his boss before he leaves the office.

4 They needn't   D take sandwiches with them because Jenny's cooking lunch.

5 Konrad should   E to send them our new address because they already have it.

6 Should you   F fill in my application form now? I'm busy at the moment.

7 Lewis needs   G spend so much time playing computer games.

8 Do they need   H carry that suitcase with your bad back?

3 Alex has made some silly mistakes recently, but he's decided to tell his parents and ask for help. Write what he says, using *should/shouldn't have* and the past participle of the verbs in the box.

ask ~~keep~~ lie lock revise

1 He lost his expensive new phone.

I ___*should have kept*___ it somewhere safe.

2 He didn't look after his bike carefully and someone stole it.

I _____ it.

3 He borrowed some money from a schoolfriend.

I _____ you for money.

4 He made up a story about why he hadn't done his homework.

I _____ about my homework.

5 He didn't prepare for his exams and he failed.

I _____ thoroughly.

I'll do better in future, I promise. Please can I have a new phone and a new bike?

4 Read this article about a pop star. Complete the sentences below.

The diary column

Pop star Lee Divine travelled from London to New York yesterday by plane.

Lee had visited his hairdresser before he went to the airport and wore his latest designer clothes, as he likes to look his best in photos. Press photographers usually follow him wherever he goes but the weather was very bad yesterday and, to Lee's obvious disappointment, there were no photographers at the airport.

Because he is famous, he didn't stand in the queue and his bodyguard carried his luggage for him. Although most people have to walk from the car park, Lee has a driver who drove him right to the door. Even this did not seem to make him happy. Lee got angry with his driver on the way because he said she wasn't driving fast enough. Of course, they arrived at the airport in plenty of time.

1 He needn't have ___visited his hairdresser___ .

2 He needn't have _____ .

3 He didn't need to _____ .

4 He didn't need to _____ .

5 He didn't need to _____ .

6 He needn't have _____ .

5 Rewrite these sentences using the correct form of *must, need, should* or *have to*.

1 It's her fault that she's lost her watch because she didn't look after it.

She _____ should have looked after her watch _____ .

2 I don't expect you to phone me before you come.

You _____ .

3 It is essential for students to buy a good dictionary.

Students _____ .

4 It was wrong of you to take money from my purse without asking.

You _____ .

5 I was getting ready to drive to the station to pick up my sister when she arrived in a taxi.

I _____ .

6 It's not fair that I do the washing-up on my own.

You _____ .

7 Students aren't allowed to use their phones during classes.

Students _____ .

8 She turned the music down to avoid disturbing her neighbours but they'd gone out.

She _____ .

9 I think she's wrong to make promises which she doesn't keep.

She _____ .

10 You can give the tour guide a tip but it is not necessary.

You _____ .

Exam practice

Reading and Use of English Part 6

You are going to read a magazine article about schools. Six sentences have been removed from the article. Choose from the sentences **A–G** the one which fits each gap (**1–6**). There is one extra sentence which you do not need to use.

Find your energy again

Even the best designed of today's schools and colleges represent artificial environments where it can be difficult to stay positive and bursting with energy. Complaints about feeling tired or ill or having no energy are commonplace.

Students and teachers often say that health problems are the inevitable consequences of being in a school all day long. **1** [ ] While there may be little you can do about the noise or the behaviour of those around you, you don't have to feel unwell. There is plenty you can do to restore those energy levels and feelings of well-being.

The first thing you must address is tiredness. If at the weekend you stay up late with your friends, going to parties or playing games online, and then sleep all the following morning, you can't expect your body to adjust on a Monday morning to a completely different routine. **2** [ ] For most of us, however, it's a very bad idea.

Our diets are another way we mistreat ourselves. Many teachers, and even some children, say they don't have breakfast – but you really should eat something, however small, before you leave home. And if you don't eat a proper lunch, or worse, you skip it altogether because you're busy, you will get to the evening and suddenly realise how hungry you are. **3** [ ] The sooner you do, the better because nothing is more important than eating and drinking regularly.

You should also take exercise regularly in the evenings. **4** [ ] Recent American research has established that frequent, vigorous exercise is a good way of improving your mood and that the effects last far longer than the session itself. It has to be vigorous, though – walking or tennis have to be kept up for at least an hour to have a positive effect.

All the advice on exercise says you should choose something you like doing. **5** [ ] If you don't want to fall into the same trap, you need to keep reminding yourself of the advantages. You should also spend as much time as possible in daylight – advice which is often ignored. We now know that lack of sunlight can cause depression. Time spent out of doors, even if it's only a few minutes, is never wasted.

You may be bothered by some of your friends' or classmates' negative attitudes towards staying healthy. Take a few moments to think about how they affect your own state of mind. **6** [ ] You are much more likely to enjoy your free time if you leave school feeling positive and it's the same for your friends. Take steps to make sure school is a place where you look forward to going. You will spend many hours of your life there!

Exam practice

A   Most people start off with good intentions but soon lose interest.

B   This is, of course, a disastrous way for anyone to run their life and you need to realise that.

C   Always remember that you don't need to behave in the same way.

D   That solution to the problem may not work for everyone.

E   However, this is not the case.

F   This will help you to get to sleep later that night and wake up refreshed.

G   Some people seem to be able to keep this up without any negative effects on their health.

 Exam tip

If you think two sentences fit in a gap, leave it and continue with the other questions. Then go back and fill in the ones you are unsure about.

Grammar focus task

Look at these sentences and find expressions in the text (including sentences A–G) which mean the same.

1   It is not necessary for you to feel ill.

You don't have to feel unwell.

2   It is essential first of all for you to deal with tiredness.

3   It is important that you exercise regularly after school.

4   It is essential that the exercise you take is vigorous.

5   It is essential to walk or play tennis for at least an hour.

6   It is important that you do a form of exercise that you enjoy.

7   It is necessary that you don't forget the positive things.

8   It is not necessary for you to behave like them.

12 Pronouns and determiners

Possessives; reflexive pronouns and *own*; *each other* and *one another*; *there* and *it*; *someone*, etc.; *all*, *most*, *some*, *no* and *none*; *each* and *every*; *both*, *neither* and *either*

A Context listening

1 You are going to hear a man talking to a woman on a holiday website helpline. Before you listen, look at the picture of the two people and the photos of places below.

1 Where do you think the woman went last year? _____

2 Which place do you think the man would prefer? _____

2 ▶16 Listen and check if you were right.

3 ▶16 Listen again and fill in the gaps. Stop the recording when you need to.

1 Have you looked at any of our special deals? Are you interested in ____anywhere____ in particular?

2 I went to a fantastic place _____ last year with some friends _____ .

3 _____ of those would suit me.

4 Are you going on your own? Yes, I'll be _____ .

5 That's better, because you get to know _____ really well.

6 All I want is _____ quiet.

7 _____ of these holidays appeals to me at all.

B Grammar

1 Possessive 's and *of*

We use *'s* with people, countries and animals:
*The **girl's** clothes were very dirty.* (**not** ~~the clothes of the girl~~)
***Britain's** roads get more crowded every year.*
*I nearly trod on the **cat's** tail.*

and with time expressions:
*I want to go on a **week's** holiday.*   *They're last **year's** tours.*

but we usually use *of* instead of *'s* with things:
*What's the price **of that holiday**?* (**not** ~~the holiday's price~~)

⚠ The position of the apostrophe is important:
*my **brother's** friends* (= one brother)   *my **brothers'** friends* (= more than one brother)

When we speak we often omit the second noun if we are referring to someone's home or business:
*I stayed at **Simon's**.* (*house* is omitted)   *I stopped at the **newsagent's**.* (*shop* is omitted)

2 Possessive adjectives and pronouns

Possessive adjectives:	my	your	his	her	its	our	their
Possessive pronouns:	mine	yours	his	hers	–	ours	theirs

Possessive adjectives are used before a noun:
*Those are **your** keys.*   *Where's **my** phone?*

Possessive pronouns take the place of a possessive adjective + noun, usually to avoid repeating the noun:
*There's a coat on the chair. Is it **yours**?* (= your coat)
*That's not your umbrella, it's **mine**.* (= my umbrella)

We use a possessive adjective rather than *the* with parts of the body and clothes:
*My father broke **his** leg.* (**not** ~~My father broke the leg.~~)
*She tore **her** favourite jeans.* (**not** ~~She tore the favourite jeans.~~)

We sometimes use *of* + possessive pronoun or possessive form of a noun instead of a possessive adjective:
*I went with some friends **of mine/yours/Tim's**.* (**not** ~~friends of me/you/Tim~~) (= some of my/your/Tim's friends)

3 Reflexive pronouns and *own*

Reflexive pronouns:	myself	yourself	himself	herself	itself	ourselves	themselves

We use a reflexive pronoun:
- to make it clear that we are talking about the subject of the verb:
  *Amy blamed **herself** for what had happened.*
  but *Amy blamed **her** for what had happened.* (= Amy blamed another person, not herself)
- for emphasis:
  *I went to this place **myself** to see what it was really like.*
- with a number of common expressions like *by (your)self, enjoy (your)self, behave (your)self, help (your)self, make (your)self at home*:
  *You can **help yourself** to as much food as you want.*
  *The resort's got everything you need to **enjoy yourself**.*

⚠ We only use a reflexive pronoun after *wash*, *shave* and *dress* for emphasis:
She dressed quickly. but *The little girl managed to dress **herself**.* (= it was difficult for her)

We use a possessive adjective + *own* to emphasise possession:
*I'd rather have **my own** apartment.* or *I'd rather have an apartment **of my own**.* (= belonging just to me)

On (your) own means 'alone' and can be used instead of *by (your)self*:
*I went diving **on my own**.* or *I went diving **by myself**.*

4 *each other* and *one another*

There is a difference between the reflexive pronouns and *each other / one another*:
*The two boys hurt **themselves**.* (= e.g. when they fell off their bicycles)
*The two boys hurt **each other / one another**.* (= e.g. when they had a fight)
*The two boys hurt **someone else**.* (= e.g. when their football hit a man on the head)

There is also a possessive form of *each other / one another*:
*They borrow **each other's / one another's** shoes because they take the same size.*

5 *there* and *it* + the verb *to be*

We use *there* + the verb *to be*:
- to say that somebody/something exists, especially when we refer to somebody/something for the first time:
__There are__ some lovely apartments.   *__There's__ a tour guide.*

⚠ Note that the verb after *there* agrees with the noun which follows.

We use *it* + the verb *to be*:
- to refer to a particular thing, action, situation or place already mentioned:
*There's a page called Walking Tours. **It is** full of useful tips.*

- to introduce information about time, weather and distance:
__It's__ twenty past five and __it's__ sunny here in New York.
__It's__ only a few metres from here to the beach.

- to avoid using a phrase with *-ing* or *to* infinitive as the subject:
__It's__ surprising to see you here. (= to see you here is surprising)
__It's__ a waste of time looking at your website. (= looking at your website is a waste of time)

6 *someone, anywhere, everybody*, etc.

Words like *someone*, *anywhere*, etc. follow the same rules as *some* and *any*.

Some is used in positive sentences:
*I want to go **somewhere** sunny.*

Some is sometimes used in questions, especially requests and offers, when we expect the answer *yes*:
*Can I have **something** cold to drink?*
*Would you like **something** to eat?*

Any is used in questions and negative sentences:
*Are you interested in **anywhere** in particular?*
*We haven't got **anything** like that this year.*

Any is also used in positive statements to show 'it doesn't matter which thing/person/place':
__Anywhere__ that I can relax will be fine.

⚠ Words like *someone*, *everybody*, etc. are followed by a singular verb:
__Everyone's__ going for them this year.
__Nobody wants__ to go on those tours.

7 *all*, *most*, *some*, *no* and *none*

These words are all used with plural and uncountable nouns. *No* can also be used with a singular noun.

Things/people in general	Things/people in a particular group
all + noun: **All** *hotels have bedrooms.* (= hotels throughout the world)	*all (of)* + *the/my/this/those* (etc.) + noun: **All (of) the** *hotels (in this street) have a restaurant.* We can omit *of* after *all*, but not after *some*, *most* or *none*.
most/some + noun: **Most** *hotels provide breakfast.* **Some** *hotels have a private beach.*	*most/some of* + *the/my/this/those* (etc.) + noun: **Most of the** *hotels (in this town) are expensive.* **Some of the** *hotels (on the website) have a pool.*
no + noun: **No** *hotels are perfect.* **No** *hotel is perfect.*	*none of* + *the/my/this/those* (etc.) + noun: **None of the** *rooms (in this hotel) has/have a balcony.* When *none of* is followed by a plural noun, the verb can be singular or plural – both forms are correct.

We can use *all/most/some/none* + *of* + pronoun:
Some of them *have a private beach.* (**not** ~~Some them~~)

All can sometimes stand alone:
All *I want is somewhere quiet.* (= the only thing)

Most, *some* and *none* can also stand alone, but only if the noun they refer to has just been mentioned:
The rooms are well furnished, but **some** *are rather dark.* (= some of the rooms)

Whole is used instead of *all* before a singular noun:
The **whole** *trip was spoilt by the weather.* (**not** ~~all the trip~~)

8 *each* and *every*

Each and *every* can be used with the same meaning:
Every/Each *apartment has a balcony.*

but sometimes they have different meanings:

- *Each* is used for individual things or people in a group:
  Each *child drew a picture of her own parents.*   *The customs officer checked* **each** *passport in turn.*
- *Every* emphasises that all the people or things in a group are included:
  Every *holiday you've mentioned is the kind of holiday I'd hate.*

Each (but not *every*) can be followed by *of* + a plural noun or pronoun:
Each of *the apartments /* **Each of** *them has a balcony.* (**not** ~~Every of the apartments~~ / ~~Every of them~~)

⚠ Notice the difference between *every* and *all*:
He sat by the river **every** *morning.* (= regularly)   *He sat by the river* **all** *morning.* (= one complete morning)

9 *both*, *neither* and *either*

We use *both*, *neither* and *either* when we refer to two items. We use a plural verb after *both*:
Both *places* **are** *too noisy.* or **Both (of) the** *places* **are** ... or **Both of** *them* **are** ...

We use a singular verb after *either* and *neither*:
Either/Neither *place* **suits** *me.* or **Either/Neither of** *the places / them* **suits** *me.*

We use *both ... and*, *neither ... nor* and *either ... or* to connect two things or actions:
Both *the Hotel Flora* **and** *the Grand Hotel* **have** *good restaurants.* (= the Flora and the Grand)
Neither *the Hotel Flora* **nor** *the Grand Hotel* **has** *a good restaurant.* (= not the Flora or the Grand)
We could stay at **either** *the Hotel Flora* **or** *the Grand Hotel.* (= the Flora or the Grand)

C Grammar exercises

1   Fill in the gaps with *it is*, *there is* or *there are*.

Sometimes I dream of a place where I'd like to live.
(1) _____*It is*_____ at the top of a mountain and on the
south-facing side **(2)** _____ a little house.
(3) _____ very pretty and **(4)** _____
flowers all around it. **(5)** _____ no other houses
nearby but **(6)** _____ lots of sheep and goats and
wonderful vegetables growing. **(7)** _____ always
sunny and warm and it only rains at night. **(8)** _____
not far from a little village where **(9)** _____
a restaurant which serves my favourite food. Unfortunately
(10) _____ just a dream!

2   Choose the correct sentence from each pair.

1   a   I saw your advertisement in yesterdays' newspaper.

    b   I saw your advertisement in yesterday's newspaper. ✓

2   a   I always enjoy when I visit my friends in Madrid.

    b   I always enjoy myself when I visit my friends in Madrid.

3   a   A friend of mine recommended this film.

    b   A friend of me recommended this film.

4   a   The college decided to publish the students' results online because they had done so well.

    b   The college decided to publish the student's results online because they had done so well.

5   a   Nobody wanted to come to the cinema with me so I went on myself.

    b   Nobody wanted to come to the cinema with me so I went by myself.

3   Choose the correct words.

I'm going to tell you about a party game you might want to play with a new class of students. It's a
game **(1)** *most* / *most of* people enjoy and it's a good way for people to get to know **(2)** *each other* /
themselves when they first arrive.

You have a pile of cards and **(3)** *all* / *every* card has the name of a famous person on it. **(4)** *Every* / *Each*
of the famous people has a partner; for example, Romeo's partner is Juliet. It's important that they're
people that **(5)** *all* / *everyone* has heard of. **(6)** *Everyone* / *Someone* has one of these cards pinned to
their back and they have to find out who they are by questioning **(7)** *every* / *all* the other people in the
room. The first two students to find **(8)** *each other* / *the other* get a prize. **(9)** *The whole* / *All* the game
takes about twenty minutes and by the end **(10)** *nobody* / *anybody* is feeling shy any longer.

4 **Fill in the gaps with the words in the box.**

all   each   every   most   no   none   some   ~~whole~~

Tickets going fast for Bimblers tournament

Next week sees the start of Bimblers tennis tournament, which has become increasingly well-known since it was first held five years ago. The **(1)** _____whole_____ tournament lasts ten days and there is great demand for tickets throughout. Up to sixty players take part and **(2)** _____ of them pays €50 to enter. Although it is not a professional competition, **(3)** _____ the umpires have professional qualifications. The prize money is not an enormous sum, but winning the tournament is seen as a great achievement, so competition is fierce and **(4)** _____ of the players likes losing.

It's a great social event as well and **(5)** _____ competitor is invited to a pre-tournament party and a final celebration dinner. The facilities for spectators are good, and they're guaranteed some exciting matches. From time to time, **(6)** _____ of the spectators shout rudely at the players, but **(7)** _____ of them clap and cheer politely. To avoid disturbing the concentration of the players, **(8)** _____ spectators may enter or leave while play is in progress.

5 **Look at the pictures of three brothers, Pete, John and Rob. Use the words in the box to complete the sentences describing them.**

beard   earring   ~~fair hair~~   glasses
moustache   short hair

Pete   John   Rob

1 Both __John__ and ___Rob have fair hair___ .
2 Both _____ and _____ .
3 Neither _____ nor _____ .
4 All of them _____ .
5 They all _____ .
6 None of them _____ .

6 👁 **Correct the mistake in each of the following sentences by Cambridge First candidates.**

1 I can lend you some swimming trunks if you have forgotten ~~your~~.   _____yours_____

2 I'd rather have a computer of mine than share with my sister.   _____

3 It was hard working together until we all knew us.   _____

4 There is a great thing to have someone you can rely on.   _____

5 I feel myself very close to nature and I know that a lot of people are like me.   _____

6 Suddenly she woke up. It was a strange noise coming from downstairs.   _____

Exam practice

Reading and Use of English Part 2

For questions **1–8**, read the text below and think of the word which best fits each gap. Use only **one** word in each gap. There is an example at the beginning **(0)**.

Names

If, like me, you're called John Smith and live in England, you have the same name **(0)** _____as_____ thousands of other people. As a child, I thought that **(2)** _____ in the world had their **(2)** _____ names, but when I started school I found **(3)** _____ were other boys with my name. In fact, one of them became a close friend of **(4)** _____ .

Strangers often think they have met me before, but then realise that they're thinking of somebody **(5)** _____ – another John Smith. In hotels or banks, people often look at me suspiciously when I give my name as **(6)** _____ is often the name used by people who don't want to give their real one!

On the whole, though, I've decided it's better to have a common name. I recently met two people called Honey Moon and Holly Bush! **(7)** _____ of them appeared to mind having an unusual name although they **(8)** _____ agreed that people sometimes did not take them seriously.

> 💡 *Exam tip*
>
> Think about what kind of word is needed in the gap and read the whole sentence to make sure the word you choose fits grammatically.

Grammar focus task

Look at these phrases and find expressions with the same meaning in the completed text above.

1	all the people	_everyone/everybody_
2	names that were unique to individuals	_____
3	one of my best friends	_____
4	a different person	_____
5	both of them seemed happy	_____
6	two people said the same thing	_____

Modals (2)

Permission; requests; offers; suggestions; orders; advice

A Context listening

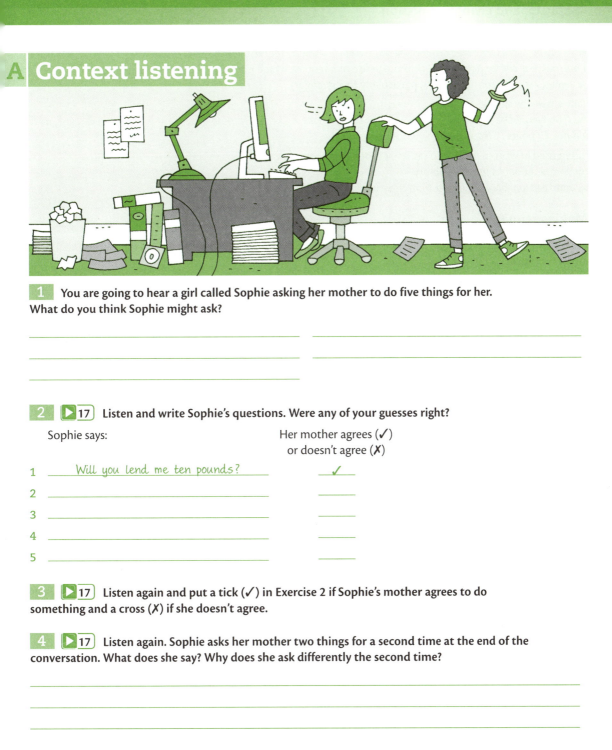

1 You are going to hear a girl called Sophie asking her mother to do five things for her. What do you think Sophie might ask?

_____   _____

_____   _____

_____

2 ▶17 Listen and write Sophie's questions. Were any of your guesses right?

Sophie says: Her mother agrees (✓)
                                                  or doesn't agree (✗)

1 _____Will you lend me ten pounds?_____   ____✓____

2 _____   _____

3 _____   _____

4 _____   _____

5 _____   _____

3 ▶17 Listen again and put a tick (✓) in Exercise 2 if Sophie's mother agrees to do something and a cross (✗) if she doesn't agree.

4 ▶17 Listen again. Sophie asks her mother two things for a second time at the end of the conversation. What does she say? Why does she ask differently the second time?

_____

_____

_____

B Grammar

1 Asking for and giving permission

We can ask for permission by saying *Can I? Could I?* or *May I?*:
Can I leave my bag here while I look round the museum? (= a simple request which expects the answer *yes*)
Could I borrow your car for a few days? (= more polite or a request which is less sure of the answer being *yes*)
May I sit here? (= a more formal request, particularly to a stranger)

We usually answer by saying:
Of course (you can). / OK. / Certainly.
I'm afraid not. (= polite) / *No, you can't.* (= not very polite)

May is often used in written notices to say what is or is not allowed:
*You **may** borrow six books from the library.*
*You **may not** keep any book for longer than three weeks.*

2 Making requests

We use *Can you?, Will you?, Could you?, Do you think you could?, Would you? Would you mind?* to ask someone else to do something.

We often use *Can you?* or *Will you?*, especially in informal conversation:
Can you pass me the bread?
Will you get me some stamps from the post office?

To be more polite, we use *Could you?* and *Would you?*:
Could you tell me where the station is?
Would you lend me your camera?

We usually answer by saying:
(Yes) of course (I can/will). or *OK.* or *Maybe.*
I'm sorry, I'm afraid I can't. (**not** ~~No, I won't~~, which sounds rude)

We often use *Do you think you could?* (**not** ~~Do you think you can?~~) to make requests:
Do you think you could move your things off the table?

⚠ We never use *May you?* to ask someone to do something.
(**not** ~~May you give me a lift?~~)

We use *Would you mind (not) -ing?* when we want to be very polite:
Would you mind moving to another seat?
Would you mind not talking so loudly?

⚠ The reply to a question with *Would you mind?* is negative:
Not at all. (= I don't mind moving to another seat. / We don't mind talking more quietly.)

3 Making offers

There are several ways of offering help to someone:
Can I/we help you to cook dinner?
Shall I/we clean the car for you?
I can / I could / I'll lend you some money.
Why don't I carry that bag for you?
Would you like me to do the washing up?

4   Making suggestions

To make a suggestion, we can use all the following expressions:

Let's	**drive** to the city centre today.
Shall I/we **Why don't I/we/you**	**drive** to the city centre today?
How about **What about**	**driving** to the city centre today?

If we are less sure of what we are suggesting, we can say:
*I/We/You **could drive** to the city centre today.*

5   Giving orders and advice

To give orders and advice, we use:

must	**had better**	**ought to/should**	**could**

stronger   less strong

*You really **must** start looking for a job.* (= an order – I am telling you to do this, or this is my opinion which I feel very strongly about)
*You**'d better** start looking for a job.* (= advice – otherwise you may regret it)
*You **should / ought t**o start looking for a job.* (= advice)
*You **could** start looking for a job.* (= this is only a suggestion)

For the negative we normally use *had better not* or *shouldn't. Ought not to* is also possible but less common:
*You**'d better not** forget to send that application form.*
*You **shouldn't / ought not to** wear those clothes for the interview.*

⚠ We don't use *mustn't* or *couldn't* when giving advice.

To talk about the past we say:
*You **should have / ought to have** accepted that job.* (= it was a good idea to accept it but you didn't)

For the negative we say:
*You **shouldn't have** worn those clothes.* (= you wore them but it wasn't a good idea)

We can use all these verbs to talk about the right thing to do:
*I **must** try harder not to be late.*
*She **should / ought to** be more thoughtful.*
*He**'d better** go and say sorry.*
*I**'d better not** upset her today.*
*They **shouldn't / ought not to** talk so much.*

To talk about the right thing to do in the past we say:
*They **shouldn't have** talked so much.*

(➤ See also Unit 11, B2 for more on these modal verbs)

13 Modals (2)

C Grammar exercises

1 Mark the sentences on the left A (advice/warning), O (offer), P (asking permission), R (request) or S (suggestion). Then match them with the replies on the right.

1 May I check my email on your laptop? ___P___   a Yes, let's. This one isn't very good.

2 Would you mind buying me a sandwich? _____   b Of course. Let me just save this document first.

3 Shall I make you a copy of my notes? _____   c Of course not. What sort would you like?

4 How about going out for a coffee? _____   d Oh thanks, that'll save me a long walk.

5 You ought to buy a new dress for your cousin's engagement party. _____   e OK, I could do with a break.

  f Well, I just can't afford one.

6 Can you text me after the exam? _____   g I'm afraid not, I forgot to charge it.

7 I can give you a lift in my car if you need one. _____   h OK, I won't.

8 Could I use your phone to make a call, please? _____   i I'm sorry, I can't. We're not allowed to take phones with us.

9 You'd better not touch anything on the desk. _____

10 Why don't we try a different website? _____   j No, it's OK. I've got all the information I need.

2 Choose the correct words in these sentences.

1 Students *ought / may* not use phones in any part of the library.

2 Why don't you *send / sending* me a text when you finish your class?

3 Please *may / can* you cut me another slice of bread?

4 How about *spend / spending* the weekend at my parents' beach house?

5 We shouldn't have *given / gave* our address to that salesman.

6 Your brother really *shouldn't / ought not* to eat so much ice cream!

7 *Shall / Could* they meet us on the beach, or is that too far from their house?

8 I knew I *should / better* have brought a warmer coat with me – I'm freezing!

3 Fill in the gaps in these sentences. There is more than one possible answer for most of these.

1 ___Can___ I leave my scooter in your garage?

2 I'm sorry to bother you. _____ I look at your timetable, please?

3 _____ cycling to town today for a change? It will be good for us.

4 We _____ ask Paula if she'd like to come riding with us. What do you think? I think she'd enjoy it.

5 _____ you get that tin down from the shelf for me, Dad? I can't quite reach.

6 I _____ post your parcel on my way to work if you want.

7 _____ we go sailing at the weekend? The weather's going to be fine.

8 Excuse me, _____ you tell me where the nearest tube station is?

9 *Passenger:* _____ I take this bottle onto the plane?

   Security officer: No, I'm afraid not.

10 _____ turning that television down? I need to use the phone.

4   Complete the dialogue with the phrases in the box.

Can I do	~~Can I help~~	Could I see	I'm afraid	Shall I ask	Would you exchange	You can't have
You could give	You'd better not	You should ask	You shouldn't have done	

Assistant: (1) _____Can I help_____ you?
Laura: I'd like to get a refund on these headphones. (2) _____ that at this checkout?
Assistant: Yes, you can. (3) _____ the receipt, please?
Laura: (4) _____ not. I haven't got one, you see, because they were a present.
Assistant: Sorry. (5) _____ a refund without the receipt.
Laura: (6) _____ them for something else, then?
Assistant: What brand are they? Oh, but you've taken them out of their box. (7) _____ that if you wanted to return them.
Laura: Christabel did that before she gave them to me.
Assistant: Did you say Christabel? Does she work here at weekends?
Laura: I don't know. She's got dark hair and glasses.
Assistant: (8) _____ her where she got them. She was probably given them free because they haven't got a price on them. (9) _____ the manager what he thinks?
Laura: (10) _____ do that. I don't want to get Christabel into trouble.
Assistant: (11) _____ them to someone else for their birthday or something, I suppose.

5   What would you say in the following situations? Write sentences using the words in brackets.

1   You have just started work in a new office and you want to know how the coffee machine works. Ask someone.
  (could) _____Could you tell me how the coffee machine works, please?_____

2   Your sister has just moved into a new flat and you offer to help her clean it.
  (shall) _____

3   Your friend is trying to decide what to buy her mother for her birthday. Suggest she buys her some perfume.
  (what about) _____

4   Your brother puts lots of salt on his food. Advise him not to use so much.
  (ought) _____

5   You want a book which you can't find in your local bookshop. Ask the assistant to order it for you.
  (could) _____

6   You are buying something in a market and you want to pay by credit card. Ask the assistant if this is possible.
  (can) _____

7   Your friend is always missing calls because he forgets to charge his phone. Advise him to charge it every night.
  (should) _____

8   You've been at a party at a friend's house and the kitchen is in a terrible mess. Offer to help clear up.
  (would / like) _____

9   Your sister is going shopping. You need a tube of sun cream. Ask her to get some for you.
  (can) _____

10   You need a lift home. Your friend has a car but lives in the other direction. Ask him politely for a lift.
  (would / mind) _____

Exam practice

Listening Part 3

▶18 You will hear five short extracts in which people are talking about advice they received. For questions **1–5**, choose from the list **(A–H)** what each speaker says about it. Use the letters only once. There are three extra letters which you do not need to use.

A   I didn't listen carefully enough to the advice.

B   I received advice I didn't ask for.

C   It was a mistake to follow the advice.

D   I didn't get the advice I'd hoped for.

E   I wish I'd taken the advice.

F   The advice was too confusing.

G   I was given the advice too late.

H   The advice wasn't relevant to me.

Speaker 1	**1**
Speaker 2	**2**
Speaker 3	**3**
Speaker 4	**4**
Speaker 5	**5**

> 💡 **Exam tip**
>
> Read the options before you listen.

Grammar focus task

▶18 What advice were the people on the recording given? Rewrite the sentences below using the words given. Listen again to check whether your new sentence is the same as what the speaker said.

1   What about going skiing in Whistler?

(*really should*) _____ You really should go skiing in Whistler._

2   Why not go hiking in Cape Breton?

(*could*) _____

3   I advise you not to do that course.

(*shouldn't*) _____

4   It's not a good idea to cycle along those roads.

(*better not*) _____

5   I suggest you take these tracks accoss the fields instead.

(*don't*) _____

6   That was the wrong thing to do.

(*have*) _____

7   It is essential that you wear your life jacket.

(*must*) _____

Modals (3)

Ability; deduction: certainty and possibility; expectations

A Context listening

1 You are going to hear two college students called Clare and Fiona. They're on their way to college when they see someone sitting in a café. Before you listen, look at the picture. Do you think the man is with his sister, his girlfriend or his mother?

_____

2 ▶19 Listen and check if you were right.

3 ▶19 Listen again and answer these questions.

1 Who does Clare think Danni is with at first? _____

2 Fiona doesn't agree. Why not? _____

3 What do the two girls decide to do? _____

4 What does Clare want to get? _____

5 Why doesn't Fiona want to? _____

6 What does Fiona want to sell? _____

7 What is Clare's opinion of Fiona's idea? _____

4 ▶19 Listen again and fill in the gaps.

1 Clare: It ____might be____ Danni.

2 Clare: She _____ his mother.

3 Fiona: She _____ his mother.

4 Fiona: He _____ me on my own.

5 Fiona: She _____ his girlfriend.

6 Fiona: It _____ him after all.

5 Look at the sentences in Exercise 4. In which sentences does the speaker:

1 seem sure that something is true? _____

2 think something is possible, but isn't sure? _____

14 Modals (3)

B Grammar

1 Ability

can and be able to – present forms

+	can + verb	*I can swim.*
–	can't + verb	*She can't swim.*
?	can ... + verb?	*Can you swim?*

+	am/is/are able to + verb	*I'm able to swim.*
–	am/is/are not able to + verb	*He's not able to swim.*
?	am/is/are ... able to + verb?	*Are you able to swim?*

We use *can* or *be able to* to say that someone has the ability to do something. *Can* is more common than *be able to* in the present.

We usually use *can*:
- to talk about an ability in a general way:
  James can play chess, although he's only six years old.
  Humans can't see very well in the dark.
- to talk about a situation which makes someone able to do something. This may refer to the future as well as the present:
  The manager can't see you right now – she's in a meeting.
  You can get tickets to the festival on this website.
  I can meet you tomorrow because I have a day off.

can and be able to – past forms

+	could + verb	*I could swim.*
–	couldn't + verb	*She couldn't swim.*
?	could ... + verb?	*Could you swim?*

+	was/were able to + verb	*I was able to swim.*
–	was/were not able to + verb	*I wasn't able to swim.*
?	was/were ... able to + verb?	*Were you able to swim?*

We use *could* or *was/were able to*:
- to talk about someone's ability in the past:
  He could / was able to read when he was three but he couldn't / wasn't able to catch a ball when he started school.
- to talk about a situation which made someone able to do something:
  I was able to meet them yesterday because I had a day off.

⚠ We do not use *could* to talk about one situation in the past, but we can use *couldn't*:
She was able to (not could) come to the meeting but she couldn't / wasn't able to stay for lunch.
They were able to (not could) see the match because they had a day off.

be able to – other tenses

For ability and situations which makes someone able to do something, *can* is only used in the present tense and *could* is only used in the past. In all other tenses we use *be able to*:
We'll be able to sell the photo to a newspaper. (will future)
They haven't been able to contact Mary because of the storms. (present perfect)
If you saved enough money, you would be able to visit me in New Zealand. (conditional)
They hope to be able to visit me next year. (infinitive)

2 Deduction: certainty and possibility

Talking about the present
Certainty

We use:

- *must* when we are sure something is true:
  It **must be** *from Steven because he's in Australia.*
  (= I'm certain it's from Steven)
- *can't/couldn't* when we are sure something is not true:
  It **can't be / couldn't be** *from Steven because that's not*
  his writing. (= I'm certain it's not from Steven)

Possibility

To talk about possibility, we can use *may*, *might* or *could*. The meaning is usually the same, but *might* sounds
a little less certain than *may* or *could*.
She **may be** *his sister.* (= I think there's a good possibility that she is his sister)
They **might have** *some money.* (= I think there's a slight possibility that they have some money)

We use:

- *may*, *might* or *could* when we think something is possibly true:
  The parcel **may be / might be / could be** *from Dad's friend Tony, because he moved to Australia recently.*
  (= it is possible, not certain, that the parcel is from him)
- *may not / might not* (but not ~~could not~~) when we think something is possibly not true:
  It **may not be / might not be** *from someone we know.* (= it is possible that it is not)

Present	True	Not true
Certainty	*must* + infinitive without *to*	*can't/couldn't* + infinitive without *to*
Possibility	*might/may/could* + infinitive without *to*	*might not/may not* + infinitive without *to*

⚠ Notice that *could* means the same as *might* and *may*, but *couldn't* is different from *might not* and *may not*.

All the verbs in the table above can also be followed by *be* + verb + *-ing* for a situation which we think is
happening now:
Steven **might be travelling** *home at this moment.*
He **must be looking** *forward to seeing his friends and family.*

Talking about the past
Certainty

We use:

- *must have* + past participle when we are sure something
  is true:
  Steven **must have arrived** *in Perth by now.* (= I'm certain
  he has arrived)
- *can't/couldn't have* + past participle when we are sure
  something is not true:
  He **can't/couldn't have got** *there yet because it will take*
  at least two weeks. (= I'm certain he hasn't got there)

Possibility

We use:

- *might have / may have / could have* when we think something is possibly true:
  He **might/may/could have stopped** *for a few days on the way.* (= it is possible that he stopped)
- *might not have / may not have* when we think something is possibly not true:
  He **might/may not have had** *time to do everything he wanted.* (= it is possible he didn't have time)

Past	True	Not true
Certainty	*must have* + past participle	*can't have / couldn't have* + past participle
Possibility	*might have / may have / could have* + past participle	*might not have / may not have* + past participle

⚠ Notice that *could have* means the same as *might have* and *may have*, but *couldn't have* is different from *might not have* and *may not have*.

Talking about the future

We also use *might (not)*, *may (not)* and *could* (but not ~~could not~~) when we are talking about a possibility in the future:

*James **may go** out to see Steven in Australia next month.*
*We **might get** into a lot of trouble, in my opinion.*
*I think there **could be** a storm tonight.*
*Should we get a bigger bag for the potatoes? This one **might/may not be** strong enough.* (**not** ~~could not be~~)

3 Expectations

When we expect something will happen, we can use *should (not)* + infinitive without *to*:

*Steven **should email** us soon.* (= I expect he will email)
*It **shouldn't be** too long before we hear from Steven.* (= I expect it will not be too long)

We also use *should* when we discover that a situation is not as we expected:

*This email from Steven says he's in Melbourne but he **should be** in Sydney this week.* (= I'm surprised because I expected him to be in Sydney)

When we talk about a past situation, we use *should (not) have* + past participle:

*He **should have left** Alice Springs several days ago.* (= I expect he left Alice Springs)
*He **shouldn't have had** any trouble finding places to stay.* (= I expect he didn't have any trouble)

C Grammar exercises

1   Complete the article with *can, can't, could, couldn't* or the correct form of *be able to*. Sometimes there are two possible answers.

THE MATHS GENIUS

Rhiannon Kennedy speaks to Nick Evans about her amazing talent.

'One day when I was four years old, my father was telling my mother how much money he'd spent and while he was talking I added it all up. They didn't believe that I (1) _____could_____ do that because I (2) _____ read or write. I'm now at university and I (3) _____ still add up complicated sums in my head. I did a maths exam once which I finished so quickly that I (4) _____ eat a meal in the canteen before the others had finished.

'Next year we have to write essays and I'm not sure whether I (5) _____ do that because I (6) _____ (*never*) spell very well. I would like (7) _____ use my mathematical skill in a job but I haven't decided what yet. I (8) _____ be a maths teacher – I'd enjoy the maths but I'm not sure about the children! I entered a maths quiz show on TV once but when they asked me the questions I (9) _____ think of the answers because I was just too nervous. So I (10) _____ imagine myself as a TV star. I (11) _____ always get work in a supermarket when the tills break down, I suppose!'

2   Read about what has happened on a camping trip.

Two teenage boys are camping with their families near a lake. One day they find an old boat and decide to row out to an uninhabited island. They explore the island until suddenly they realise it's getting dark. They run to find the boat, but it's gone.

Here are some of the things their families say when they don't come back. Decide if each sentence refers to the present, past or future.

1   There can't be much to eat on the island. ____present____

2   People may have seen them rowing across the lake. _____

3   They could be stuck there for days. _____

4   Someone in a fishing boat might see them. _____

5   They must have forgotten how late it was. _____

6   They must be getting scared. _____

7   There may be a cave or hut they can shelter in. _____

8   The boat could have sunk. _____

9   Someone may have taken the boat. _____

10   They can't have tied the boat up properly. _____

Now write the number of each sentence next to the correct meaning, A or B.

A   I feel certain about this. _1,_____   B   I think this is possible. _____

14 Modals (3)

3 **Complete these sentences with a modal verb and the correct form of the verb in brackets.**

1 Jenny's brother _____ *can't be* _____ (*be*) a doctor because he's only 18.

2 Samantha said she'd go for a swim as soon as she reached the seaside so she _____ (*swim*) in the sea right now.

3 I can't think what's happened to Annie. She left home hours ago so she _____ (*be*) here by now.

4 These football boots don't fit me any more. My feet _____ (*grow*).

5 My neighbour remembers when there were fields here instead of houses so he _____ (*be*) very old.

6 Alan _____ (*forget*) that it was my birthday yesterday because it's the same as his!

4 **Complete these dialogues with a modal verb and the correct form of the verb in brackets.**

1 **A:** I can't get the TV to record any programmes.

   B: You _____ *must be doing* _____ (*do*) something wrong.

   A: OK. Where are the instructions?

2 **A:** I don't seem to have my wallet.

   B: Did you forget to bring it?

   A: No, I _____ (*leave*) it at home because I had it when I paid for my train ticket.

3 **A:** I sent Camilla a text an hour ago but she hasn't got back to me yet.

   B: She _____ (*not see*) it if she's at work today.

4 **A:** I found this watch in the changing rooms.

   B: It _____ (*be*) Peter's. I think he's got one like that.

5 **A:** I don't really like James. Why did you invite him?

   B: Well, you don't have to talk to him and he _____ (*not come*) anyway. He said he wasn't sure what his plans were.

6 **A:** Did your team win their match yesterday?

   B: Yes, we did! We _____ (*lose*) really, but their best player hurt herself in the first five minutes so they only had ten players. She _____ (*be*) furious with herself!

   A: That was lucky for you, though.

5 Read this police report about a stolen painting.

Crime report

Theft:
The Celebration by James Patrone – a 17th century painting, 15 x 20 centimetres, worth £150,000

Location:
Sidcombe Art Gallery

Time:
between 6.00 and 7.30 on Friday evening

Suspects (all have keys to the art gallery):

The caretaker, Sam Willis
Sam, who has worked at the gallery for 32 years, locked up at 6.30 as usual after the cleaners had left.

The director, William Rees
William was on the phone in his office between 6.00 and 7.00. He says he left the gallery at 7.15 but nobody saw him leave.

A cleaner, Sandra Thompson
Sandra cleaned the offices and the galleries with two other cleaners. They finished at 6.00 and had a chat in the cloakroom before leaving together at 6.15. She says the picture was still there at 6.00.

A research student, Daniel Foreman
When the gallery shut at 5.30 Daniel begged the caretaker to let him stay a bit longer to finish his work. The caretaker saw him coming out of the toilets at 6.30 and told him to leave. He bought an expensive car on Saturday.

The shop manager, Sophie Christie
Sophie closed the museum shop at 5.30, but had to stay and wait for a delivery. The driver got delayed in the traffic and arrived at 6.05. He left straight away and Sophie said she left at about 6.15 but nobody saw her leave the building.

The cloakroom attendant, Josie McCartney
The cloakroom closed at 5.30 and Josie tidied up. She was just leaving when the cleaners arrived and she stopped to have a chat with them. They all left together at 6.15.

Who had the opportunity to steal the painting? Complete these sentences using *must have, can't have, couldn't have, might have, may have* and *could have*. Use each structure once.

1 Sam Willis _____*might have stolen*_____ the painting because he was there until 6.30.

2 Sandra Thompson _____ the painting because _____
_____ .

3 Sophie Christie _____ the painting because _____
_____ .

4 William Rees _____ the painting because _____
_____ .

5 Daniel Foreman _____ the painting because _____
_____ .

6 Josie McCartney _____ the painting because _____
_____ .

Exam practice

Reading and Use and English Part 3

For questions **1–8**, read the text below. Use the word given in capitals at the end of some of the lines to form a word that fits in the gap **in the same line**. There is an example at the beginning (**0**).

The woman on the hill

A (**0**) _____mysterious_____ woman has lived completely alone in a large house on a hill in north Yorkshire for the last fifty years. She (**1**) _____ visits the nearby village to buy fruit. She walks (**2**) _____ down the main street but she only speaks briefly to one shop assistant. She doesn't (**3**) _____ with anyone at all and no one has ever been to visit her. Local people say that she receives (**4**) _____ of food and fuel but they assume she makes all her orders and (**5**) _____ online, so they don't even know her name.

MYSTERY
OCCASION
CONFIDENCE

SOCIAL
DELIVER
PAY

She gives the (**6**) _____ from the way she behaves that she might once have been famous. She must have been very (**7**) _____ when she was young but she appears to be well over 70 now. Nobody in the village knows who she is and they are (**8**) _____ ever to find out.

IMPRESS
ATTRACT

LIKE

Grammar focus task

What do you think the villagers say about the woman on the hill? Complete the sentences using *must*, *might (not)*, *may (not)*, *could(n't)* or *can't*.

1   I'm sure she isn't happy. = She _____can't be_____ happy.

2   I think perhaps she's shy. = She _____ shy.

3   I strongly believe she's lonely. = She _____ lonely.

4   It's not possible that she has any family nearby. = She _____ any family nearby.

5   No doubt she moved there when she was very young. = She _____ here when she was very young.

6   She probably has an interesting background. = She _____ an interesting background.

15 Reported speech

Tense changes in reported speech; reporting in the same tense;
verbs for reporting; verbs for reporting with to infinitive;
reporting questions; reference to time, place, etc.

A Context listening

1 You are going to hear a radio interview. Rachel,
a reporter in the studio, is talking to a man called James
Baker, who is sailing in a round-the-world yacht race.
What do you think she is asking him?

_____

2 ▶20 Listen and check if you were right.

3 ▶20 Later, Rachel tells a colleague about the conversation. Read what Rachel says, then listen again
and fill in the gaps with James's actual words.

1 Rachel: James told me he was about 100
kilometres off the coast of Australia.

   James: 'I 'm_____ about 100 kilometres
off the coast of Australia.'

2 Rachel: He said he hadn't seen another boat for
a few days.

   James: 'I _____ another boat for
a few days.'

3 Rachel: He said he thought he might win.

   James: 'I _____ win.'

4 Rachel: He said there had been a terrible storm.

   James: 'There _____ a terrible storm.'

5 Rachel: He said he hadn't slept for three days.

   James: 'I _____ for three days.'

6 Rachel: He told me the sea was calm, the sun
was shining.

   James: 'The sea _____ calm, the sun
_____.'

7 Rachel: He said that he could sometimes see
sharks and dolphins swimming.

   James: 'I _____ sometimes see sharks
and dolphins swimming.'

8 Rachel: He said he would spend two hours in a
hot bath.

   James: 'I _____ two hours in a
hot bath.'

9 Rachel: He said he had to get his hair cut.

   James: 'I _____ my hair cut.'

4 ▶20 Complete the questions that Rachel asked. Then listen again to check.

1 I asked him where he was. 'Where _____?'

2 I asked him if he thought he was going to win. 'Do you _____ to win?'

3 I asked him what the weather was like. 'What _____ like?'

4 I asked him if he could see dolphins there. '_____ dolphins there?'

5 Can you see any pattern to the changes to the tenses in Exercises 3 and 4?

B Grammar

1 Tense changes in reported speech

When we report what someone else said, we are usually reporting at a later time so we change the tenses used by the original speaker.

Direct speech	Reported speech
present simple 'I**'m (am)** about 100 km from Australia.'	**past simple** He said (that) he **was** about 100 km from Australia.
present continuous 'The sun**'s (is)** shining.'	**past continuous** He said (that) the sun **was shining**.
past simple 'There **was** a terrible storm.'	**past perfect** He said (that) there **had been** a terrible storm.
present perfect 'I **haven't (have not) seen** another boat.'	**past perfect** He said (that) he **hadn't (had not) seen** another boat.
past perfect 'I **hadn't (had not) expected** the storm.'	**past perfect** He said (that) he **hadn't (had not) expected** the storm.
am/is/are going to 'I**'m (am) going to** win.'	*was/were going to* He said (that) he **was going to** win.
will future 'I**'ll (will) spend** two hours in a bath.'	*would* He said (that) he**'d (would) spend** two hours in a bath.
can 'I **can** see sharks and dolphins.'	*could* He said (that) he **could** see sharks and dolphins.
may 'I **may** win.'	*might* He said (that) he **might** win.
might 'I **might** win.'	*might* He said (that) he **might** win.
must 'I **must** get my hair cut.'	*had to* He said (that) he **had to** get his hair cut.

⚠ The following verbs do not change when they are reported at a later time:
could, would, should, might, ought to, used to and verbs in the past perfect
*You **ought to** buy a new coat in the sale.* → *My mum said I **ought to** buy a new coat in the sale.*
*They **used to** live in California.* → *He said they **used to** live in California.*

When we report *must*, we can use either *must* or *had to* in the reported speech but *had to* is more common:
*Kate: 'I **must** buy some fruit.'* → *Kate said she **had to / must** buy some fruit.*

⚠ We use *must*, not *had to*, when we report:
- a negative:
  *Paul: 'You **mustn't** tell Sally our secret.'* → *Paul said we **mustn't** tell Sally our secret.*
- a deduction:
  *Sarah: 'Jim **must** be tired after the flight.'* → *Sarah said Jim **must** be tired after the flight.*

2 Reporting in the same tense

If the reporting verb is in the present tense (e.g. *says*), we use the same tenses as the original speaker:
Amy: *'I've missed the bus so I'll be a bit late.'* → Amy **says** she**'s missed** the bus so she'll be a bit late.

If the reporting verb is in the past (e.g. *said*), we sometimes use the same tenses as the original speaker if the situation is still true:
Robert: *'I have three sisters.'*
→ *Robert said he* **has** *three sisters.* or *Robert said he* **had** *three sisters.*

Carlo: *'I'm getting married in June.'*
If we report what Carlo said before June we can say:
→ *Carlo said he* **is getting** *married in June.* or *Carlo said he* **was getting** *married in June.*

⚠ But if we report after June, we must change the tense:
Carlo said he **was getting** *married in June.*

3 Verbs for reporting

We often use *say* and *tell* to report what somebody said:

With *say*, we must use *to* if we mention the person spoken to:
He **said to me** *(that) he was going to win.* (**not** *He said me*)

Tell is always used without *to*, and it must be followed by the person spoken to:
He **told them** *(that) he was going to win.* (**not** *He told to them* / *He told that*)

⚠ With *say* and *tell*, we usually omit *that*, especially in spoken English.

We can use other reporting verbs instead of *say* and *tell*. Some verbs are like *tell*:
He **reminded me** *(that) it was his birthday.*
She **persuaded me** *(that) I should buy a different car.*
He **informed me** *(that) he had a new job.*
They **warned us** *(that) the bridge was in a dangerous condition.*

Some verbs are nearly always followed by *that* and we use *to* if mentioning the person spoken to:
I **mentioned** (**to** *my uncle*) **that** *Nicholas had found a new job.*
The attendant **pointed out that** *the pool would be closed on Saturday.*
She **complained** (**to** *the waiter*) **that** *the food was cold.*
He **explained** (**to** *us*) **that** *volcanic activity often caused earthquakes.*

After *agree* we use *with* for the person spoken to:
Jack **agreed** (**with** *me*) **that** *the film was brilliant.*

Some verbs are nearly always followed by *that* but do not mention the person spoken to:
He **answered that** *he had already read the report.*
She **replied that** *she didn't know my cousin.*

4 Verbs for reporting with *to* infinitive

We usually report orders and requests by using *tell* or *ask* + object + *to* infinitive:

'Be quiet!' → The teacher **told us to be** quiet. (= an order)
'Don't stay out late.' → Dad **told me not to stay** out late. (= an order)
'Please help me!' → He **asked us to help** him. (= a request)
'Could you carry my bag, please?' → She **asked me to carry** her bag. (a request)

Some other reporting verbs are also used with the *to* infinitive (➤ see also Unit 18):

'You should vote for me.' → He **advised us to vote** for him.
'We could help you.' → They **offered to help** me.
'I'll be a good leader.' → He **promised to be** a good leader.
'OK. I'll help you do the shopping.' → He **agreed to help** me do the shopping.

5 Reporting questions

Questions are reported using the word order of a statement rather than a question.

Questions with question words (*who, what*, etc.) keep these words in the reported speech:

'How **do you feel**?' → Rachel asked James how **he felt**. (**not** *how did he feel*)
'What**'s the weather** like?' → She asked (him) what **the weather was** like. (**not** *what was the weather like*)

Yes/*no* questions are reported with *if* or *whether*:

'**Can you hear** me?' → Rachel asked James **if/whether he could hear** her.
'**Is the sea** calm?' → Rachel wanted to know **if/whether the sea was** calm.

⚠ We use the same structure when we ask politely for information:
Can you tell me what time **the next train leaves**?
I'd like to know **if there's** a flight to Australia next Thursday.

6 References to time, place, etc.

Depending on how close in time we are to the original situation, we often have to change references to time when we report what someone said:

yesterday	→	the day before / the previous day
today	→	that day / the same day
tomorrow	→	the next/following day
next week	→	the next/following week
now	→	(right) then / right away, immediately, etc.

'We didn't do any work **yesterday**.' → They admitted that they hadn't done any work **the day before**.
'Will the library be open **tomorrow**?' → She enquired whether the library would be open **the following day**.
'I have to go **now** or I'll miss my bus.' → He explained that he had to go **right then** or he'd miss his bus.

Other changes may include:

here	→	there
this	→	that/the

'I saw him **here** yesterday.' → She explained that she had seen him **there** the day before.
'What's **this** red box?' → He wanted to know what **the** red box was.

C Grammar exercises

1 You talk on the phone to a friend, Luke. This is what he says.

1 'I've given up my job.'

2 'I can easily find another one.'

3 'I'm going to travel round Africa.'

4 'I lived there as a child.'

5 'I might get a part-time job there.'

6 'I'm packing my bag.'

7 'I'm really excited.'

8 'I'll be away for a year.'

9 'I may stay longer.'

10 'You could come too.'

After your conversation with Luke, you tell another friend what he said. Change the verbs above to complete the sentences below.

1 He said he _____ *had given up his job* _____ .

2 He said he _____ .

3 He said he _____ .

4 He said he _____ .

5 He said he _____ .

6 He said he _____ .

7 He said he _____ .

8 He said he _____ .

9 He said he _____ .

10 He said I _____ .

Is it possible to report what Luke said without changing the verbs? Why?

2 Match the beginnings and endings of these sentences.

1 She told   A   I could help my neighbour mend his car.

2 My sister asked   B   whether my sister could give me a lift.

3 I said   C   me she couldn't afford to come to the theatre.

4 My parents said   D   to phone home regularly.

5 My teacher advised   E   to me, 'You shouldn't watch so much TV.'

6 I wanted to know   F   if I wanted to go on holiday with her.

7 I told   G   the dentist that Thursday was the only day I was free.

8 My brother promised   H   me to revise my work more thoroughly.

3   **Last year you worked at a children's holiday camp. During your interview for the job the organiser asked you the following questions.**

1   Are you married?

2   How old are you?

3   Which university are you studying at?

4   Where do you come from?

5   Have you worked with children before?

6   What sports do you play?

7   Will you work for at least two months?

8   Can you start immediately?

9   Do you need accommodation?

10   Would you like any more information?

> ## Work abroad
>
> We are looking for enthusiastic and lively young people to work in a children's holiday camp over the summer.

A friend of yours called Miguel is going to apply for a job at the same camp. Complete the email, telling him what questions you were asked.

Hi Miguel

Good luck with the job application! These are the things the organiser asked me about – he'll probably ask you the same sorts of questions.

He asked me **(1)** _if I was married_ . He wanted to know **(2)** ———————— , which university **(3)** ———————— at and where **(4)** ———————— . Then he asked **(5)** ———————— with children before and what sports **(6)** ———————— . He wanted to know **(7)** ———————— for at least two months and **(8)** ———————— immediately. He asked **(9)** ———————— accommodation and wondered **(10)** ———————— any more information.

Let me know how you get on.

---

4   **Correct the mistake in each of the following sentences by Cambridge First candidates.**

1   I didn't know she had ~~said~~ you about the problem with my university.   _told_

2   I asked him how he did feel about it, but he hasn't replied to my email.   ————

3   I told her not to worry about the damage, but she replied me that it was her father's car.   ————

4   Juan asked me if you did wanted to come.   ————

5   She asked me did I want to go to the cinema.   ————

6   He asked me for giving information about an interesting place to visit in London.   ————

7   I reminded him he told me that there was a ghost in the castle.   ————

8   He asked me if I will go to the dance with him.   ————

5 A teacher is talking to Andy, a student. Later, Andy tells a friend what the teacher said. Complete his sentences.

> **1** You need to work harder.

> **2** You could do well.

> **3** Do you study every evening?

> **4** What time do you go to bed?

> **5** You won't get good marks.

> **6** You spend too much time with your friends.

> **7** Have you decided on a career yet?

1 She said I needed to work harder .

2 She told _____ .

3 She wanted to know _____ .

4 She wondered _____ .

5 She warned _____ .

6 She complained _____ .

7 She asked _____ .

6 Read what happened to Suzie the other day. Then write the conversation that she actually had.

I travel to college on the same bus every day. The other day when I got on the bus I realised that I had left my purse at home and didn't have the money for the bus fare. But the woman sitting behind me told me not to worry because she would lend me some money. She said the same thing had happened to her the day before. I asked her what she had done. She said someone had lent her the fare and she was going to give it back that afternoon on the bus, so she was happy to do the same for me. She told me I could give the money back to her the following day. I thanked her very much and told her I was very glad she was there.

Woman: Don't worry, I'll lend you some money.

_____

Suzie: _____

Woman: _____

_____

_____

_____

_____

Suzie: _____

_____

Exam practice

Reading and Use of English Part 4

For questions **1–6**, complete the second sentence so that it has a similar meaning to the first sentence, using the word given. **Do not change the word given.** You must use between **two** and **five** words, including the word given. Here is an example (**0**).

---

0   The tourist guide said to us: 'Take a map if you go walking in the hills.'

ADVISED

The tourist guide _____ *advised us to take* _____ a map if we went walking in the hills.

1   The weatherman forecast that it would be sunny all day.

SHINE

The weatherman said: 'The _____ all day.'

2   'I haven't heard from Helen for a long time,' Paul said to me.

TOLD

Paul _____ not heard from Helen for a long time.

3   'Did you book a room with a balcony?' I asked my mother.

IF

I asked my mother _____ a room with a balcony.

4   Jack wanted to know what time they would leave the next day to catch the train.

WE

Jack asked: 'What time _____ to catch the train?'

5   The little boy said he could dress himself without any help.

I

The little boy said: '_____ without any help.'

6   'Are we meeting David in the morning or the afternoon?' Karen asked.

WHETHER

Karen wondered _____ in the morning or the afternoon.

Grammar focus task

In three of the sentences above, the reporting verbs can be replaced with *complain*, *insist* and *predict*. Write the reported sentences again using these verbs.

_____

_____

_____

A Context listening

1 You are going to hear a radio news bulletin. Before you listen, look at the pictures and decide what happened. Put the pictures in the correct order.

1 _____   2 _____   3 _____   4 _____

2 ▶21 Listen and check if you were right.

3 ▶21 Read this article from a news website. Then listen again and fill in the gaps. Stop the recording when you need to.

Burglars' 'luck' was well planned

FOUR BURGLARS have escaped from custody only hours after (1) _____*being*_____ sentenced to ten years in prison. They (2) _____ transferred from the law courts in Manchester to Strangeways Prison. They (3) _____ found guilty of stealing electrical goods and money from shops in the Manchester area. It (4) _____ thought that they were all members of the same gang. They escaped from the van in which they (5) _____ transported, when the driver (6) _____ forced to stop because of a tree across the road. It (7) _____ believed that the tree (8) _____ placed there by other members of the gang, who (9) _____ informed of the route (10) _____ taken by the van. A full investigation of the events leading to the escape (11) _____ ordered and anyone with information (12) _____ asked to contact the police to help with their inquiries.

4 How many of the verbs that you completed in Exercise 3 are in the passive? _____

16 The passive

B Grammar

1 The passive

How the passive is formed
We form the passive by using the verb *to be* followed by the past participle:

Active:
*The police officer **saw** the robber at the airport.*
*She**'s following** him.*
*She**'ll catch** him soon.*

Passive:
*The robber **was seen** at the airport.*
*He**'s being followed**.*
*He**'ll be caught** soon.*

Active		Passive
to catch	→	to be caught
to have caught	→	to have been caught
catching	→	being caught
having caught	→	having been caught
catch(es)	→	am/are/is caught
am/are is catching	→	am/are/is being caught
will catch	→	will be caught
am/are/is going to catch	→	am/are/is going to be caught
has/have caught	→	has/have been caught
caught	→	was/were caught
was catching	→	was being caught
had caught	→	had been caught
would catch	→	would be caught
would have caught	→	would have been caught

When the passive is used
The passive is used quite often in English, both in speech and writing. We use the passive when:

- we don't know who or what did something:
  *My phone **has been stolen**.* (= Someone has stolen my phone.)
  *The first tools **were made** in Africa two million years ago.* (= People made the first tools …)
- the action is more important than who did it:
  *Income tax **was introduced** in England in 1798.*
- it is obvious who or what did something:
  *The thief **has been arrested**.*

We can use *by* + person/thing to show who/what did the action if this information is important:
*The robber was seen **by the police officer**. (= The police officer saw the robber.)*

Verbs with two objects
Some verbs (e.g. *give, send, buy, bring*) can have two objects:
Active: *A witness **gave** the police some information.*
  *A witness **gave** some information to the police.*

  *Lots of fans **sent** the footballer birthday cards.*
  *Lots of fans **sent** birthday cards to the footballer.*

Either of the objects can be the subject of a passive sentence:

Passive: *The police **were given** some information by a witness.*
  *Some information **was given** to the police by a witness.*

  *The footballer **was sent** birthday cards by lots of fans.*
  *Birthday cards **were sent** to the footballer by lots of fans.*

2 *to have/get something done*

When we ask someone else to do something for us, we often use the structure *to have something done*.
It is not usually necessary to say who did the action:
*The president **had** his speeches **written** (by his staff). (= The president's staff wrote his speeches.)*
*I **had** my hair **cut**. (= The hairdresser cut my hair.)*
*I'm **having** my kitchen **painted**. (= The decorator is painting my kitchen.)*
*They want to **have** their car **fixed**. (= They want the garage to fix their car.)*

In informal speech, we often use *get* instead of *have*:
*I **got** my hair **cut**. (= I had my hair cut.)*
*When **are** you **getting** that window **repaired**?*
*We need to **get** something **done** about this leak in the roof.*

3 *It is said that ...*

We often use *it* + passive + *that* when we report what people in general say or believe:
*It **is believed that** the tree was placed there by other members of the gang. (= Everyone believes that ...)*

We can use a number of verbs in this pattern, e.g. *agree, announce, believe, decide, report, say, think*:
*It's **(is) said that** a famous singer used to live in this house. (= People say that ...)*
*It **was agreed that** the theatre must be closed. (= The theatre's owners agreed that ...)*
*It's **(is) reported that** the damage will cost millions of pounds to repair. (= The news media report that ...)*
*It's **(has) been announced that** a new road will be built along the river. (= The council has announced ...)*
*Until the 16th century **it was thought that** the sun revolved around the Earth. (= People generally thought that ...)*

C Grammar exercises

1 Choose the correct words.

1 The children wanted to <u>be</u> / *been* allowed to stay up late and see the fireworks.

2 Our flight was *delaying* / *delayed* by fog and we missed our connection.

3 Lauren was sulking because she *wasn't* / *hadn't been* invited to Ralph's party.

4 By the time we arrived at the market, the best fruit *had be* / *had been* sold.

5 While the meal was *being* / *been* prepared, we had a drink on the terrace.

6 The new library will be *open* / *opened* by the Mayor next Saturday.

7 The rock star was sent a chocolate cake *by* / *of* one of his fans.

2 Fill in the gaps with the passive form of the verbs.

1 A government minister _____was found_____ (*find*) guilty of fraud yesterday.

2 It was a lovely surprise to find that all the washing-up _____ (*do*) while I was asleep.

3 These souvenirs _____ (*make*) by children from the local school in their last summer holidays.

4 Wait for me! I don't want _____ (*leave*) on my own!

5 It _____ (*say*) that the Prime Minister's husband plays the piano quite well.

6 The votes _____ (*count*) right now and we should know the result before midnight.

7 As he _____ (*sack*) from his previous job, he found it hard to get another.

8 In the past, it _____ (*think*) that the population of the world would always increase but now it _____ (*agree*) that this may not be true.

9 The judges still have to decide which design _____ (*award*) the top prize.

10 This parcel appears _____ (*open*) before it _____ (*deliver*).

3 Match the two halves of the conversations and fill in the gaps with the correct form of the verbs in brackets.

1 I thought those chairs were broken.

2 Your bike's got a flat tyre!

3 This carpet's filthy.

4 What's happened to your hair?

5 I don't like this room. It's too dark.

6 These trousers are much too loose.

7 What a beautiful garden!

8 Why is your car at the garage?

A I _____ (*have / colour*).

B Yes, you need to _____ (*have / take in*).

C I can _____ (*get / fix*) at the cycle shop.

D Yes, we should _____ (*have / redecorate*).

E I've __had them mended__ (*have / mend*).

F We _____ (*have / check*) before we go away.

G We must _____ (*get / clean*).

H Thanks! We _____ (*have / design*) by an expert.

4 Read this report in the *Cybernian News*.

CYBERNIAN NEWS

22 October 3008

Victory for Cybernia!

The victorious Cybernian Inter-galactic Forces report:

Yesterday we invaded Planet Upstart with a large force. We have completely crushed the year-old rebellion there. Our space ships have destroyed ninety per cent of the Upstart space fleet. A special Cybernian task force landed near the central communications building and captured it without difficulty. Our spokesperson immediately broadcast a message to the population. We announced that we had liberated them from the illegal Upstart government and we asked them to cooperate with the new government of their planet. We have arrested the rebel leaders and we are taking them back to Cybernia where the government will put them on trial.

Complete the report below so it matches the report in the *Cybernian News*. Use the passive form of the verbs.

UPSTART NEWS...22 OCTOBER 3008...

Defeat for Upstarts

Yesterday our planet (1) ____*wasp invaded*____ (*invade*) by a large force from Cybernia. Our year-old rebellion (2) _____ (*crush*).

Ninety per cent of our space fleet (3) _____ (*destroy*). The central communications building (4) _____ (*capture*) without difficulty by a special Cybernian task force and a message (5) _____ (*broadcast*). It (6) _____ (*announce*) that we (7) _____ (*liberate*), and we (8) _____ (*ask*) to cooperate with our new government. Our leaders (9) _____ (*arrest*) and they (10) _____ (*take*) to Cybernia where it (11) _____ (*claim*) that they (12) _____ (*put*) on trial.

---

5 Correct the mistake in each of the following sentences by Cambridge First candidates.

1 The mark on the ceiling ~~was appeared~~ last week.   ____*appeared*____

2 He escaped without having being recognised by anyone.   _____

3 A shopping mall was been built in the town centre about 20 years ago.   _____

4 Most of the problems was happened when we arrived at the hotel.   _____

5 Yesterday I went to your barber's shop to cut my hair and I was very disappointed.   _____

6 I can get my computer fixing at the shop next to the bank.   _____

Exam practice

Reading and Use of English Part 4

For questions **1–6**, complete the second sentence so that it has a similar meaning to the first sentence, using the word given. **Do not change the word given.** You must use between two and five words, including the word given. Here is an example (**0**).

---

0 My grandfather hasn't spoken to me since Sunday.

SPOKE

My grandfather _____ *last spoke to me on* _____ Sunday.

1 The students gave a concert after their exams.

WAS

A concert _____ students after their exams.

2 My computer needs to be repaired before the weekend.

HAVE

I must _____ before the weekend.

3 We heard reports last week that the dictator had fled the country.

IT

Last week _____ the dictator had fled the country.

4 No one gave my message to the shop manager.

NOT

My message _____ the shop manager.

5 The teacher said Simon had cheated.

ACCUSED

Simon _____ his teacher.

6 The address the tourist office gave us for the hotel was wrong so we got lost.

RIGHT

We _____ address for the hotel by the tourist office so we got lost.

Grammar focus task

1 Which of the sentences can these phrases be added to?

   a *by an expert* _____   **b** *by the foreign press* _____

2 What effect does this have on their meaning?

   a _____

   b _____

17 Conditionals (1)

Zero, first, second and third conditionals; mixed conditionals

A Context listening

1 You are going to hear a spy, known as Double X, talking to his boss, Mrs Seymour, about a photograph which she gives him. Mrs Seymour is asking Double X to do something. Before you listen, guess what she is asking.

_____

_____

2 ▶22 Listen to the beginning of the conversation and check if you were right.

3 ▶22 Listen to the whole conversation and answer these questions. Stop the recording when you need to.

1   What is wrong with the photo? _____

2   Why doesn't Mrs Seymour give Double X a better photo? _____

3   Who sent the photo to Mrs Seymour? _____

4   How is it possible to make the picture clearer? _____

5   Who is in the photo? _____

6   Can you guess why the photo was sent to Mrs Seymour? _____

4 ▶22 Listen again and fill in the gaps.

1   If you _____*find*_____ him, I _____ extremely pleased.

2   If we _____ a better picture, we _____ it to you.

3   If she _____ us that, I _____ to ask for your help.

4   It _____ me somewhere to start if I _____ her phone number.

5   It _____ a bit clearer if you _____ at it with your eyes half closed.

5 Look at Exercise 4 and complete these sentences.

1   In sentence 5, the _____ tense is used after _if_.

2   In sentence 1, the _____ tense is used after _if_.

3   In sentences 2 and 4, the _____ tense is used after _if_.

4   In sentence 3, the _____ tense is used after _if_.

B Grammar

Conditional sentences tell us a condition (*if* ...)* and its consequence. The tenses we use depend on:
- whether the condition and its consequence are possible, unlikely or imaginary.
- whether they are generally true or are linked to a particular event.

➤ *For other words like *if* which introduce conditions, see Unit 19.

Often the condition comes before the consequence and in this case the condition is followed by a comma:
If you ring that bell, *someone will come to the door.*

Sometimes the consequence comes first and in this case we don't use a comma:
Someone will come to the door *if you ring that bell.*

We can divide conditionals into four groups.

1 Zero conditional

> *If* + present tense, + consequence using present tense
> **If** *the economy* **is** *bad, there* **are** *few jobs for young people.*
>
> Consequence in present tense + *if* + present tense
> *There* **are** *few jobs for young people* **if** *the economy* **is** *bad.*

We use this to state general truths. *If* means the same as *when* in zero conditional sentences:
If/When *you're in love, nothing else* **matters**. = *Nothing else* **matters** **if/when** *you're in love.*
If/When *it* **rains**, *we* **get** *terrible traffic jams*. = *We* **get** *terrible traffic jams* **if/when** *it* **rains**.
If/When *we* **heat** *ice, it* **melts**. = *Ice* **melts if/when** *we* **heat** *it.*

2 First conditional

> *If* + present tense, + consequence using future tense
> **If** *I* **pass** *this exam, my parents* **will give** *me a motorbike.*
>
> Consequence in future tense + *if* + present tense
> *My parents* **will give** *me a motorbike* **if** *I* **pass** *this exam.*

We use this for a condition which we believe is possible. We use a present tense after *if* even though we are very often referring to a future possibility:
If you visit me, I'll take *you to the Tower of London.* (**not** ~~If you'll visit~~) (= it's possible you will visit me)
If it snows, we'll go *skiing.* (= it's possible that it will snow, we can't be certain)
If I see *Ruth, I'll give her your message* (= it's possible I'll see her but I might not)

If does not mean the same as *when* in sentences like these:
When *you visit me, I'll take you to the Tower of London.* (= I know you're going to visit me)
When *it snows, we'll go skiing.* (= it will definitely snow, I'm certain)
When *I see Ruth, I'll give her your message.* (= I know I'm going to see her)

Sometimes we use the imperative followed by *and* to express this kind of condition (the imperative always comes first). This form is more common in spoken English. We usually use it for promises and threats:
Pass *this exam and we'll give you a motorbike.*
Wait *a minute and I'll be able to help you.*
Break *that jug and you'll have to pay for it.*

3 Second conditional

> *If* + past tense, + consequence using *would* + verb
> **If** you **lived** in London, I **would visit** you at weekends.
>
> Consequence using *would* + verb + *if* + past tense
> I **would visit** you at weekends **if** you **lived** in London.

We use this for an imaginary condition, which we believe to be impossible or very improbable.
We use the past tense after *if* even though we are referring to the present or future:
*The world **would seem** wonderful **if** you **were** in love.* (= but you're not in love, so the world doesn't seem wonderful)
*If it **snowed**, we'd **(would) go** skiing.* (= I think it's very unlikely that it will snow)

⚠ We often use *were* instead of *was* in the *if* clause, especially when we write. It is more formal:
*If I **wasn't/weren't** so tired, I'd go out with my friends this evening.*
*The product would attract more customers if it **was/were** less expensive.*

We always use *were* in the phrase *If I were you*, used to give advice:
If I were you, I wouldn't phone him.

4 Third conditional

> *If* + past perfect, + consequence using *would have* + past participle
> *If I'**d (had) seen** Karen, I'd **(would) have given** her your message.*
>
> Consequence using *would have* + past participle + *if* + past perfect
> *I'd **(would) have given** Karen your message **if** I'd **(had) seen** her.*

We use this to talk about past events which cannot be changed, so we know that the condition is impossible and its consequence is imaginary:
*The world **would have seemed** wonderful **if** you'd **(had) been** in love.* (= but you weren't in love so the world didn't seem wonderful)
*If it **had snowed**, we'd **(would) have gone** skiing.* (= but it didn't snow, so we didn't go skiing)
*I'd **(would) have visited** you every weekend **if** you'd **(had) invited** me.* (= but you didn't invite me, so I didn't visit you.)

⚠ Other modal verbs like *might* and *could* are sometimes used instead of *would* in second and third conditional sentences:
*I **might** visit you **if** you **invited** me.*
*I **could have** visited you **if** you'd **(had) invited** me.*
*If it **had snowed**, we **could have gone** skiing.*

5 Mixed conditionals

We sometimes meet sentences which contain a mixture of second and third conditionals because of their particular context:
*If you **lived** in London, I'd **have visited** you by now.* (= but you don't live in London so I haven't visited you)
*If the weather **had been fine** last week, there **would be** roses in my garden.* (= but the weather was bad last week so there are no roses in my garden now)
*Lesley **wouldn't have missed** the bus **if** she **was** better organised.* (= she missed the bus because she is a badly organised person)
*You **could have used** my car yesterday **if** the battery **wasn't** flat.* (= the battery is still flat)

C Grammar exercises

1 Match the beginnings and endings of these sentences.

1 The house wouldn't have been such a mess	A if she wasn't such a jealous type.
2 If Mike had listened to his father,	B I'd probably try to get into a local team.
3 I would quite like Juno	C they usually wait until the weather is good.
4 If Dave didn't work so much,	D and you'll never forget his face.
5 We would have arrived early	E he wouldn't have got into trouble.
6 If I were as good at tennis as Nancy,	F I still wouldn't love you!
7 If people want to have a barbecue,	G she'll get a nasty surprise.
8 If Sally opens that door,	H if the roads had been less busy.
9 Take one look at Alan	I he wouldn't get so tired.
10 If you were as handsome as a film star,	J if the guests hadn't been careless.

2 Put the verbs in brackets into the correct form.

1 I won't help you with your homework if you _____don't tidy_____ (*not tidy*) your bedroom.

2 You'll need a visa if you _____ (*want*) to travel to China.

3 If he _____ (*care*) about other people's feelings, he wouldn't behave that way.

4 She _____ (*not be*) successful if she doesn't learn to control her temper.

5 If I'd known you were such a gossip, I _____ (*not tell*) you my secret.

6 They would work harder if they _____ (*not be*) so tired.

7 The boss _____ (*be*) furious if he'd found out what you were up to.

8 If the temperature _____ (*fall*) below freezing, water turns to ice.

9 If they _____ (*not expect*) delays, they wouldn't have set off so early.

10 Open the envelope and you _____ (*discover*) what prize you've won.

3 Complete the sentence for each picture using the third conditional, to show how missing her bus one day resulted in a new job for Zoe.

1 If she hadn't missed her bus, she _____ wouldn't have gone into the café _____ .

2 If there had been a free table, she _____ .

3 _____ , she wouldn't have had to wait for her coffee.

4 _____ , she wouldn't have picked up the magazine.

5 If she hadn't noticed the advertisement, she _____ .

4 👁 Complete the following sentences by Cambridge First candidates with the correct form of these verbs.

| apply | be | come | earn | get | go | ~~have~~ | stay | take |

1 If I _____ had _____ to choose a present, I would like to have a new skirt.

2 If he hadn't been interested in the job, he _____ (*not*) for it in the first place.

3 If I _____ you, I would try to organise water skiing for my students.

4 If we had seen her during the holidays, we _____ her to the castle.

5 If I _____ more money, I would buy a new phone.

6 I'll be really happy if you _____ to my birthday party.

7 If she _____ at home on Saturday, she wouldn't have met Andrei at the party.

8 If I _____ camping with my father, we will probably go fishing.

9 If I watch too much TV before school, my father _____ angry with me.

Exam practice

Reading and Use of English Part 6

You are going to read a magazine article about a young woman who works in a nursery school. Six sentences have been removed from the article. Choose from the sentences **A–G** the one which fits each gap (**1–6**). There is one extra sentence which you do not need to use.

CHANCES

Nursery school teacher Sarah Oliver tells how a chance meeting changed her life.

I really enjoy my job, it makes me feel good at the beginning of every week, because I love working with small children and I enjoy the challenges that arise. But there was a time when I thought I would never have that sort of career.

I wasn't very good at school: I mean, I didn't like studying much, so I didn't try very hard. I thought I was the sort of person who couldn't do school work, I suppose. **1** [ ] But in my final term I started thinking what I might do and I realised that I didn't have much to offer. If I'd worked harder, I would have had better grades, but it was too late. I just accepted that I wasn't the type to have a career.

Then I thought, well, I've spent every holiday for the past five years helping my mum – I've got two brothers and a sister, all much younger than me. **2** [ ] Their father worked abroad and their mother had some high-powered job in an insurance company. I did most of the housework and I had a lot of responsibility for the children although I was only sixteen.

The problems began really when I agreed to live in, so that I would be there if my boss had to go out for business in the evening. What was supposed to happen was, if I had to work extra hours one week, she'd give me time off the next. But unfortunately, it didn't often work out. **3** [ ] I felt trapped, because if I walked out, there wouldn't be anyone to look after them.

Anyway, one Sunday I was in the park with them, while their parents were on yet another business trip, and I met a girl called Megan I used to be at school with. **4** [ ] I was telling her how I loved the kids but hated the job and she said, 'If you want to work with children, you ought to do a course and get a qualification.'

I thought you couldn't do courses if you hadn't done all sorts of exams at school, but she persuaded me to phone the local college and they were really helpful. My experience counted for a lot and I got on a part-time course. **5** [ ] I was really short of money and I even had to get an evening job as a waitress for a while. But it was worth it in the end.

Now I've got a full-time job. Most of the children in this school come from families where there are problems like unemployment or poor housing. **6** [ ] The children benefit, but also the parents. It gives them time to sort things out, go for training or job interviews, and so on. I'll always be grateful to Megan. If I hadn't bumped into her, I would have stayed on where I was, getting more and more fed up.

Exam practice

A	I had to leave my job with the family, but I got work helping out at a nursery school.
B	I find that the work we do helps in lots of ways.
C	I was getting more and more tired and fed up, because I had too many late nights and early mornings with the little ones.
D	So I found myself a job as a nanny, looking after two little girls.
E	We weren't particularly friendly before, but we chatted about what we were doing.
F	If I'd had more confidence, I would have done that.
G	I was just impatient to leave as soon as I could.

Grammar focus task

Without looking back at the text, match the beginnings and endings of these extracts.

1	I thought you couldn't do courses	**A**	there wouldn't be anyone to look after them.
2	If I'd worked harder,	**B**	you ought to do a course and get a qualification.
3	If I hadn't bumped into her,	**C**	I would have done that.
4	If I'd had more confidence,	**D**	she'd give me time off the next.
5	If you want to work with children,	**E**	I would have stayed on where I was.
6	If I walked out,	**F**	I would have had better grades.
7	If I had to work extra hours one week,	**G**	if you hadn't done all sorts of exams at school.

The *to* infinitive and *-ing*

Verb + to infinitive; verb + infinitive without to; verb + -ing;
verb + *that* clause; adjective + to infinitive

A Context listening

1 You are going to hear a TV chef telling a group of people how to cook something. Look at the picture, which shows the things he uses. Can you guess what he is going to make? _____

2 ▶23 Listen and check if you were right.

3 ▶23 Listen again and fill in the gaps. Stop the recording when you need to.

1 Continue _____*doing*_____ this until the mixture begins to look pale and fluffy.

2 Avoid _____ the eggs all at the same time.

3 Keep _____ all the time.

4 Don't forget _____ the baking powder.

5 I recommend _____ sultanas and apricots.

6 If you prefer _____ dates or raisins, that's fine.

7 Some people like _____ some nuts too.

8 If you decide _____ nuts, chop them up small.

9 Remember _____ if the fruit cake is ready after about an hour.

10 I suggest _____ a little lemon juice as well.

11 Don't try _____ the cake until it's completely cold.

12 Don't expect _____ much fruit cake left after a couple of hours.

4 What do you notice about the forms of the verbs you have filled in?

B Grammar

When one verb follows another, the second verb is always either an *-ing* form or an infinitive, with or without *to*. The form of the second verb depends on the first verb.

All the verbs in this unit marked * can also normally be followed by a *that* clause with the same meaning (➤ see B7).

1 Verb + *to* infinitive

> (can/can't) afford *agree aim appear *arrange attempt choose
> *decide *demand deserve fail *hope learn manage neglect
> offer omit plan prepare *pretend refuse seem tend
> threaten (can't) wait wish

*If you **decide to add** nuts ...*
*I **hope to see** you later.*

Notice how the negative is formed:
*If you **decide not to ice** it ...*

The following verbs + *to* infinitive **always** have an object before the *to* infinitive:

> *advise allow encourage forbid force invite order permit
> *persuade *remind *teach *tell *warn

*Her father **taught** <u>her</u> **to play** tennis.*
*The teacher **reminded** <u>the children</u> **to bring** their swimming things.*
*The school **allows** <u>students</u> **to wear** jeans.*

Advise, allow, encourage, forbid and *permit* can also be followed by *-ing* when there is no object:
*I **advise** <u>you</u> **to add** nuts.* or *I **advise adding** nuts.*

The following verbs + *to* infinitive **sometimes** have an object:

> ask beg *expect help *intend *promise want

*We **expected to be** late.* or *We **expected** <u>Tom</u> **to be** late.*
*We **wanted to stay** longer.* or *We **wanted** <u>them</u> **to stay** longer.*

⚠ *Would like, would love, would prefer,* etc. are also followed by the *to* infinitive (➤ see B4).

2 Verb + infinitive without *to*

Modal verbs (*can, could, may, might, must, needn't, shall, should, will, would*), *had better* and *would rather* are followed by the infinitive without *to* (➤ see also Units 11, 13 and 14):
*You **should add** the eggs slowly.*
*You **needn't include** nuts.*

Help can be followed by the infinitive with or without *to*:
*We **helped** them **(to) start** their car.*

Make and *let* (always with an object) are followed by the infinitive without *to*:
***Let** <u>the cake</u> **cool** for half an hour.*
*I **made** <u>my sister</u> **help** with the cooking.* (= I forced or obliged her to help)

3 Verb + *-ing*

*admit   avoid   can't face   can't help   can't stand   carry on   *consider   delay   *deny   detest   dislike   enjoy   fancy   feel like   finish   give up   *imagine   involve   keep (on)   *mention   (not) mind   miss   postpone   practise   put off   *recommend   risk   resist   *suggest

*I **enjoy making** it.*
***Avoid adding** the eggs all at the same time.*
***Keep beating** the eggs.*
*I **suggest adding** a little lemon juice.*

Notice how the negative is formed:
*If you don't leave immediately, you **risk not catching** your plane.*
*Can you **imagine not having** a car nowadays?*

4 Verb + *to* infinitive or *-ing* (with no difference in meaning)

begin   can't bear   continue   hate   dislike   like   love   prefer   *propose   start

***Continue adding** the flour.* or ***Continue to add** the flour.*
*I **prefer using** apricots.* or *I **prefer to use** apricots.*
*I **love making** cakes.* or *I **love to make** cakes.*

Two *-ing* forms do not usually follow each other:
*I was **starting to make** a cake when the phone rang.* (**not** ~~I was starting making~~)

⚠ *Like, prefer, hate* and *love* can be followed by the *to* infinitive or *-ing,* but *would like, would prefer, would hate* and *would love* are always followed by the *to* infinitive:
*She **would like to go** out but we **would prefer to stay** in.*

⚠ *Like* + *to* infinitive has a slightly different meaning from *like* + *-ing*:
*I **like to catch** the early bus on Mondays.* (= this is a good thing to do or it's a habit, but not necessarily something I enjoy)
*I **like dancing**.* (= I enjoy it)

5 Verb + *to* infinitive or *-ing* (with a difference in meaning)

The following verbs have two different meanings depending on the verb form that follows:

*remember   *forget   *regret   try   stop   mean   go on

Verb + *to* infinitive	Verb + *-ing*
***Remember to check** whether the cake is ready.* (= remember an action you need to do)	*I **remember checking** that I had my keys when I left the house.* (= have a memory of a past action)
*Don't **forget to add** the baking powder.* (= fail to remember something you need to do)	*I'll never **forget going** to school on my own for the first time.* (= lose the memory of something you did)
*I **regret to inform** you that your application was unsuccessful.* (= I am sorry to tell you …)	*We **regret sending** our daughter to that school.* (= we wish we hadn't)
*She **stopped to have** a rest.* (= in order to have a rest)	***Stop beating** when the mixture is pale and fluffy.* (= finish doing it)

*They don't **mean to upset** you.* (= they don't intend to)	*If you go by train, that **means taking** a taxi to the station.* (= it involves)
*He **went on to tell** us how to make a different cake.* (= the next thing he did was to tell us ...)	*They **went on cycling** until they reached the farm.* (= they continued)
***Try to ice** the cake quickly.* (= attempt to do it quickly if you can)	***Try adding** nuts as it will improve the flavour.* (= do it as an experiment)

6 Verb + *-ing* or infinitive without *to* (with a difference in meaning)

The following verbs connected with the senses may be followed by an object and either *-ing* or the infinitive without *to*:

> feel   hear   notice   see   watch

Notice the difference in meaning between verb + *-ing* and verb + infinitive without *to*:
*I **watched** <u>the boys</u> **playing** football.* (= an activity continuing over a period of time)
*I **watched** <u>the boy</u> **kick** the football into the road.* (= a short completed action)

*She **heard** <u>her mother</u> **singing** as she came downstairs.* (= a continuing action)
*She **heard** <u>the doorbell</u> **ring**.* (= a short completed action)

7 Verb + *that* clause

All the verbs marked * in this unit can also be followed by a *that* clause with the same meaning:
*She **admitted taking** the money.* = *She **admitted (that) she had taken** the money.*
***Imagine sitting** on a tropical beach with a cool drink.* = ***Imagine (that) you're sitting** on a tropical beach ...*
*I **suggest adding** some lemon juice.* = *I **suggest (that) you add** some lemon juice.*
*I **recommend using** sultanas and apricots.* = *I **recommend (that) you use** sultanas and apricots.*
*They **agreed to leave** early.* = *They **agreed (that) they would leave** early.*

8 Adjective + *to* infinitive

Many adjectives can be followed by the *to* infinitive. These are some common ones:

> afraid   cheap   *dangerous   delighted   *difficult   *easy
> expensive   happy   *hard   impossible   interesting   *nice
> pleased   possible   safe   sorry   surprised

*I'm **surprised to see** you here.*
*The book was **hard to understand** and at times I found it almost **impossible to read**.*

The adjectives marked * can sometimes also be followed by *-ing* with the same meaning:
*It's **nice meeting** friends after school.*   or   *It's **nice to meet** friends after school.*

➤ See also Unit 21, B1 for adjectives followed by a preposition + *-ing* or a noun.

C Grammar exercises

1 **Complete this conversation using the verbs in brackets.**

Andy: I've decided **(1)** ___to leave___ (*leave*) my job next month.

Sally: But I thought you enjoyed **(2)** _____ (*work*) in an architect's office.

Andy: Oh, I do. But I feel like **(3)** _____ (*do*) something different for a while.

Sally: Didn't you promise **(4)** _____ (*stay*) there at least two years?

Andy: Yes, I did but I just can't stand **(5)** _____ (*work*) with those people. One of them refuses **(6)** _____ (*stop*) talking while she works, another one keeps **(7)** _____ (*sing*) to himself. And then there's a man who attempts **(8)** _____ (*tell*) awful jokes all the time, which he always gets wrong. I detest **(9)** _____ (*work*) with all that noise around me.

Sally: It sounds quite a cheerful place to me. Can't you manage **(10)** _____ (*ignore*) them and get on with your work?

Andy: No, I can't. I just can't carry on **(11)** _____ (*go*) there every day. I'm hoping **(12)** _____ (*go*) abroad for a bit.

Sally: Well, good luck.

2 **Choose the correct form of the verb.**

1   I noticed the man *drop* / *dropping* / *to drop* his ticket so I picked it up for him.

2   The tour guide advised the tourists not *take* / *taking* / *to take* too much money out of the hotel with them.

3   I heard the horses *come* / *coming* / *to come* down the lane so I waited for them to pass before driving on.

4   The old man said he would love *have* / *having* / *to have* the chance to fly in an aeroplane again.

5   Don't make the children *come* / *coming* / *to come* with us to the shops if they don't want to.

6   I saw the boy *jump* / *jumping* / *to jump* into the lake before anyone could stop him.

7   I recommend *phone* / *phoning* / *to phone* the restaurant before you set off.

8   We were so pleased *hear* / *hearing* / *to hear* that Josh can come to the wedding after all.

9   The school only allows students *eat* / *eating* / *to eat* in the dining room.

10   It was my drama teacher who encouraged me *become* / *becoming* / *to become* an actor.

3 **Fill in the gaps with the correct form of the verbs in the box.**

| book | ~~buy~~ | chat | finish | get | go | inform | leave | lend | make | send | throw | watch | wear | write |

1 If I go to my friend's wedding it will mean _____buying_____ a new dress.

2 Please try _____ to the airport in good time – I'll be nervous if I don't see you when I come into the arrivals hall.

3 Will you stop _____ that noise? I'm trying _____ this book before I go to bed.

4 I forgot _____ a table at the restaurant and it was full when we got there, so we had to wait for ages.

5 The children went on _____ their ball against the wall, although they had been told several times to stop.

6 We regret _____ you that the course you applied for is now full.

7 Tommy says he doesn't know where my jacket is, but I clearly remember _____ it to him.

8 When you go out of the hotel, remember _____ the room key with reception because we've only got one between us.

9 Why don't you try _____ sunglasses? Then you might not get so many headaches.

10 I saw Philip when I was in the park so I stopped _____ to him.

11 I meant _____ you a text when I got to the hotel but I didn't have time.

12 I regret not _____ to Egypt with my sister because she says it was a really great trip.

13 After getting a degree in biology, my son went on _____ a book about monkeys.

14 I'll never forget _____ the sun come up over the mountains when I was in the Himalayas.

4 👁 **Some of these sentences by Cambridge First candidates have mistakes. If a sentence is correct, mark it with a tick (✓). If it is incorrect, mark it with a cross (✗) and correct it.**

1 Not all of the students can afford ~~going~~ abroad on the trip.   _✗ to go_

2 I hope to visit the museum the next time I visit you.   _✓_

3 He pretended knowing nothing about it, but I knew he did.   _____

4 The guard refused to sell me a half-price ticket for the journey.   _____

5 I didn't feel well, but I managed getting downstairs.   _____

6 Famous people deserve to have a private life without journalists following them everywhere.   _____

7 He wrote the letter because he wanted to avoid to be found out.   _____

8 I don't know why the teachers delayed to tell us the results.   _____

9 I don't feel like going camping because I like holidays where I can relax.   _____

10 I think that a lot of women dislike going shopping.   _____

11 I've put off writing you this letter for months, but finally here it is.   _____

12 They suggested to take the trip to Williamstown on the first day.   _____

Exam practice

Reading and Use of English Part 1

For questions **1–8**, read the text below and decide which answer (**A, B, C** or **D**) best fits each gap. There is an example at the beginning (**0**).

Balloon adventure

Brian Jones and Bertrand Piccard were the first team to go (**0**) _____A_____ the world in a balloon. Nobody (**1**) _____ them to finish their astonishing 19-day expedition, especially as they had to (**2**) _____ with poisonous fumes and temperatures of –50℃.

Brian had run a business, but he got tired of it and (**3**) _____ to buy a balloon. Before long he was one of the country's (**4**) _____ balloon instructors and pilots. Why did he risk everything for one trip? He says he was not a very confident child: 'When I was seven a friend (**5**) _____ me go down a water slide with him. I still (**6**) _____ being absolutely terrified. I've never learnt to swim properly.' He thinks everyone should face their greatest (**7**) _____ and that is one reason why he went up in the balloon. Six of the 19 days were spent over the Pacific Ocean. Brian says he won't (**8**) _____ to do it again because there are so many other things he wants to do.

0	(A)	round	B	through	C	across	D	above
1	A	expected	B	hoped	C	intended	D	admitted
2	A	do away	B	get along	C	keep up	D	put up
3	A	thought	B	considered	C	afforded	D	decided
4	A	unique	B	preferable	C	leading	D	suitable
5	A	demanded	B	made	C	encouraged	D	persuaded
6	A	forget	B	remind	C	remember	D	regret
7	A	fears	B	suspicions	C	disturbances	D	frights
8	A	delay	B	imagine	C	attempt	D	suggest

Grammar focus task

These are some verbs from the exam task. Without looking back, put them into the table below. Three of the verbs can go in two columns.

> ~~afford~~ ~~admit~~ attempt consider decide delay demand ~~encourage~~
> expect hope imagine learn persuade remind suggest want

Verb + *to* infinitive	Verb + *-ing*	Verb + object + *to* infinitive
afford	admit, encourage	encourage

19 Conditionals (2)

unless; in case; provided/providing that and as/so long as;
I wish and if only; it's time; would rather; otherwise and or else

A Context listening

1 You are going to hear a man talking to a group of people about something they are going to do tomorrow. Here are some of the things they are taking with them. What do you think they are going to do?

_____

2 ▶24 Listen and check if you were right.

3 ▶24 Listen again and fill in the gaps. Stop the recording when you need to.

1 We're going _____*unless*_____ the weather gets much worse.

2 _____ that it doesn't snow too heavily tonight, I'll see you back here at six o'clock.

3 We won't reach the top of the mountain _____ we set out early.

4 You need a whistle _____ you get separated from the rest of the group.

5 _____ you didn't bring large cameras.

6 _____ we all stay together, we'll have a great time.

7 I _____ you'd come a few weeks ago.

8 _____ we had dinner now!

4 Look at sentences 1, 2, 3, 4 and 6 in Exercise 3. What do you notice about the tense of the verbs which follow the words in the gaps?

_____

B Grammar

1 unless

Unless means 'if not' and is used with the present tense to talk about a condition in the present or future:
*We're going **unless** the weather **gets** much worse.* (= if the weather doesn't get much worse)
*We won't have time to reach the top of the mountain **unless** we **set** out early.* (= if we don't set out early)
***Unless** you **drive** more slowly, I'll be sick.* (= if you don't drive more slowly)
*This water isn't safe to drink **unless** you **boil** it.* (= if you don't boil it)

2 in case

In case shows that an action is taken to prepare for a possible event or situation.

We use the present tense after *in case* when we explain that a present action prepares us for a future event:
*Take a whistle **in case** you **get** separated.* (= there's a chance you might get separated and a whistle will help us find you)
*Make sure you have my phone number **in case** you **miss** the bus.* (= I expect you'll get the bus, but if you miss it, you'll need to phone me)

We use the past simple after *in case* to explain a past action. It often shows that you did something because another thing might happen later:
*He took his surfboard **in case** they **went** to the beach.* (= he took his surfboard because he thought they might go to the beach)
*I had taken plenty of cash with me **in case** the shop **didn't accept** credit cards.*

⚠ *In case* does not mean the same as *if*. Compare:
*I'll cook a meal **in case** Sarah comes over tonight.* (= I'll cook a meal now because Sarah might visit us later)
*I'll cook a meal **if** Sarah comes over tonight.* (= I won't cook a meal now because Sarah might not visit us)

3 provided/providing that and as/so long as

These expressions are used with a present tense to talk about the future. They have a similar meaning to *if*:
***As long as** we all **stay** together, we'll have a great time.*
*You'll do very well in your interview, **so long as** you don't talk too fast.*
***Provided (that)** it doesn't snow too heavily, I'll see you here at six o'clock.*
*My father says he'll meet us at the airport, **providing (that)** we let him know our arrival time.*

⚠ *If, unless, in case, provided/providing that* and *as/so long as* are all followed by the present tense to talk about the future. Some conjunctions (*when, until, after, before, as soon as*) are also followed by the present tense to talk about the future (➤ see Unit 6, B3).

4 I wish and if only

I wish and *if only* are both used to express a wish for something. They have the same meaning, but *if only* is less common and is usually stronger.

Wish / if only + the past simple is used when we express a wish about a present situation:
***I wish** you **loved** me.* (= but you don't love me)
***I wish** I **knew** the answer.* (= but I don't know the answer)
***If only** he **could** drive.* (= but he can't drive)
***If only** we **had** a bigger flat!* (= but our flat is small)

⚠ Notice that we use the past tense, even though we are talking about now.

We can use *were* instead of *was* after *I* and *he/she/it*:
***I wish** I **was/were** clever like you.* (= but I'm not clever)
***I wish** the weather **wasn't/weren't** so wet here.* (= but it is wet)
***If only** my sister **was/were** here!* (= but she isn't here)

Wish / if only + the past perfect is used when we express a wish or regret about the past. It's like the third conditional – the event can't be changed:
*She **wishes** she**'d (had) never met** him.* (= but she did meet him)
***I wish** we**'d (had) come** a few weeks ago.* (= but we didn't come)
***If only** I **hadn't broken** that priceless vase!* (= but I did break it)

Wish / if only + *would* is used when we express a wish:

- for something to happen now or in the future:
  ***I wish** you **would stay** longer.*
  ***If only** the rain **would stop**!*

- for someone to do something (often when we are annoyed):
  ***I wish** you **wouldn't leave** your bag in the doorway.*
  ***I wish** the waiter **would hurry** up. I'm so hungry!*

Notice the difference between *I hope* + *will* and *I wish* + *would* when talking about the future:
***I hope** he **will** phone.* (= there's a good chance he will phone)
***I wish** he **would** phone.* (= it's unlikely he will phone)

5 *it's time* and *would rather (not)*

These expressions are followed by the past simple with a present meaning:
***It's time** we **ate** dinner now.*
***It's time** I **went** home.*
***I'd rather** you **didn't bring** large cameras.*
***We'd rather** the flat **was** bigger, but it's all we can afford.*

⚠ When the subject of *would rather* is the same as the subject of the following verb, we normally use the infinitive without *to*:
*They**'d rather eat** at home as they have a small baby.*
*I**'d rather go** home by taxi at this time of night.*
*We**'d rather not spend** too much money as we're saving for a new car.*

6 *otherwise* and *or else*

These words mean 'because if not':
*I have to go to bed early, **otherwise** I get too tired.* (= if I don't go to bed early, I get too tired)
*Back up your work as you go along, **otherwise** you could lose it all.* (= if you don't back up your work, you could lose it all)
*Carry that tray with both hands **or else** you'll drop it.* (= if you don't carry it with both hands, you'll drop it)
*They have to have a car **or else** they wouldn't be able to get to work.* (= if they didn't have a car, they wouldn't be able to get to work)

C Grammar exercises

1 Rewrite these sentences using *unless* instead of *if not*.

1 Sam will pass his driving test if he doesn't drive too fast.
   Sam will pass his driving test unless he drives too fast.

2 They'll be here soon if their plane isn't delayed.

3 If you're not in a hurry, you could take the bus.

4 I won't be able to come to see you tomorrow if my brother can't give me a lift.

5 If the factory doesn't increase its production, it will close down.

6 If you don't write your address down for me, I'll forget it.

7 I won't stay in that hotel if it hasn't got a good restaurant.

8 If I don't hear from you, I'll meet you at six.

2 Fill in the gaps with *in case* or *if*.

1 Elaine will post the letters _____ *if* _____ she goes out.
2 I'll go for a swim _____ I finish college early.
3 I'll teach you to windsurf _____ you teach me to play golf.
4 I always check my phone when I come out of school _____ I've missed a call.
5 I'll take Tim's address with me _____ I have time to visit him while I'm in London.
6 Our team will win the match _____ our goalkeeper plays like he did last week.
7 It's a good idea to back up your contacts list _____ you lose your phone.
8 I'll leave these films here _____ you have time to watch them.

3 Choose the correct words in these sentences by Cambridge First candidates.

1 The journey doesn't take too long <u>unless</u> / if it rains, and then it takes ages.
2 I think it's safe for children to go to school by bike *unless* / *provided that* they don't live too far away.
3 The police gave the orders to close all the doors *as long as* / *in case* the robbers were still hiding in the building.
4 Zoos should be allowed *unless* / *as long as* the animals are well looked after.
5 Bring your passport *provided that* / *in case* we go to Copenhagen on the boat.
6 People don't work more than ten hours a day *unless* / *provided that* it is really necessary.

4 Chloe is on holiday in a foreign city. She's been so busy admiring the sights that she has got lost. **What is she thinking? Complete her sentences.**

1 I haven't got a map. I wish _I had a map_ .

2 The streets all look the same. If only _the streets didn't all look the same_ .

3 I didn't bring my phone. I wish _____ .

4 I can't speak the language. If only _____ .

5 I didn't buy a phrase book. If only _____ .

6 I'm hot and thirsty. I wish _____ .

7 I came here alone. I wish _____ .

8 I need someone to help me. If only _____ .

9 I'm sorry I came here. I wish _____ .

10 I want to be back in my hotel. If only _____ .

5 Complete the email with the correct form of these verbs. You will need to make some of the verbs negative.

be	be	behave	bring	can	change	finish	~~have~~	learn	know	miss	use

---

To: Joe
Subject: Party!

Hi Joe

I'm having a birthday party on Saturday in my uncle's flat. I wish I **(1)** ___had___ a bigger
flat myself but I haven't. Of course I'd rather **(2)** _____ my own place but anyway,
my uncle has offered me his flat so long as there **(3)** _____ no more than thirty people
and provided that the party **(4)** _____ by midnight. So please come and bring a friend,
but I'd rather you **(5)** _____ Matthew with you because he always causes trouble.
I wish he **(6)** _____ to behave better. I had to work hard to persuade my uncle and
unless everyone **(7)** _____ well, he won't let me use his place again.

I'm attaching a map in case you **(8)** _____ the road where my uncle lives. If you
(9) _____ find it, just ring me. So I'll see you on Saturday unless my uncle
(10) _____ his mind!

By the way, has Katherine changed her phone number? I can't get hold of her. I wish
I **(11)** _____ rude to her last week,
as she's not speaking to me now.

Must go or else I **(12)** _____
the bus to college! See you Saturday.

Robin

Exam practice

Reading and Use of English Part 4

For questions **1–6**, complete the second sentence so that it has a similar meaning to the first sentence, using the word given. **Do not change the word given.** You must use between **two** and **five** words, including the word given. Here is an example (**0**).

0   Simon now regrets doing a part-time course.

    WISHES

    Simon now _____ *wishes he hadn't done* _____ a part-time course.

1   The engine won't start if you don't press both buttons.

    UNLESS

    The engine won't start _____ both buttons.

2   We arrived in good time as we were afraid the coach might leave without us.

    CASE

    We arrived in good time _____ without us.

3   You can use my laptop but I must have it back by ten o'clock.

    PROVIDED

    You can use my laptop _____ it back to me by ten o'clock.

4   If we don't start cooking now, the food won't be ready in time.

    ELSE

    It's time we _____ the food won't be ready in time.

5   Stop playing your drums at night, otherwise the neighbours will complain.

    KEEP

    The neighbours will complain _____ your drums at night.

6   The students don't really like eating in the school canteen.

    RATHER

    The students _____ in the school canteen.

Grammar focus task

Compare these sentences with the sentence pairs above. Is the meaning the same (S) or different (D)?

1   You must press both buttons or else the engine won't start.   S

2   We arrived at the correct time because we were worried the coach might leave without us. _____

3   It's essential that I have my laptop at ten o'clock, but you can use it till then. _____

4   It's a pity the food won't be ready in time. _____

5   Keep playing your drums at night unless the neighbours complain. _____

6   The students aren't very keen on eating in the school canteen. _____

20 Prepositions (1)

Prepositions of place and time

A Context listening

1 You are going to hear a news broadcast. Before you listen, look at the pictures and guess what the news stories are about.

A _____   C _____

B _____   D _____

2 ▶25 Listen and check if you were right. As you listen, put the pictures in the order in which you hear the stories.

1 _____   2 _____   3 _____   4 _____

3 ▶25 Listen again and answer these questions. Stop the recording when you need to.

1 Where will the Prime Minister be for the next two days? ___*at a conference in Washington*___

2 When will he fly to Mexico? _____

3 Where did Moira MacNab's plane hit bad weather? _____

4 When does she say she will be quite well? _____

5 How far do the traffic jams stretch? _____

6 How long will part of the motorway remain closed? _____

7 Where was the security man? _____

8 When was the manager released? _____

4 Look at your answers to Exercise 3.

1 Which prepositions are used in the answers about time? _____

2 Which prepositions are used in the answers about place? _____

B Grammar

1 Prepositions of place

in, at and on

In is used:

- for someone or something inside a limited area (e.g. a town, a country, a garden):
  *The Prime Minister is **in** Washington.*
  *She is due to appear **in** Edinburgh.*
  *There are some lovely trees **in** this park.*

- for someone or something inside a building, room or container:
  *They heard shouting **in** the manager's office.*
  *Do you keep your credit cards **in** this wallet?*

On is used:

- for a point on a fixed line (e.g. a road, the coast):
  *She's holidaying **on** the north coast of Africa.*
  *We stopped at a café **on** the road to Brighton.*

- for a point on a surface:
  *I want to hang this picture **on** the wall.*

- with *floor* and *ceiling*:
  *There's a spider **on** the ceiling.*

- for public transport vehicles, such as buses, trains or planes:
  *They met **on** a plane.*
  *I can't read **on** the bus.*
  but we use *in* for cars and taxis:
  *He came home **in** a taxi.*

At is used:

- when we think about a place in terms of its function or as a meeting place:
  *He will have talks **at** the White House.*
  *I keep my tennis racket **at** the sports club.*
  *I'll see you **at** the theatre.*

- for an event:
  *He will remain **at** the conference.*
  *There were a lot of strangers **at** the party.*

across and over

There are some places where either *across* or *over* can be used:
*a footbridge **across/over** the motorway*
*a route **across/over** the mountains*
*a view **across/over** the valley*

But compare:
*Their eyes met **across** the table.*

*Fred jumped **over** the gate.*

*The plane was flying **across** the Mediterranean.*

above and over

Above or *over* is used if one thing is higher than another:
*They built an extra room **above/over** the garage.*

Over is used when one thing covers another:
*Put this rug **over** that old chair.*

Above is used when the two things are not directly on top of each other:
*The hotel is **above** the beach.*

Above is used in documents:
*Please don't write **above** the line.*

under and below

Under or *below* is used if one thing is lower than another:
*The garage is **below/under** the workshop.*

Under is the opposite of *over*:
*There's a beautiful old chair **under** that rug.*

Below is the opposite of *above*:
*The beach is **below** the hotel.*

Below is used in documents:
*Please don't write **below** the line.*

along and through

Along is used for something which follows a line:
*There were cheering crowds **along** the route of the procession.*
*We strolled **along** the river bank at dusk.*

Through means passing from one side of something to the other side of it:
*The road goes **through** Birmingham.*
*I struggled **through** the crowd to reach the café.*
*We could see the sea **through** the trees.*
*The train went **through** the tunnel.*

by and *beside*

By can be used in the same way as *beside*, meaning 'next to':
*A security man was standing **by/beside** the door.*
*I'd love to live **by/beside** a lake.*

between and *among*

Between is used when we talk about two places, things or people:
*the motorway **between** London and Oxford*
*The dictionary is **between** the grammar book and the atlas.*

Among is used to identify something as part of a group:
*Is there a dictionary somewhere **among** these books?*

beyond and *behind*

Beyond is used for something that is further away from us than something else (we may or may not be able to see it):
*Traffic jams were stretching **beyond** the motorway.*
*You can't see the lake, it's **beyond** the forest.*

Behind is used for something that is partly or completely hidden by an object in front of it:
*The robber stood **behind** the door, hoping he wouldn't be seen.*

2 Prepositions of time

at, *on* and *in*

At is used:
- for a point of time:
  at the start of her tour of Europe
- for the time of day:
  *at six o'clock, **at** dawn, **at** lunchtime*
- for seasonal holidays:
  *at Christmas, **at** Easter*
- in the following expressions:
  *at the weekend, **at** first, **at** last, **at** present (= now), **at** the moment (= now), **at** times (= sometimes), **at** once (= immediately)*

On is used for dates and days (including special days):
*on Monday, **on** 3rd December (note that we say 'on **the** third of December'), **on** New Year's Day, **on** Christmas Day, **on** my wedding anniversary*

In is used for all or part of a period of time:
*in the afternoon, **in** winter, **in** the twenty-first century, **in** the Middle Ages*

by and *until*

By means that something happens not later than, and probably before, the time mentioned:
*She intends to be in Chile **by** the end of the year. (= on 31st December at the latest, but probably before that)*
*Can we finish this work **by** four o'clock? (= not later than four o'clock)*

Until means that something continues up to, but not later than, the time mentioned:
*Part of the motorway will remain closed **until** this afternoon. (= it will open this afternoon)*

Until is often used with a negative, meaning 'not before':
*We **can't** eat **until** all the guests arrive. (= we can eat when they are all here)*

⚠ *Till* is often used instead of *until* in informal speech:
*We can't eat **till** all the guests arrive.*

in, *during* and *for*

In and *during* are often used with the same meaning:
***In/During** the summer we often go for long walks.*

but *during* shows a particular event against the background of a period of time:
*The manager was released **during** the night.*

especially if it is an interruption:
*They walked out of the hall **during** the politician's speech. (= while the politician was giving a speech)*

For shows how long something lasts:
*He will remain at the conference **for** two days.*
*We went to Spain **for** the summer.*

In shows how soon something happens:
***In** less than an hour we had heard all about his adventures.*
*I'll meet you **in** ten minutes.*

C Grammar exercises

1 Choose the correct word in each sentence.

1 She hid *below* / *under* the bed until the visitors had gone.

2 We arrived at our destination *at* / *in* dawn.

3 During the night, we heard strange noises in the room *over* / *above* us.

4 The gymnast sailed *through* / *along* the air and landed lightly on the mat.

5 The detective found an earring on the path *along* / *between* the pool and the house.

6 I need to get some cash so I'll see you at the cinema *in* / *by* ten minutes.

2 Sara is on the train and she's phoning her friend Rebecca. Complete the conversations with the prepositions in the box.

at	at	by	by	during	for	in	in	~~on~~	over	till

In Rebecca's office, 11.30 am.
Rebecca: Rebecca White.
Sara: Hi, it's Sara. I'm **(1)** ——on—— the train.
Can you meet me **(2)** ——————— the station?
Rebecca: What time?
Sara: Three.
Rebecca: I think so. The car's got a puncture. If I can arrange to get it fixed **(3)** ——————— my break, I'll be there.
Sara: Thanks, that's great.

At the garage, 1.40 pm.
Rebecca: Can you fix this puncture for me?
Mechanic: Yes, probably. But my assistant won't be back from lunch **(4)** ——————— half an hour and I'll be working on this other job **(5)** ——————— then.
Rebecca: Well, I've got to collect someone from the station **(6)** ——————— three.
Mechanic: Oh, that's no problem. We'll have it done **(7)** ——————— half past two easily.
Rebecca: Thanks. I'll be back **(8)** ——————— an hour, OK?
Mechanic: Fine. See you then.

On the train, 2.10 pm.
Sara: Hello?
Rebecca: The car's being fixed now. I'll wait for you **(9)** ——————— the main door of the station, so I can help carry your stuff.
Sara: No, don't worry. I haven't got anything heavy. I'll see you **(10)** ——————— the car park. It's just **(11)** ——————— the footbridge, isn't it?
Rebecca: Yes, all right. See you there.
Sara: Bye.

3 Fill in the gaps in this email with suitable prepositions.

Hi everyone!

How are you? We're having a great time in Thailand. **(1)** _____At_____ the moment we're still **(2)** _____ the north of the country. This evening we're flying to Bangkok where we'll visit the amazing palaces **(3)** _____ the morning and then we'll probably go shopping **(4)** _____ a few hours.

(5) _____ the weekend we're heading south to Phuket. We're going to book a morning flight so we'll be there **(6)** _____ midday at the latest. We'll go to Phi Phi island from there **(7)** _____ Monday. We've booked a bungalow. The tourist office says it's **(8)** _____ the end of a long beach, **(9)** _____ the middle of gardens which lie **(10)** _____ the beach and the hillside. We're going to go snorkelling and we can't wait to go swimming **(11)** _____ the tropical fish! We're staying there **(12)** _____ about a week and then it will be time to come home. See you all then!

Love,
Emmy and Sam

4 A hotel owner is showing visitors round his new premises.
Fill in the gaps with prepositions.

We're now standing **(1)** ___in___ the lounge, a beautiful room, with paintings **(2)** _____ the ceiling and a view **(3)** _____ the park to the hills **(4)** _____ it. The cellar is being decorated **(5)** _____ present and we're going to open it as a restaurant **(6)** _____ a few months' time. **(7)** _____ then we are serving meals **(8)** _____ the dining room only.

Do you see the trees planted **(9)** _____ the sides of the road up to the front door? They're going to be hung with coloured lights **(10)** _____ special occasions. If we go **(11)** _____ that wooden door, we'll reach the rose garden, where you can see some interesting sculptures on display **(12)** _____ the bushes.

5 👁 Correct the mistake in each of the following sentences by Cambridge First candidates.

1 I am going to see an English film ~~in~~ the cinema this evening. _____at_____

2 I look forward to seeing you in the weekend. _____

3 Both of the courses are in the same day, so I will have to miss one. _____

4 A TV company was on our school yesterday. _____

5 I'll come to your house in the holidays during a few days. _____

6 I want to know why the departure of the train was delayed by 8:15 pm. _____

7 I advise you to have a rest during a week and then start again. _____

8 I need to finish this letter because I must post it until 3 o'clock. _____

9 I enjoyed meeting your family for my short stay at your house. _____

10 I was travelling from Latvia at 10th December. _____

Exam practice

Reading and Use of English Part 2

For questions **1–8**, read the text below and think of the word which best fits each gap. Use only **one** word in each gap. There is an example at the beginning (**0**).

New residents on the farm

There is a new arts centre on the road between Salisbury and Winchester on what (**0**) _____*used*_____ to be a farm. The old farm buildings have been made (**1**) _____ artists' studios and workshops for people producing a variety of work such (**2**) _____ pottery, furniture and jewellery.

One barn has been made into an attractive gallery, displaying work produced at the arts centre, in (**3**) _____ to holding exhibitions by more famous artists. (**4**) _____ present there is a lovely exhibition of modern glass from Scotland.

When the artists are in their studios, visitors can talk to them about (**5**) _____ they are doing. For artists, who can feel lonely at times, (**6**) _____ is good to be in a place where they are among people who understand their work. They can go across the yard for coffee and share their problems with (**7**) _____ other.

The centre is open to visitors (**8**) _____ weekdays and at weekends from 12.00 to 4.00.

Grammar focus task

After you have checked your answers to the exam task, read the text once more. Then, without looking back at the text, complete these sentences with the correct prepositions.

1   The arts centre is _____*on*_____ the road _____ Salisbury and Winchester.
2   There is an attractive gallery displaying work produced _____ the arts centre.
3   When the artists are _____ their studios, visitors can talk to them.
4   Artists can feel lonely _____ times.
5   It's good to be in a place where they are _____ people who understand their work.
6   They can go _____ the yard for coffee.

Prepositions (2)

Prepositions which follow verbs and adjectives; prepositions
to express who, how and why; expressions with prepositions

A Context listening

1 You are going to hear a man called Andy telling his wife Dawn about a fire. Before you listen, look at the pictures. What is happening in each one?

A _____

B _____

C _____

2 ▶26 Listen and decide which picture best fits what Andy tells Dawn. What is wrong with the other two pictures?

_____

_____

3 ▶26 Listen again and fill in the gaps.

1   What's happened ___*to*___ your jacket?

2   There's no need to shout _____ me.

3   I had a bit of an adventure _____ the way home.

4   I called the fire brigade _____ my phone.

5   I got in _____ breaking a window.

6   I smashed a window _____ hitting it with a hammer.

7   I covered my face _____ a handkerchief.

8   You could have been _____ real danger.

9   Then the fire brigade were _____ control.

10 I hope they thanked you _____ saving their property.

11 Do you forgive me _____ being late?

12 I can't be angry _____ you now.

4 Look at your answers to questions 5 and 6 in Exercise 3. Which preposition is used to show how something is done? _____

B Grammar

1 Prepositions which follow verbs and adjectives

Verb + preposition

Some verbs are nearly always followed by a particular preposition. These include:

- *approve of:* Yasmina doesn't **approve of** children having too many toys.
- *enquire about:* I am writing to **enquire about** your advertisement.
- *insist on:* She **insisted on** paying for the taxi.
- *look forward to:* I'm really **looking forward to** eating it.
- *succeed in:* Did Pierre **succeed in** finding accommodation?

Notice that prepositions are followed by a noun or by the *-ing* form of a verb:
We enquired **about** our **reservation** at the hotel.   We enquired **about booking** a room.

Verb + object + preposition

Some verbs are nearly always followed by an object and a particular preposition. These include:

- *accuse someone of:* The rock group **accused** their manager **of** stealing their money.
- *congratulate someone on:* Heidi **congratulated** me **on** my exam results.
- *forgive someone for:* She can't **forgive** Maurice **for** all the lies he told.
- *prevent someone/something from:* The bus strike hasn't **prevented** people **from** coming to work.
- *suspect someone of:* I **suspect** Maryann **of** being dishonest.

Verb + different prepositions

Some verbs can be followed by different prepositions with a change in the meaning. These include:

- *agree with someone* and *agree about something:*
  I quite **agree with** you, I think you're right. (= with a person)
  My father and I don't **agree about** politics. (= about a subject)
- *ask for something* and *ask about something:*
  He **asked** me **for** some money. (= he requested)
  She **asked** me **about** my plans for the summer. (= she enquired)
- *laugh about* and *laugh at:*
  I was late but he wasn't angry, he just **laughed about** it. (= found it funny)
  I can't wear this hat. Everyone will **laugh at** me. (= make fun of)
- *think of* and *think about:*
  'What do you **think of** my new jacket?' 'It's great.' (= what is your opinion?)
  'What **are** you **thinking about**?' 'Lunch – I'm hungry!' (= what is on your mind?)
- *throw at* and *throw to* (also *shout at / shout to* and *point at / point to*):
  The little boy **threw** the ball **to** his father. (= expecting him to catch it)
  Don't **throw** toys **at** your sister – you might hurt her. (= intending to hit her)

to be + adjective + preposition

Some adjectives are usually followed by particular prepositions, for example:

- *angry about (something):* She's **angry about** the theft of her purse.
- *angry with (someone):* He's very **angry with** his assistant.
- *good/bad at (something):* She's **good at** drawing flowers.
- *pleased about (something):* My parents weren't **pleased about** my bad report.
- *pleased with (something or someone):* Granny was very **pleased with** the book you sent her.
- *rude / polite / (un)kind to (someone):* Don't be **rude to** anyone at the party.

2 **Prepositions used to express who, how and why**

by, *with* and *for*

We use *by* with passive verbs, for the person or thing which does the action:
*The window was smashed **by Andy**.*
*The fire was started **by an electrical fault**.*

We use *by + -ing* to show how something is done:
*He smashed the window **by hitting** it with a hammer.*
*He got in **by breaking** a window.*

We use *with* + noun for a tool (or other object used for a purpose):
*He smashed the window **with a hammer**.*
*He covered his face **with his handkerchief**.*

We use *for + -ing* or a noun to explain the purpose of a tool or other object:
*Hammers are normally **for knocking** in nails, not **for smashing** windows!*
*He keeps a bag of tools in his car **for emergencies**.*

We can also use *for + -ing* or a noun to explain the reason for something:
*The owners of the house thanked him **for saving** their property.*
*He received an award **for bravery**.*

3 **Expressions with prepositions**

We use prepositions in the following fixed expressions:
* ways of travelling:
  ***by** air, **by** plane, **by** road, **by** car, **by** bus, **by** rail, **by** train* but ***on** foot*
* ways of contacting people:
  ***by** post, **by** email, **by** phone* but *to be **on** the phone* (= using the phone)
* ways things can happen:
  ***by** chance, **by** accident, **by** mistake* but ***on** purpose*
* conditions and circumstances:
  ***in** love, **in** trouble, **in** debt, **in** charge (of)*
  ***in** secret, **in** private, **in** public*
  ***in / out of** control, **in / out of** sight, **in / out of** danger, **in / out of** difficulties*
  ***in** a hurry, **in** a temper*
  ***at** peace, **at** war, **at** work, **at** home*
  ***on** holiday, **on/off** duty, **on** business*

⚠ Don't make mistakes with these expressions:
* *on the way* and *in the way*:
  *I'm going to my office so I'll call and see you **on the way**.* (= between two points on a journey)
  *I can't move the table because that chair's **in the way**.* (= blocking a path between objects/people)
* *on time* and *in time*:
  *If the train's **on time**, I'll be home at six.* (= punctual)
  *If we leave now, we'll be home **in time** to see the news.* (= at or before the correct time)
* *in the end* and *at the end*:
  *She didn't want to come with us, but **in the end** we persuaded her.* (= the final result)
  *It was a great show and the audience applauded loudly **at the end**.* (= the last thing to happen)

C Grammar exercises

1 Write sentences describing what happened in each of the pictures, starting with the words given and using a preposition from the box.

A — Henry, you've been reading my diary!

B — Well done, Laura! You certainly deserved to win the tournament.

C — Can you tell me what trains there are to Scotland?

D — CLUB — No, young man, you can't come in here.

E — Liz, I'm so sorry I forgot to phone you. — It's OK, Mike. I'm not angry.

F — I didn't enjoy that book at all. — No, I didn't either.

about	about	for	from	~~of~~	on

1 She accused _____ *Henry of reading her diary* _____ .

2 She congratulated _____ .

3 He enquired _____ .

4 They prevented _____ .

5 Liz forgave _____ .

6 They agreed _____ .

2 Choose the correct preposition in each sentence.

1 You know you shouldn't phone me *in* / <u>*at*</u> work!

2 Yvonne doesn't approve *of* / *on* wearing real fur.

3 The mermaid was combing her hair *with* / *by* a silver comb.

4 I had to tidy my room *in* / *with* a hurry before I went out.

5 Did you drop that dish *by* / *on* purpose?

6 What do you think *of* / *about* Matt's new hairstyle?

3 Fill in the gaps in these news articles with suitable prepositions.

A

The wedding took place last Saturday of a couple who fell **(1)** _____in_____ love through the internet. Penny and Peter O'Donnell communicated **(2)** _____ email for six months until they discovered **(3)** _____ accident that they worked **(4)** _____ the same building. 'Actually, I had noticed her before and liked her, but I was too shy to speak to her **(5)** _____ public,' said blushing Peter. 'When I realised she was my internet friend, at first I suspected her **(6)** _____ laughing **(7)** _____ me, and I was quite angry **(8)** _____ it. But luckily she succeeded **(9)** _____ persuading me that I was wrong. Now we're looking forward **(10)** _____ spending our lives together.'

B

An elderly brother and sister were reunited today for the first time since they were children. Mia and David's parents had been **(1)** _____ debt and the children had been put in children's care homes until their family was **(2)** _____ difficulties. But the country was **(3)** _____ war, the children were separated, and their papers were lost.

David's daughter began trying to find Mia five years ago. 'It was hard, but **(4)** _____ last I found the daughter of the woman who had been **(5)** _____

charge of the home where Mia was. She said that some of the girls were sent abroad to be **(6)** _____ danger during the war and many of them never returned. When I thought I'd found Mia in Canada, I wanted to tell Dad immediately, but I decided to meet her **(7)** _____ secret first, in case I was wrong. But I was right.'

Two days ago, David travelled **(8)** _____ air for the first time **(9)** _____ his life to meet his sister. 'We've got a lot of catching up to do,' he said.

4 ◉ Correct the mistake in each of the following sentences by Cambridge First candidates.

1 I didn't go because his parents didn't approve ~~with~~ me.   _____of_____

2 I am not sure why your brother is always rude with me.   _____

3 Maria insisted in driving him home.   _____

4 I accused him about cheating in the game.   _____

5 Many people will feel angry of cars being banned in the city centre.   _____

6 Could you please forgive me with being late in sending this letter to you?   _____

7 We didn't succeed on winning the competition.   _____

8 He congratulated my sister with passing her exams.   _____

Exam practice

Reading and Use of English Part 3

For questions **1–8**, read the text below. Use the word given in capitals at the end of some of the lines to form a word that fits in the gap **in the same line**. There is an example at the beginning (**0**).

The clothes we choose to wear

The clothes we wear can be a form of (**0**) _communication_. Clothes, like   **COMMUNICATE**

a (**1**) _____ language, give out a message. This can be simple,   **SPEAK**

for example, when we choose clothing for keeping warm, to attend

a football match or (**2**) _____ ceremony, to announce our   **GRADUATE**

(**3**) _____ views or just to look attractive.   **POLITICS**

It isn't always this simple, however. As with speech, our reasons for making any

statement have a (**4**) _____ to be quite complex. The man who   **TEND**

buys an expensive coat may want it not only to offer (**5**) _____   **PROTECT**

from bad weather but also to magically surround him with the qualities of

an international film star. (**6**) _____ , people rarely succeed in   **NATURE**

satisfying both these requirements at once. Even (**7**) _____ that   **SUPPOSE**

both these statements could actually be made by one single coat, this ideal item

of clothing may not be available and, if it is, it may be (**8**) _____   **AFFORD**

for people who have limited money to spend on clothes.

Grammar focus task

Without looking back at the text, complete these sentences with the correct prepositions.

1   The clothes we wear can be a form _____ _of_ _____ communication.

2   Our reasons _____ making any statement have a tendency to be complex.

3   He wants it to magically surround him _____ the qualities of a film star.

4   People rarely succeed _____ satisfying both these requirements.

5   Both these statements could actually be made _____ one single coat.

6   It may be unaffordable _____ people who have limited money.

Relative clauses

Defining and non-defining relative clauses; relative pronouns and prepositions

A Context listening

1   You are going to hear a man showing some visitors round the castle where he lives. He's talking about some paintings. Before you listen, look at each painting and answer these questions.

1   Can you guess when the people lived?   2   Do you think they were members of the same family?

2   ▶27   Listen and check if you were right. As you listen, match the corect names with the paintings.

Andrew   Edmund   George   Henry   Jane   Jasper   Margaret   William

A _____   B _____   C _____ and _____

D _____ and _____ with their children

3   ▶27   Listen again and complete the answers to these questions. Stop the recording when you need to.

1   What do we learn about the ship in the picture of Edmund?

It's the one <u>which he commanded during a famous naval battle</u> .

2   Which is the picture of Henry and William?

It's the picture _____ .

3   How do we know who William is?

He's the one _____ .

4   Which side did Henry support in the Civil War?

It was the side _____ .

5   In which year was the picture of Jane and her children painted?

It was the year _____ .

4   Underline the first word in each of the answers to Exercise 3. They are all words which can introduce relative clauses. What does each word refer to?

1 _____   2 _____   3 _____   4 _____   5 _____

B Grammar

1 Defining relative clauses with *who*, *which* and *that*

Defining relative clauses tell us some essential information about the things or people they refer to:

*The picture **that hangs next to Margaret's portrait** is the one I like best.*

If we remove the words *that hangs next to Margaret's portrait*, we don't know which picture Jasper is talking about.

Defining relative clauses:

- use the relative pronouns *who* for people, *which* for things and *that* for things and people:
  *There's the woman **who** sold me the bracelet.*
  *I'm looking for a website **which** has the words of pop songs.*
  *Where did you get the coat **that** you were wearing?*
  *They're the people **that** run the local café.*

- may have *who*, *which* or *that* as the subject or object of the relative clause:
  *The picture **which/that** hangs next to Margaret's portrait ...* (*which/that* is the subject of the relative clause)
  *She's the woman **who/that** <u>he</u> married.* (*who/that* is the object of the relative clause, and *he* is the subject)

- very often omit the relative pronoun when it is the object of the relative clause:
  The painting we're looking at shows Edmund.
  or *The painting **which/that** we're looking at shows Edmund.*

- are never separated from the rest of the sentence by commas:
  (**not** *The painting, that we're looking at, shows Edmund.*)

- are used in writing and speaking.

2 Non-defining relative clauses with *who* and *which*

Non-defining relative clauses tell us some extra information about the things or people they refer to:

*The next painting shows Edmund's wife Margaret, **who he married in 1605**.*

If we remove the words *who he married in 1605*, we still know who Jasper is talking about. It is Edmund's wife Margaret.

Non-defining relative clauses:

- always use the relative pronouns *who* for people and *which* for things:
  *My friend Tom, **who** works for a software company, earns a good salary.*
  *This company makes all kinds of phones and chargers, **which** are sold in fifty different countries.*

- may have *who* or *which* (but never *that*) as the subject or object of the relative clause:
  *The building, **which** is very old, costs a lot of money to repair.* (**not** *that is very old*)
  *The castle's owner, **who** <u>we</u>'ve just seen, enjoys meeting visitors.* (**not** *that we've just seen*)

- never omit the relative pronoun:
  *This small café, **which** was opened three years ago, has the best coffee in town.*

- must be separated from the rest of the sentence by commas:
  My best friend, who works at the café on Saturdays, says it's always busy.

- are more common in writing than in speaking.

⚠ The relative pronoun refers back to a person/thing mentioned previously. We do not add any extra pronoun in the relative clause:
*This is the painting **that I like best**.* (**not** *the painting that I like it best*)
*The painting shows Edmund's wife, **who he married in 1605**.* (**not** *Edmund's wife, who he married her*)
*This café, **which opened two years ago**, has the best coffee in town.* (**not** *This café, which it opened*)

3 *whose, whom, when, where* and *why* in relative clauses

Both defining and non-defining relative clauses can:
- begin with *whose* (instead of *his/her/their*), *when* (for times) and *where* (for places):
  *William, **whose wife Jane was a famous beauty**, had nine children.*
  *Here they are in this picture from the year **when the youngest was born**.*
  *This has been my family's home, **where we've lived for over 400 years**, since the time of Edmund Claremont.*
- begin with *whom* (for people) as the object of the clause (this is mainly in written English, and is increasingly rare):
  *The man **whom we asked for directions** was extremely helpful.*
  *His girlfriend, **whom he neglected**, became very depressed.*

A defining relative clause can:
- begin with *why* after the words *the reason*:
  *This victory was the reason **why he became a national hero**.*
- often omit the words *when* and *why* (but not *where*):
  *I remember the day **(when) I met you**.*
  *That was the reason **(why) we went there**.*
  *She returned to the village **where she was born**.* (**not** ~~the village she was born~~)

4 **Prepositions in relative clauses**

When there is a preposition attached to a relative pronoun:
- we usually put the preposition at the end of the clause:
  *I had a friend I shared everything **with**.*
  *Peter Frost, who (or whom) my father used to work **for**, has become a government minister.*
- in formal English, we sometimes put the preposition at the beginning of the clause, followed by *which* (for things) or *whom* (for people):
  *I had a friend **with whom** I shared everything.*
  *Peter Jones, **for whom** my father used to work, has become a government minister.*
  *The family history, **about which** I cared very little, was Jasper's main interest.*
  *There may be a fault in the cable **to which** the printer is connected.*

⚠ We cannot use *that* after a preposition in a relative clause:
*The Conference Room, **in which** the meeting was held, was not really big enough.* (**not** ~~in that the meeting was held~~)

We can sometimes use preposition + *which* instead of *where*:
*This is the house **where** Jasper used to live. = the house **in which** Jasper used to live / the house **(which)** Jasper used to live in.* (**not** ~~the house which Jasper used to live~~)
*She showed us the town **where** she was born. = the town **in which** she was born / the town **(which)** she was born in.* (**not** ~~the town which she was born~~)

5 **Numbers and pronouns +** *of whom / of which*

Non-defining relative clauses can start with a number or a pronoun such as *all, some, most, none, each, a few, neither + of whom* or *of which*. This is more common in writing than in speech:
*The castle contained a lot of paintings, **two of which** were extremely valuable.*
*The best students, **all of whom** are over eighteen, will go to university in the autumn.*
*Free tickets were given out to a group of football fans, **one of whom** was my brother.*
*The cakes, **each of which** was decorated in a different colour, looked very appetising.*
*My uncle's stories, **most of which** I'd heard before, were extremely boring.*
*I was offered a choice of two rooms, **neither of which** looked very clean.*

C Grammar exercises

1 Complete this email with *who* or *which*. If *who* or *which* can be left out, put it in brackets.

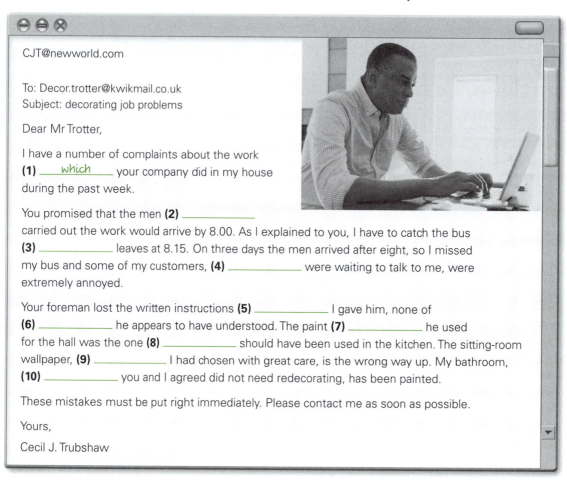

CJT@newworld.com

To: Decor.trotter@kwikmail.co.uk
Subject: decorating job problems

Dear Mr Trotter,

I have a number of complaints about the work
(1) _____which_____ your company did in my house
during the past week.

You promised that the men **(2)** _____
carried out the work would arrive by 8.00. As I explained to you, I have to catch the bus
(3) _____ leaves at 8.15. On three days the men arrived after eight, so I missed
my bus and some of my customers, **(4)** _____ were waiting to talk to me, were
extremely annoyed.

Your foreman lost the written instructions **(5)** _____ I gave him, none of
(6) _____ he appears to have understood. The paint **(7)** _____ he used
for the hall was the one **(8)** _____ should have been used in the kitchen. The sitting-room
wallpaper, **(9)** _____ I had chosen with great care, is the wrong way up. My bathroom,
(10) _____ you and I agreed did not need redecorating, has been painted.

These mistakes must be put right immediately. Please contact me as soon as possible.

Yours,

Cecil J. Trubshaw

2 Use a relative pronoun from the box and match the two halves of these sentences.

| where | when | ~~which~~ | which | which | who | whose | why |

1 I don't really enjoy films _____which_____   A you didn't tell me about your engagement.
2 I often go to parties _____   B I was late for school?
3 My teacher usually explains vocabulary _____   C show a lot of violence.
4 Can you remember any occasion _____   D speaks five languages?
5 I can't understand the reason _____   E involved working in the evenings.
6 Have you ever met anyone _____   F they play very loud music.
7 I envy people _____   G I don't understand.
8 I would hate to have a job _____   H parents buy a car for them.

3 Choose the correct sentence from each pair.

1 a Have you ever been back to the town where you were born in?
  b Have you ever been back to the town where you were born? ✓

2 a My left ankle which I broke last winter is still giving me trouble.
  b My left ankle, which I broke last winter, is still giving me trouble.

3 a Is that the man you were talking about?
  b Is that the man you were talking about him?

4 a I'm looking for the book you lent me last week.
  b I'm looking for the book what you lent me last week.

5 a This expensive silk jacket, that I only bought last week, has lost three buttons.
  b This expensive silk jacket, which I only bought last week, has lost three buttons.

6 a The laptops, two of which belonged to teachers, were taken from the school office.
  b The laptops, two of them belonged to teachers, were taken from the school office.

7 a The friend that I want to introduce you to her is away this weekend.
  b The friend I want to introduce you to is away this weekend.

4 Combine each pair of sentences by making the second sentence into a non-defining relative clause.

1 My aunt loves ice cream with chocolate sauce. She is rather greedy.
  My aunt, who is rather greedy, loves ice cream with chocolate sauce.

2 My uncle's cottage has been damaged by floods. We usually spend our holidays there.
  _____

3 The chemistry exam was actually quite easy. We had been worrying about it.
  _____

4 My brother got into a fight near the school. His classmates had been teasing him.
  _____

5 There are dreadful traffic jams during the summer. Everyone goes on holiday then.
  _____

6 My parents enjoyed that film very much. They don't often go to the cinema.
  _____

5 Complete the sentences with these phrases.

~~all of whom~~   none of whom   most of which   neither of which   one of which

1 The company was founded by three brothers, _____all of whom_____ became millionaires.
2 The thieves took my bike and my sister's, _____ was insured.
3 The four students, _____ spoke Spanish, had travelled all over South America.
4 We bought several computer games, _____ we had to return as it didn't work.
5 The in-flight entertainment consisted of foreign films, _____ had subtitles.

Reading and Use of English Part 4

For questions **1–6**, complete the second sentence so that it has a similar meaning to the first sentence, using the word given. **Do not change the word given.** You must use between **two** and **five** words, including the word given. Here is an example (**0**).

---

0   The same person bought the three paintings Katie had put in the exhibition.

  WHICH

  Katie had put three paintings in the exhibition,   *all of which were bought*   by the same person.

1   That's the hotel where we had lunch last Sunday.

  IN

  That's the hotel _____ last Sunday.

2   Being an airline employee, my sister sometimes gets cheap flights.

  WORKS

  My sister, _____, sometimes gets cheap flights.

3   I don't like Jim because he's so mean.

  REASON

  Jim's meanness _____ I don't like him.

4   Last week Gerry borrowed the book from me and now he's lost it.

  I

  Gerry's lost the _____ last week.

5   The concert which Ben took me to wasn't very enjoyable.

  WENT

  I didn't enjoy _____ to with Ben.

6   The mother of that boy is a well-known actress.

  WHOSE

  That's _____ a well-known actress.

Grammar focus task

Look at your answers to the exam task.

1   Which of the sentences you have written contain relative clauses? _____

2   Are they defining or non-defining relative clauses? _____

3   How do you know? _____

Linking words (1)

*because, as and since; so and therefore; in order to, to + infinitive
and so (that); so and such; enough and too*

A Context listening

1   You are going to hear two friends, Josie and Adam, talking at their sports club. Before you listen, look at the picture. Can you guess which sports they take part in?

_____

2   ▶28   Listen and check if you were right.

3   ▶28   Listen again and fill in the gaps. Stop the recording when you need to.

1   Josie thinks Tom Castle was chosen _____*because*_____ he's the coach's nephew.

2   Adam believes that Tom is certainly _____ to be captain.

3   Adam suggests Josie ought to be in the team herself _____ she seems to know so much about the subject.

4   Josie objects that she isn't _____ to play volleyball.

5   Adam points out that Melanie is _____ that she's one of the best players.

6   Josie says that going to judo once a week gives her _____ .

7   She thinks that volleyball would take _____ .

8   She adds that they have _____ after school.

9   Adam says that he has been training every day _____ be really fit.

10   The coach told Adam that he plays _____ .

11   Some of the older players may drop out _____ they've got _____ to do.

4   Look at your answers to questions 2, 4, 6 and 10 in Exercise 3. What do you notice about the position of the word *enough*?

_____

B Grammar

1 Expressing reason and result

because, **as** and **since**

Because, as and *since* introduce the reason for an action or situation. They can go at the beginning or in the middle of a sentence:

They had to choose him **as/because/since** *he's the coach's nephew.*
As/Because/Since *he's the coach's nephew, they had to choose him.*

Notice that if they go at the beginning, there is usually a comma at the end of the clause:
As/Because/Since *I hadn't done my homework, I didn't understand the lesson.*

⚠ *Because* (but not *as* or *since*) can be used to begin the answer to a question with *Why*:
Question: **Why** *didn't you understand the lesson?*
Answer: **Because** *I hadn't done my homework.* (**not** ~~As/Since I hadn't~~ ...)

so and **therefore**

So and *therefore* introduce the result of an action or situation.

So usually goes in the middle of a sentence:
They may need a new goalkeeper **so** *I want to be ready.*

Therefore goes at the beginning of a new sentence:
They may need a new goalkeeper. **Therefore** *I want to be ready.*

We could also say:
I want to be ready **because** *they may need a new goalkeeper.*

Compare these sentences, which have the same meaning:
I hadn't done my homework **so** *I didn't understand the lesson.*
I hadn't done my homework. **Therefore** *I didn't understand the lesson.*
As/Since/Because *I hadn't done my homework, I didn't understand the lesson.*

So is more common in speaking. *Therefore* is more common in writing.

2 Expressing purpose

(in order) to + infinitive and **so (that)** + verb

(In order) to and *so (that)* are used to link an action and its purpose.

So always goes in the middle of a sentence, and is followed by a clause, often with *will, would, can* or *could*:
I've been training every day **so (that)** *I'll be really fit.*
I joined the tennis club **so (that)** *I could play whenever I wanted.*
I phoned to say the train was late **so (that)** *my parents wouldn't worry.*

(In order) to goes in the middle, or occasionally at the beginning, of a sentence and is followed by the infinitive:
I've been training every day **(in order) to be** *really fit.*
(In order) to be *really fit, I've been training every day.*

In order to and *so that* are more formal than *to* and *so* on their own. *To* and *so* are more usual in spoken English.

⚠ Remember, in sentences like these we do not use *for* to express purpose:
(**not** ~~I have been training every day for to be really fit.~~)

⚠ Sentences with *so* can sometimes have two meanings, depending on their context, for example:
I've been training every day **so** *I'll be ready for the next match.*
This could express purpose: *I've been training every day* **in order to be** *ready for the next match.*
or it could express result: *I've been training every day.* **Therefore** *I'll be ready for the next match.* (➤ See B1.)

3 Explaining cause and effect

so and *such*

So and *such* mean 'as much as this'. We can use them before a *that* clause to talk about cause and effect:
He walked **so slowly that** *we arrived late.* (= we arrived late because he walked very slowly)
He was **such a slow walker** *that we arrived late.*

We often omit *that*, especially in speech:
It was **such an untidy office** *we couldn't find our books.* = *It was* **such an untidy office that** *we couldn't find our books.*

We can use *so* and *such* for emphasis, often after *because*:
Her teachers sent her home because she had behaved **so badly**.
I love those shoes. They're **so cool**!
Her teachers sent her home because she was **such a naughty child**.
Did you hear what he said? He's **such an idiot**!

So is followed by:
- an adjective or an adverb:
  Her father is **so rich** *(that) she's never travelled by bus.*
  He spoke to her **so rudely** *(that) she walked out of the room.*
- the words *many*, *much* and *few*, with or without a noun:
  He's invited **so many people** *to the party (that) there's nowhere to sit down.*
  I've got **so few books** *(that) I can keep them on one shelf.*
  You complain **so much** *(that) everyone gets bored.*

Such is followed by:
- *a/an* (if necessary) + adjective + noun:
  Her father is **such a rich man** *(that) she goes everywhere by taxi.*
  The café always charges **such high prices** *(that) students can't afford to eat there.*
  We weren't used to **such luxurious accommodation**.
- *a/an* (if necessary) + noun only:
  They were treated with **such kindness** *(that) they were reluctant to leave.*
  The concert was **such a success** *(that) they decided to give another.*
- the expression *a lot (of)*, with or without a noun:
  He's invited **such a lot of people** *to the party (that) there's nowhere to sit down.*
  I spent **such a lot** *last night (that) I can't afford to go out at the weekend.*

➤ See Unit 8, B4 for other words which modify adjectives and adverbs.

Very and *so/such* can be used with a similar meaning for emphasis:
She is **very** *annoying. / She is* **so** *annoying. / She is* **such** *an annoying person.*

But *very* is not followed by a *that* clause:
The sun was **so** *hot* **(that)** *we had to sit in the shade all day.* (**not** ~~The sun was very hot (that) we had to sit ...~~)

enough and *too*

Enough means 'sufficient, the right quantity'. *Too* means 'more than enough'.
*I don't want to swim in the sea today – it's **too cold** / it isn't **warm enough**.*

Phrases with *too* and *enough* are often followed by:
*   *to* + infinitive:
    *This bag is **too heavy to carry**.*
    *I'm not **strong enough to carry** this bag.*
    *He wasn't running **quickly enough to catch** us.*
*   *for* something/someone:
    *This bikini is **too small for** me.*
    *Have you got **enough money for** the car park?*
    *There isn't **enough cake for** everybody to have a piece.*
    *It was raining **too heavily for** the match to continue.*

Enough goes:
*   before a noun:
    *I've got **enough sandwiches** for lunch.* (= as many sandwiches as I need)
    *We haven't got **enough time** to go to the café before the film.*
*   after an adverb:
    *Are we speaking **loudly enough** to be heard?* (= Can everyone hear us?)
*   after an adjective:
    *This room is **warm enough** for me.* (= the right temperature)

Too goes:
*   before *many/much* + a noun:
    *There are **too many books** for me to carry.* (= I can't carry all of them)
    *I've got **too much work**.* (= I can't do it all)
*   before an adverb:
    *Are we speaking **too loudly**?* (= Are we disturbing the other students?)
*   before an adjective:
    *This room is **too warm** for me.* (= the temperature is uncomfortably high)

⚠ *Very* does not mean the same as *too*:
    *This jacket is **very** expensive, but I can afford it.*
    *This jacket is **too** expensive, so I can't afford it.*

C Grammar exercises

1 Fill in the gaps with the words and phrases in the box.

as	~~because~~	enough	in order to	so	so	so that	too

1 A: Why are you staring at me like that?

   B: _Because_   you've got a large black mark on the end of your nose!

2 A: It's only eleven o'clock. Why aren't you still at school?

   B: We've been sent home early _____ revise for our exam tomorrow.

3 A: How was the trip to the museum?

   B: _____ several galleries were closed for repairs, it was rather disappointing.

4 A: What are all those students doing in the park?

   B: The university term has ended _____ they're having a picnic to celebrate.

5 A: Come on! If we run fast _____ , we'll catch the early train.

   B: Sorry, I've got _____ many bags I can't run.

   A: Oh, never mind. If we're _____ late for that train, we can have a drink while we wait for the next one.

6 A: Why are you working late today?

   B: I want to finish this essay _____ I'll be free to go out tomorrow.

2 Do these pairs of sentences have the same meaning? Write S (same) or D (different).

1 a It was such a sad film I couldn't stop crying at the end.

  b The film was so sad I couldn't stop crying at the end.   _S_

2 a We're packing our cases tonight as we're leaving very early tomorrow.

  b We're leaving very early tomorrow so we're packing our cases tonight.   _____

3 a My father says I'm too young to have a motorbike.

  b My father says I'm very young to have a motorbike.   _____

4 a I've lost weight. Therefore I can wear this tight skirt at my party.

  b I can wear this tight skirt at my party because I've lost weight.   _____

5 a Since I've never been to New York, I can't tell you much about it.

  b I can't tell you much about New York as I've never been there.   _____

6 a She's been given so much advice that she doesn't know what to do.

  b She's been given enough advice so she knows what to do.   _____

7 a He was speaking too softly for us to hear him properly.

  b He wasn't speaking loudly enough for us to hear him properly.   _____

8 a I revise in the college library so that I can concentrate on my work.

  b In order to concentrate on my work, I revise in the college library.   _____

3   Match the beginnings and endings of these sentences.

1	Tessa's got so much homework	A	he should be in bed.
2	Stephen's so arrogant that	B	to make sandwiches for us all.
3	Jessie has so many hobbies that	C	he can buy any clothes he wants.
4	The lecture wasn't too difficult	D	she neglects her schoolwork.
5	Saskia hasn't got enough money	E	for us to understand.
6	Keith earns so much money	F	to come on holiday with us.
7	I think there's enough bread	G	he thinks every girl fancies him.
8	Peter has such a bad cold	H	she can't come out with us.

4   👁 Choose the correct words in these sentences by Cambridge First candidates.

1   The city's quite interesting but it isn't *enough big* / *big enough* to get lost in.

2   It would be lovely if you came here *therefore* / *since* we could do millions of interesting things.

3   The concert was *such* / *so* exciting that the time went by very quickly.

4   We should apply to work there *so* / *as* it would be a good way for us to practise English.

5   They think the project is a waste of time. *Therefore* / *Because* it will be cancelled.

6   It has been *so* / *such* a long time since I last wrote to you.

7   Why is shopping so popular? *Because* / *As* it can help us to relax.

5   Complete the second sentence so that it means the same as the first, using *enough* and any other words you need.

1   The hall only had two hundred seats but two hundred and fifty people came to the show.

There weren't ____enough seats for____ all the people who came to the show.

2   Jim couldn't keep up with the other runners because he was unfit.

Jim wasn't _____ keep up with the other runners.

3   Can the whole team travel in that little minibus?

Is there _____ the whole team to travel in that little minibus?

4   Nicky is sixteen now so she can fly to New York on her own.

Nicky is _____ fly to New York on her own.

Do the same with these sentences, using *too* and any other words you need.

5   I can't afford to buy designer jeans.

Designer jeans are _____ buy.

6   He's such a good player I can't beat him.

He plays _____ beat him.

7   We weren't able to walk to the beach because it was a long way away.

The beach was _____ walk to.

8   The wind's extremely strong today so the ferry can't operate.

It's _____ operate today.

Exam practice

Reading and Use of English Part 1

For questions **1–8**, read the text below and decide which answer (**A**, **B**, **C** or **D**) best fits each gap. There is an example at the beginning (**0**).

World English

The term 'World English' has been **(0)** ___A___ by some people to describe the kind of English used all around the world. If we read English language newspapers or **(1)** _____ to newsreaders who use English in different **(2)** _____ of the world, we may gain the impression that one kind of English is so **(3)** _____ used that it will soon unite all the different varieties.

Is there enough **(4)** _____ to support this impression? In fact, a version of English which is exactly the same throughout the world does not yet **(5)** _____ . For one thing, people whose first language is English are **(6)** _____ of their particular version of the language. Therefore they try to **(7)** _____ it from the influence of other forms of English. Moreover, there are too many regional differences in vocabulary for the language to be the same everywhere, as people need specialised words in order to **(8)** _____ local politics, culture and natural history.

0	Ⓐ proposed	B offered	C presented	D allowed
1	A look	B listen	C watch	D hear
2	A divisions	B parts	C sections	D places
3	A widely	B extremely	C totally	D normally
4	A knowledge	B witness	C belief	D evidence
5	A exist	B happen	C arrive	D occur
6	A confident	B jealous	C proud	D attached
7	A hold	B possess	C preserve	D insure
8	A argue	B talk	C mention	D discuss

Grammar focus task

Without looking back, complete these extracts with the words in the box.

enough   in order to   so   that   therefore   to   too

1   One kind of English is ___so___ widely used _____ it will unite all the different varieties.

2   Is there _____ evidence _____ support this impression?

3   People are proud of their particular version of the language. _____ they try to preserve it.

4   There are _____ many regional differences for the language to be the same everywhere.

5   People need specialised words _____ discuss local politics, business, culture and natural history.

Linking words (2)

in spite of and *despite*; *but*, *although* and *though*; *even though* and *even if*; participle clauses; *before* and *after* + *-ing*; *when*, *while* and *since* + *-ing*

A Context listening

1 ▶29 You are going to hear an interview with a young woman. Look at the newspaper headlines from two years earlier. One of the headlines has the correct facts, the rest are wrong. Listen to the interview and tick the correct headline.

A
New star signs contract to make three films in a year

B
15-year-old given leading role in new film

C
TEENAGE FILM ACTOR WINS STARRING PART

D
GIRL WITH NO ACTING EXPERIENCE IS NEW FILM STAR

2 ▶29 Listen again and fill in the gaps. Stop the recording when you need to.

1 You've been world famous ____*since making*____ the film *Starshine* two years ago.

2 I got the part _____ no film experience.

3 The director chose me to play the part _____ several schools.

4 I had a long talk with my parents _____ it.

5 I was offered two more films _____ *Starshine* …

6 … but _____ far from home, I sometimes felt very lonely.

7 I'd be happy to do another film later, _____ booked up for the next few months.

8 It's actually a comedy, _____ called *Dark Days*.

3 What form of the verb follows *since*, *in spite of*, *despite*, *after*, *before* and *while* in the sentences in Exercise 2?

_____

B Grammar

1 *in spite of* and *despite*

These words:

- are used to explain an unexpected event:
  *I got the part **in spite of** having no experience.*
  *We enjoyed the trip **despite** the bad weather.*
- go at the beginning or in the middle of the sentence:
  ***In spite of / Despite** having little money, we were very happy.* (notice the comma)
  *We were very happy **in spite of / despite** having little money.*
  If they go at the beginning, there is usually a comma in the middle of the sentence.
- are followed by *-ing* or a noun:
  *He continued to work **in spite of / despite being** ill.*
  *He continued to work **in spite of / despite** his **illness**.*
- are often followed by *the fact that* + subject + verb:
  *I got the part **in spite of the fact that** I had no experience.*
  ***Despite the fact that** I had no experience, I got the part.*

In spite of is more common in speaking than *despite*.

2 *but, although* and *though*

These words contrast two events or ideas. *Though* is more common than *although* in speaking.

But usually goes in the middle of the sentence:
*I like making films **but** I'm really a stage actor.*

Although and *though* can go in the middle or at the beginning of the sentence:
*I like making films **though/although** I'm really a stage actor.*
***Although/Though** I'm really a stage actor, I like making films.* (notice the comma)

⚠ We can't use *though/although* and *but* in the same sentence:
(**not** ~~Though / Although I'm really a stage actor, but I like making films.~~)

We sometimes use *though* at the end of a sentence:
*I like making films. I'm really a stage actor, **though**.*

3 *even though* and *even if*

Even though makes a stronger contrast than *although/though*. It emphasises the speaker's surprise that two facts are both true:
*She was given the part **even though** she had no experience.* (= it's surprising she got the part in these circumstances)

We use *even if* when we are not certain about our facts:
*I'll support my team **even if** they don't win the Cup.* (= I don't know whether they'll win the Cup, but I'll support them anyway)

4 Participle clauses

The *-ing* form or the past participle:
- can be used to combine two sentences when both sentences have the same subject.
- replaces a subject + verb:
  *I **work** far from home. + I sometimes feel lonely. → **Working** far from home, **I** sometimes feel lonely.*
  *Ali **was asked** about the play. + **Ali** said it was great. → **Asked** about the play, **Ali** said it was great.*

These structures are more common in writing than in speaking.

The *-ing* form:
- replaces an active verb:
  *He **refused** to apologise. + **He** left the room. → **Refusing** to apologise, **he** left the room.*
- links two things happening at about the same time (present or past):
  *The **girl used** all her strength. + **The girl** pushed open the heavy doors. → **Using** all her strength, **the girl** pushed open the heavy doors.*
- can begin the first or second half of the sentence:
  *She **writes** a blog. + **She** uses her experiences at work. → **She** writes a blog **using** her experiences at work.*

The past participle:
- replaces a passive verb:
  *The **boys were refused** entry to the club. + **The boys** walked slowly home. → **Refused** entry to the club, **the boys** walked slowly home.*
- links two connected events or situations:
  *'Greensleeves' **was written** in the 16th century. + '**Greensleeves**' is still a famous song. → **Written** in the sixteenth century, '**Greensleeves**' is still a famous song.*

5 *before* and *after* + *-ing*

Before and *after* + *-ing*:
- show the order in which things happen.
- are used to combine two sentences only when both sentences have the same subject.
- can replace the subject + verb of either sentence:
  *I **had** a long talk with my parents. (= first event) + **I accepted** the part. (= second event)*
  *→ I had a long talk with my parents **before accepting** the part.*
  *or → I accepted the part **after having** a long talk with my parents.*

Before and *after* + *-ing* can go at the beginning or in the middle of the sentence. If they go at the beginning, there is usually a comma before the main clause:
Before accepting the part, I had a long talk with my parents.
After having a long talk with my parents, I accepted the part.

6 *when, while* and *since* + *-ing*

We can use *when, while* and *since* + *-ing* in a similar way to *before* and *after* + *-ing*.

When + *-ing* links two actions happening at the same time:
When leaving the train, passengers should ensure that they have all their possessions with them.
You must try to make a good impression when starting a new job.

While + *-ing* links a longer action to an action which happens in the middle of it:
I was offered two more films while making 'Starshine'.
While making 'Starshine', I was offered two more films.

Since + *-ing* links an ongoing situation or action to the event or action when it began:
She hasn't been in touch once since moving to New York.
Since leaving school, she's completely changed.

C Grammar exercises

1 Match the beginnings and endings of these sentences.

1	I know Shanghai quite well,	A	you should read it carefully.
2	In spite of injuring his foot,	B	he retired to an island in the Mediterranean.
3	He doesn't earn very much,	C	he scored three goals.
4	Although he always takes his laptop,	D	in spite of being so talented.
5	Smiling broadly,	E	this book is still very useful.
6	When changing the torch battery,	F	our uncle welcomed us into his house.
7	Before signing that document,	G	but I've never been to Beijing.
8	After selling his business,	H	Dad rarely emails us when he's away.
9	Despite the fact that it is very old,	I	be careful not to damage the bulb.

2 Do these pairs of sentences have exactly the same meaning? Write S (same) or D (different).

1 a Although Sharon quite enjoys musicals, she really prefers more serious drama.

   b Sharon quite enjoys musicals, but she really prefers more serious drama.   _S_

2 a Asking for directions, Sam showed the farmer the map he'd been given.

   b Asked for directions, Sam showed the farmer the map he'd been given.   _____

3 a Brian continued to work long hours, in spite of being ill.

   b Even though he was ill, Brian continued to work long hours.   _____

4 a Chloe's father promised her a car, even though she didn't pass her final exam.

   b Chloe's father promised her a car, even if she didn't pass her final exam.   _____

5 a Despite searching everywhere, I didn't find the money.

   b I searched everywhere, but I didn't find the money.   _____

6 a Warning of storms ahead, the mountain guide led us back to the hostel.

   b Warned of storms ahead, the mountain guide led us back to the hostel.   _____

3 Combine each pair of sentences, using the *-ing* form or the past participle.

1 Arnold was faced with a difficult decision. Arnold decided to consult his boss.
   Faced with a difficult decision, Arnold decided to consult his boss.

2 The singer waved to her fans. The singer got into her car.
   _____

3 Simon grumbled about the amount of homework he had. Simon took out his grammar book.
   _____

4 The school buildings were designed by a famous architect. The school buildings won several prizes.
   _____

5 Wendy was a sensible girl. Wendy didn't panic when she cut her hand.
   _____

6 Paul heard cries for help. Paul dived into the water.
   _____

7 This song was recorded only last week. This song has already been downloaded a million times.
   _____

4 Complete the sentences with these words and phrases.

before	even if	even though	~~in spite of~~	since	though	while

1 I quite enjoy playing tennis, ___*in spite of*___ the fact that I usually lose.
2 _____ painting my room, I made quite a mess of the carpet.
3 It's essential to train regularly _____ attempting to run a marathon.
4 I hardly ever receive any emails _____ I write lots.
5 They insist they'll have a barbecue _____ it rains.
6 Jane enjoys cooking. She's not much good at making cakes, _____ .
7 _____ arriving in this country, I've made lots of new friends.

5 👁 Choose the correct version of these sentences by Cambridge First candidates.

1 a I thought the restaurant was expensive in spite the fact that the manager had told me it was cheap.
   b I thought the restaurant was expensive in spite of the fact that the manager had told me it was cheap. ✓

2 a Although I enjoyed the book, but I found the ending very disappointing.
   b Although I enjoyed the book, I found the ending very disappointing.

3 a You can think before to choose which one you will buy.
   b You can think before choosing which one you will buy.

4 a He allowed me to go into the concert despite the fact that I was an hour late.
   b He allowed me to go into the concert despite of the fact that I was an hour late.

5 a After receiving the visa, I will come and visit you in Canada.
   b After received the visa, I will come and visit you in Canada.

Exam practice

Reading and Use of English Part 2

For questions **1–8**, read the text below and think of the word which best fits each gap. Use only **one** word in each gap. There is an example at the beginning (**0**).

Antarctica

The first people known to have seen Antarctica (**0**) _____ *were* _____ hunters on ships in 1819. Two years later, Captain John Davis managed to land there, (**1**) _____ though the conditions were difficult and prevented him (**2**) _____ exploring very far. Other expeditions followed and by the late nineteenth century scientists had succeeded in mapping the coastline, in spite of the (**3**) _____ that Antarctica is almost entirely covered by a thick layer of ice (**4**) _____ stretches far beyond the edge of the land in places.

Something else attracted people to Antarctica (**5**) _____ from scientific research. This was the South Pole. Several attempts to reach it were made early in the twentieth century (**6**) _____ the first person to succeed was a Norwegian, Roald Amundsen, in 1911. Travelling with dogs (**7**) _____ pull the sledges carrying his party's supplies, he arrived at the pole five weeks before a rival British group.

(**8**) _____ the terrible weather conditions, many nations now have scientific bases in Antarctica.

Grammar focus task

Without looking back at the text, match the beginnings and endings of these extracts.

1	Captain John Davis managed to land there, even though	**A**	Antarctica is almost entirely covered by a thick layer of ice.
2	Scientists had succeeded in mapping the coast of the continent, in spite of the fact that	**B**	the conditions were difficult and prevented him from exploring very far.
3	Several attempts to reach it were made early in the twentieth century,	**C**	many nations now have scientific bases in Antarctica.
4	Travelling with dogs to pull the sledges carrying his party's supplies,	**D**	but the first person to succeed was the Norwegian Roald Amundsen.
5	Despite the terrible weather conditions,	**E**	he arrived at the pole five weeks before a rival British group.

Learning and revising vocabulary

It is a good idea to keep a record of all new words in a vocabulary notebook. Make a note of the main features of the word so that you can use your notebook for reference.

The example below records all the main features of the word. If you can't complete all the boxes when you first record the word, leave them blank and complete them later. If there is no word for this in your own language, you can leave the translation box blank.

orchard	pronunciation: /ˈɔːtʃəd/	part of speech: countable noun
definition:	an area of land where fruit trees grow	
translation:		
example sentence:	We saw some people picking apples in the orchard.	

You may need to review/use a word up to 20 times before you have really learnt it. So even if you have already recorded some of the vocabulary in a unit, it is useful to write it down again to help you revise. You can do this as you work through a unit and as you go through the wordlists as revision.

Here are some ideas:

- Draw a mind map, like this one for learning food words:

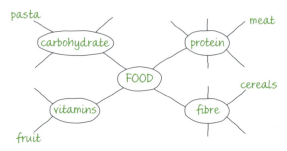

- or a word tree, for example:

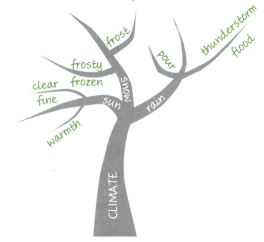

Try to put all the nouns together, all the verbs together, etc. When you think you know the words in your mind map or word tree, draw it again and try to fill it in again without looking.

- Divide words into groups and write them in circles or boxes. Some of these may overlap, for example:

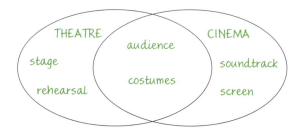

When you think you know the words, draw the circles or boxes again and see how many you can remember.

- For word-building, tables are useful, for example:

Noun	fear	amazement
Verb	to frighten	to amaze
Adjective	frightening, frightened	amazing, amazed

- Write down several phrasal verbs together, for example:

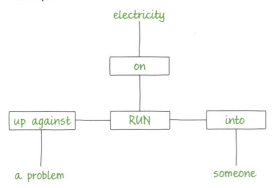

- Put the words onto a drawing, for example:

roof

- Use other simple drawings to remind you what words mean; for example, smiley faces are good for positive feelings ☺ and negative feelings ☹ or for likes and dislikes or agreeing and disagreeing.

- Many common expressions should be learnt as whole phrases rather than as individual words. When you come across expressions like this, highlight them and then write them down in your notebook.

- Some words are always followed by a preposition so write the word and the preposition together (e.g. *worried about, afraid of* in Unit 28).

- Write down words with similar meanings together, e.g. *surprised = amazed, astonished*. It is also useful to write opposites together, e.g. *hard-working ≠ lazy*.

- Choose one word and note down other words that are often used with it, for example:

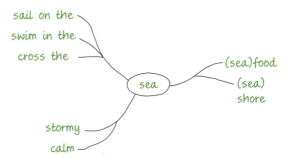

Earth, sea and sky

Geography, climate and weather

1.1 Look at photos A and B. Where do you think the places are? Choose from the list below.

Brazil   France   India   Kenya   Morocco   Thailand

1.2 Match the description below with one of the photos. Then complete it with the words in the box.

bank   orchards   ~~peaks~~   pine   slopes   springs   streams   tracks   valleys   vegetation

Manali is surrounded by towering snow-capped mountain **(1)** _____peaks_____ and dense forests of
(2) _____ trees. Shallow **(3)** _____ of clear mountain water flow into the Beas River.
Around the town the landscape is breathtaking. The **(4)** _____ which covers the gentle wooded
(5) _____ of the hillsides is mainly wild flowers and fertile apple **(6)** _____ . Above Manali,
travellers can walk along the winding **(7)** _____ through the narrow **(8)** _____ and high
mountain passes to the Himalayas or take part in the adventure sports on offer. They can also relax in the
village of Vashisht, on the left **(9)** _____ of the Beas River just a few kilometres from Manali, where
hot **(10)** _____ emerge from the rock at about 50 degrees centigrade.

1.3 ▶30 Listen to this description of the other photo and complete it with the words you hear.

This is a tropical rainforest. It's also sometimes called a **(1)** _____jungle_____ . The trees are probably very old as
they have very thick **(2)** _____ . It's usually quite dark in the forest as not much **(3)** _____
gets through the trees. The **(4)** _____ that grow under the trees tend to have large **(5)** _____
in an effort to get as much light as possible. The **(6)** _____ in the rainforest is often very poor so
the trees have shallow **(7)** _____ , but some of them still manage to grow very tall with few
(8) _____ near the bottom. They put all their energy into reaching the light! Rainforests are full of
wildlife, from **(9)** _____ and snakes on the forest floor to monkeys and **(10)** _____ higher up.

1.4 Match the adjectives with their opposites.

cultivated   ~~deep~~   mountainous   muddy   steep   straight   wide

1   shallow _____deep_____   2   narrow _____   3   winding _____   4   clear _____

5   wild _____   6   flat _____   7   gentle _____

1.5 Write two or three sentences in your notebook about the place in this photo.

 Vocabulary note

Some words can have more than one meaning, and the second meaning may be idiomatic:

I've got a mountain of work to do. (= a huge amount of work)

There was a flood of applications for the job. (= suddenly a large number of applications)

2.1 Read these sentences about two different climates. Decide which are about photo A and which are about photo B in 1.1.

1 It is always hot and humid. _B_

2 Summers are mild and wet. _____

3 As it is near the Equator, there is little difference in temperature between the warmest and coolest months. _____

4 Rain falls nearly every day and there is no dry season. _____

5 In winter it becomes cold and frosty and the temperature falls to below 0°C. _____

6 In the rainforest, as dawn breaks and the sun comes up, there is a clear blue sky. _____

7 The heavy snowfall in winter attracts skiers and tourists. _____

8 By mid-afternoon every day it pours with rain and thunderstorms are also common. _____

9 The area is often cut off because of snow. _____

10 Floods sometimes occur in July and August during the wet season. _____

11 The temperature at night is 20–25°C but during the day it rises to above 30°C. _____

12 Skies are often cloudy in the mountains, whether it is summer or winter. _____

2.2 The sentences make two separate descriptions. Which sentences can you join with *and* or *but*?

A Summers are mild and wet, but in winter ...

2.3 ▶31 Listen to a description of the climate in another country. Which part of the world do you think it is?

2.4 Using 2.1–2.3 to help you, write a list of vocabulary you can use about your country's climate.

3.1 WORD BUILDING Complete the sentences with new words made from the words in the box.

freeze globe mist ~~storm~~ tropic warm

1 Yesterday the weather was so ____stormy____ that the waves were crashing against the houses by the beach.

2 They were able to skate on the lake because it was _____ .

3 We climbed to the top of the mountain but it was so _____ we couldn't see much.

4 Everybody is staying inside as the forecast says a _____ storm is on its way.

5 We always appreciate the _____ of the sun after a long cold winter.

6 It is thought that some unusual weather is caused by _____ warming.

Reading and Use of English Part 6

You are going to read a newspaper article about a trip to South America. Six sentences have been removed from the article. Choose from the sentences **A–G** the one which fits each gap (**1–6**). There is one extra sentence which you do not need.

A trip to Patagonia

Laura Holt goes in search of pumas, the large wild cats of South America

Taking in a large area of Chile and Argentina, running along the Andes and down to where South America flicks its tail towards Antarctica, is a region called Patagonia and I was there on holiday. It was only my first day in the Torres del Paine National Park, a wild portion of Chilean Patagonia that's lavished with towering glaciers, snow-clad valleys and dramatic peaks.

Some other intrepid travellers come here to tackle the formidable 'W' circuit – an extended trek that links five key points in the national park over several days of scrambling up and down mountains. **1** [ ] I therefore planned to take a more leisurely pace, in the back of a chauffeur-driven van.

We gathered around a fire on the first night at camp. **2** [ ] A mother and her cubs had been spotted in the valley days before and a lone male had been seen casually strolling across the camp's wooden walkways. But by far the most startling tale was of a young puma cub which had found its way through an unlocked door into a hotel.

The next morning, we drove into the Patagonian plains. Overhead, majestic birds of prey carved black shadows against a brilliant blue sky. At Lake Sarmiento, oystercatchers squawked as we approached and elegant ostrich-like rheas pranced past like ballerinas. **3** [ ] It was too large to be a grey fox and too small to be a guanaco, the curious llama-like creature that roams these lands.

'Did you see that?', my guide, Felipe, pointed. 'Puma?' I replied. 'I think so,' said Felipe. A sighting of this size was so lucky. Even if it was over in a flash. But I suddenly felt vulnerable, out there in the wilderness, with nothing but a stick to defend myself if it came near. **4** [ ] Even so, I hoped I wouldn't have to put the theory to the test.

After a hearty barbecue beside the Blue Lagoon, it was time to set off again. We hurtled down unmade mountain roads at breakneck speed, past the milky green glacial flow of the Paine River. **5** [ ] But I was soon back at the camp, exhilarated and utterly exhausted.

Over the next few days, the pace picked up steadily. There was a walk up to the Mirador Cuernos, through silent valleys of grazing animals, to a startling lookout point. **6** [ ] On the way down, we watched herds of horses gallop past isolated farms with red corrugated roofs.

On the final day I said goodbye and drove out of the park. The closest I had come to seeing a puma may have been a fleeting glimpse but I realised it mattered little. For my search had made me study every crag and cave, bush and boulder in this vast, ultimately unknowable land all the more intensely.

Exam practice

A At that point, I was more focused on staying upright than spotting pumas.

B Suddenly, a fleeting shadow sent a bolt of excitement through us.

C My goal, on the other hand, was to spot Patagonia's rare big cats and other wildlife.

D The thunderclap of a distant avalanche was the only disturbance of the peace.

E But with only 50 of these large cats in a huge area, there were still no guarantees.

F Apparently, the best thing to do is stand completely still and all should be well.

G Rumours of recent puma sightings were plentiful.

> *Exam tip*
>
> Read the whole paragraph and then all the options. Make sure the one you choose fits before and after the gap.

Writing Part 2: email

You have received this email from your English friend Joe.

From: Joe
Subject: your climate

Hi, can you help me with something? We're doing a project at college about the climate in different countries. Please could you write and tell me about the climate in your country? Is the weather very different at different times of year? What do you like and dislike about it?

Thanks a lot.
Joe

Write your **email** (140–190 words).

> *Exam tip*
>
> You have several questions to answer here. Make sure you answer them all, and close your email in a friendly way. Plan your answer before you start, and make sure you write 140–190 words.

26 Living a healthy life

Health and fitness

1.1 Look at the two pictures. Why are these meals healthy or unhealthy? Use the words in the box to complete the sentences below.

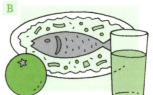

~~salt~~ fat vitamins protein fibre
carbohydrate sugar calories

Meal A is high in _salt,_____ and low in _____ .
Meal B is high in _____ and low in _____ .

1.2 ▶32 Listen to a sportsman talking about his lifestyle and underline the things he mentions.

going on a diet   eating lean meat   needing carbohydrate for energy   eating substantial portions
not putting on weight   cutting out fat   doing regular training   drinking coffee
getting enough sleep   handling stress

1.3 ▶32 Listen again. What would the sportsman say to these statements? True or false?

1 I eat lots of fruit and vegetables.   _True_

2 I've stopped eating dairy products.   _____

3 I've cut down on chocolate.   _____

4 I occasionally eat junk food.   _____

5 I go to the gym regularly.   _____

6 I've recently given up smoking.   _____

7 I drink lots of water.   _____

8 I don't get much sleep at the weekend.   _____

> **V** Vocabulary note
>
> **Diet** can mean the food and drink normally eaten by an individual or a group of people:
> *I'm an athlete so I eat a healthy diet.*
> *Rice is the staple diet of many people in India.*
>
> **Diet** is also used when particular food is eaten for medical reasons or to lose weight:
> *The doctor put me on a low-salt diet.*
> *My jeans are tight, so I'm going on a diet.*

1.4 Are the statements in 1.3 true or false for you? Rewrite any false statements to make them true for you.

1.5 PHRASAL VERBS Complete the paragraph below using the correct form of these phrasal verbs.

come down with   cut down on   get round to   go for   ~~keep to~~   live on   put on   take up

If you want to stay healthy, you need to (**1**) ___keep to___ a healthy diet. Eat plenty of fruit, vegetables and salad and (**2**) _____ salt, fat and processed sugar. And if you want to avoid (**3**) _____ weight, it's definitely best not to (**4**) _____ junk food, because it contains all those things. Also, whatever your age, it's important to (**5**) _____ doing exercise on a regular basis, so think about (**6**) _____ a sport, or (**7**) _____ a regular walk or run. By doing all these things, you should build up a healthy immune system and avoid (**8**) _____ colds all the time.

2.1 Match the phrases for minor medical problems (1–6) with the possible causes (A–F).

1	get a blister		A	You're just recovering from flu.
2	have a stomach upset		B	You've had a bad cough.
3	have a sore throat		C	You've eaten some undercooked meat.
4	feel run down		D	You've just done a long flight.
5	lose your voice		E	You're getting a cold.
6	be jet-lagged		F	You've been wearing new shoes.

2.2 Choose the correct words in these sentences.

1 If you have burnt yourself badly, you go to the <u>casualty department</u> / *local surgery*.

2 If you cut your hand and need *scars* / *stitches*, the doctor will give you a local anaesthetic.

3 If you suffer from hay fever, the doctor will give you *antihistamines* / *antibiotics*.

4 If you need medicine, the doctor will give you a *recipe* / *prescription* to take to the local pharmacy.

5 If you break your leg, the doctor will put it in *plaster* / *bandage* as soon as possible.

6 When travelling to some countries, you might need a *protection* / *vaccination* for a disease like yellow fever.

7 If you need weighing, the nurse will ask you to step on the *weights* / *scales*.

8 If the *symptoms* / *treatments* of your illness are obvious, it is easy for your doctor to decide what's wrong.

ERROR WARNING ❗

The words **prescription**, **receipt** and **recipe** are often confused.

A **prescription** is the piece of paper on which the doctor writes the medicines you need:
The doctor gave me a prescription for antibiotics.

A **receipt** is the piece of paper you receive to show you have paid:
I always keep the receipt when I buy clothes in case I want to change anything later.

A **recipe** is a set of instructions telling you how to prepare and cook food:
My mother gave me a really good recipe for bread.

3.1 **PHRASAL VERBS** Underline the phrasal verbs in 1–5 and match them with the descriptions.

1 I didn't want to play hockey, so I <u>made up</u> a story about twisting my ankle.

2 She didn't visit me when I was ill, but she made up for it by sending me some flowers.

3 Sophie didn't know which ward her brother was on, so she made for the information desk.

4 The nurse spoke so softly that I couldn't make out what she was saying about my medicine.

5 The old operating theatres are no longer used, so the hospital has made them into accommodation for nursing staff.

A Someone did something good to compensate for something they hadn't done before.

B Someone headed in a particular direction.

C Someone decided to use something in a different way.

D Someone invented a reason for something which happened to them.

E Someone was unable to understand what another person was saying.

Exam practice

Reading and Use of English Part 2

For questions **1–8**, read the text below and think of the word which best fits each gap. Use only **one** word in each gap. There is an example at the beginning (**0**).

The importance of physical activity

The pace (**0**) _____*of*_____ modern life is very fast, and most people have busy and demanding lives. Consequently, eating (**1**) _____ balanced diet and doing physical activity make a big difference to overall health. (**2**) _____ we are all aware of how important exercise is for us, from our brains to our bones, many people spend far (**3**) _____ little time exercising. The good news is that (**4**) _____ is easier than you think to fit physical activity (**5**) _____ your day because you can do it at (**6**) _____ time and wherever suits you.

Remember that your feet were made for walking, so use them (**7**) _____ you get the chance. Walk around town, ignore lifts and escalators, and build up your leg muscles by climbing stairs. Next, get out and have fun. For example, kicking a ball about is a great way to spend time together (**8**) _____ a family, or with friends.

> **Exam tip**
>
> Read the text first to get a general impression of what it is about.

Writing Part 1: essay

In your English class you have been talking about how to be fit and healthy. Now your English teacher has asked you to write an essay.

Write an essay (140–190 words) using **all** the notes and give reasons for your point of view.

What is the best way to stay fit and healthy?

Notes
Write about:
1   eating a healthy diet
2   making time to relax
3   _____ (your own idea)

> **Exam tip**
>
> Remember to read the question carefully and plan your essay before you write. When you have finished it, read it carefully and check for grammar and spelling mistakes.

27 Sound waves

Music, sounds

1.1 **Read these words. Which is the odd one out in each group? Why?**

1 choir   composer   conductor   guitarist   orchestra

2 beat   lyrics   rhythm   chapter   tune

1.2 ▶33 **Listen to a woman talking about music.**

1 Is she musical?   Yes

2 Does she come from a musical family?   _____

3 Can she play a musical instrument?   _____

4 Has she ever sung in a choir?   _____

5 Does she ever go to concerts?   _____

1.3 ▶33 **Complete the woman's statements. Then listen again to check.**

1 I've always been able to _____ sing in tune _____ .

2 The rest of us _____ our hobbies.

3 I _____ in cello and violin.

4 When I was at school, I _____ in the school choir.

5 I _____ with a friend.

6 I've _____ in the car, or else I have _____ .

2.1 **Read the music reviews below. Match the types of music with the reviews.**

rock: _____   pop: _____   classical: _____   world music: _____

1 Having produced an **album** of African rumba tunes, the group have turned to Cuba for inspiration. But instead of using the original **lyrics**, they've added their own. The rhythm and lead guitars and the variety of arrangements effectively maintain interest. A brilliant addition to their repertoire.

2 This album is built around the work of legendary **composers** Andersson and Ulvaeus, whose songs defined much of 20th century music. Yet their **fans** may be surprised by these arrangements. **Old favourites** with catchy tunes from the 1970s and 1980s are effortlessly transformed into the band's own **distinctive style** with some very pleasing **harmonies**. Buy this one for your collection!

3 This is much better than their first album, and nothing here is a **cover version**. Some of the **tracks** feature heavy metal guitar solos, and the drums are alive with rhythm. A marvellous album that gets better with every listening.

4 This is an album of Argentinian chamber songs, written in the early 1900s, and exquisitely accompanied by violins. There's everything here, from a beautiful **duet** to a passionate tango. It's all superbly recorded and packaged with an imagination and care that do the designers credit. Fantastic.

2.2 Look at the words in bold in the reviews. Find the correct words for these definitions.

1   a song sung by two people   *duet*

2   a combination of voices singing together in tune   _____

3   a collection of recordings   _____

4   people who write music   _____

5   individual recorded songs   _____

6   a re-recording of another musician's song   _____

7   the special way someone does something   _____

8   people who are really keen on a particular singer or group   _____

9   familiar songs that everyone likes   _____

10 the words written for a song   _____

2.3 Use words and expressions from 2.1 and 2.2 to write a short description of an album you particularly like.

3.1 ▶34 Listen to four people describing different kinds of music. Which type is each person describing?

> jazz   folk   rock 'n' roll   country and western

1 _____   2 _____   3 _____   4 _____

4.1 ▶35 Each of these words describes a sound, and can be used as a verb or a noun. Listen and write the correct word for each sound you hear.

> bang   ~~bark~~   smash   sneeze   snore
> splash   tap   whistle

V Vocabulary note

Many of these words can be used in a range of different contexts:
I tapped on the car window to get her attention.
She tapped her foot in time to the music.

1 _____bark_____   2 _____   3 _____   4 _____

5 _____   6 _____   7 _____   8 _____

4.2 Make sentences by matching 1–8 with A–H.

1   It was really difficult to sleep

2   There was so much dust in the house

3   As Peter fell head first into the pond

4   I knocked over the enormous vase

5   The sports instructor was very strict

6   When the wind blew

7   The tune was very catchy

8   The door slammed shut

A   it whistled through the cracks in the old front door.

B   that I started to sneeze almost as soon as I arrived.

C   with a loud bang that made everybody jump.

D   and barked out instructions to the students.

E   and I heard my dad tapping his foot to the beat.

F   because my brother snored so much.

G   there was an impressive splash.

H   and it made a terrible noise as it smashed.

Exam practice

Reading and Use of English Part 2

For questions **1–8**, read the text below and think of the word which best fits each gap. Use only **one** word in each gap. There is an example at the beginning (**0**).

Music and its effect on children

For all children, music provides an obvious opportunity for both self-expression (**0**) _____ *and* _____ creativity. But researchers have now also shown that a strong musical education provides so (**1**) _____ more. For example, music develops self-discipline: the child who devotes time to practising (**2**) _____ day is known to develop similar habits (**3**) _____ relation to other subjects as well. Organisational skills increase and the child learns (**4**) _____ is needed to be 'good' at something. In addition, band or choir members learn the importance of being a reliable member of a group and becoming a true team player, and (**5**) _____ necessarily always 'the star'.

Scientists have also discovered that learning to read music or play a musical instrument develops higher thinking skills. Any child (**6**) _____ is skilled at music also excels in problem-solving, evaluation and analysis. The part of the brain used to read music is the same (**7**) _____ the area used in mathematical thinking. This explains (**8**) _____ so many capable musicians are also good at maths.

Writing Part 1: essay

In your class you have been talking about the importance of learning to play music. Now your English teacher has asked you to write an essay.

Write an essay (140–190 words) using **all** the notes and give reasons for your point of view.

Should everyone learn to play a musical instrument?

Notes
Write about:
1. whether playing music is enjoyable
2. whether everyone can learn to play an instrument
3. _____ (your own idea)

Highs and lows

Feelings

1.1 ▶36 **Listen to a boy called Nick talking about something that happened recently. Answer these questions.**

1 Who came to watch Nick's team play? Why? _____

2 What happened after the match? _____

3 Who was chosen? _____

1.2 **Look at the adjectives below. Which are positive and which are negative? Write P above the positive adjectives and N above the negative ones.**

ashamed confident disappointed embarrassed excited guilty jealous proud relaxed upset

1.3 ▶36 **Listen again. How do you think Nick felt:**

1 after he scored the goal? _____

2 at the end of the day? _____

1.4 ▶37 **Now listen to Nick continue his story. Choose three adjectives from 1.2 to describe how he felt at the end of Saturday.**

_____   _____   _____

2.1 **Read the email. The underlined adjectives have similar meanings to those in the table below. Write them in the correct column.**

Hi Helga

Just wanted to tell you that I went to the seaside last Saturday with my friends. I was really glad that they phoned me because I was feeling fed up and I was relieved to have something to do. But when we got to the seaside I realised they were going to the theme park and I've always been scared of the big rides. I got a bit angry with them because they hadn't told me. But in the end they persuaded me to go with them. As I sat there waiting for the first ride to begin, I could feel my heart beating faster and faster, but as soon as it started I forgot to feel anxious about it because it was such fun. When I got off I was surprised to realise how much I'd enjoyed it and I went on all the other rides too! You must come with me next time.

Love, Tina

amazed	annoyed	depressed	frightened	pleased	worried
				glad	

2.2 The adjectives below also have similar meanings to the ones in the table in 2.1. Write them in the correct column. If there is one adjective in a column which is stronger than the others, underline it.

> afraid   astonished   concerned   delighted   miserable   furious   terrified

3.1 Look at the people in the picture. How are they feeling? Write as many adjectives as you can.

Paul: _____

_____

Don: _____

_____

Paul   Don

3.2 Think about something you did recently, e.g. a sports match you played in, a place you visited, a party you went to. Choose two of the phrases for feelings below and write a sentence with each one.

> worried about   surprised that   afraid of   upset that   pleased to   annoyed with

4.1 Choose the correct adjectives in these sentences.

1 I was really *boring* / *bored* on holiday. There was nothing to do.

2 Last night's show was really *disappointing* / *disappointed* – we wasted our money.

3 We were very *surprising* / *surprised* when we got to the hotel and it was closed.

4 Tom was so *exciting* / *excited* when he received your letter with the good news.

5 He hated talking in public so he felt very *worrying* / *worried* about giving a speech.

6 Rahim gave me a ride on his motorbike. It was absolutely *terrifying* / *terrified*.

7 I didn't find the holiday *relaxing* / *relaxed* because my friend wanted us to go out all the time.

V *Vocabulary note*

Many adjectives for feelings can also be followed by **(that) + subject + verb** or **infinitive (to …)**:
Maria was sorry (that) she had missed the party.
Maria was pleased to get the invitation.

4.2 Complete these tables.

Noun	fear	amazement	_____	_____	annoyance	_____
Verb	*frighten*	_____	_____	_____	_____	excite
Adjective	frightening frightened	_____ _____	embarrassing embarrassed	pleasing pleased	_____ _____	exciting excited

Noun	depression	_____	pride	anxiety	misery	_____
Adjective	_____ _____	angry	_____	_____	_____	jealous

Exam practice

Listening Part 1

 38 You will hear people talking in eight different situations. For questions **1–8**, choose the best answer (**A**, **B** or **C**).

💡 *Exam tip*

Listen carefully for words which mean the same as words in the questions, e.g. if *frightening* is in the question you might hear *scary* or *terrifying* in the recording.

1 You hear a woman telling a friend about a conversation she had with her parents.

How did her parents feel about her news?

A furious that she wouldn't complete her studies

B astonished that she hadn't consulted them

C pleased that she'd made a good decision

2 You hear a man talking about an activity holiday.

What opinion does he give of the holiday?

A It was more suitable for teenagers.

B The activities were too demanding for him.

C The teaching was disappointing.

3 You hear two people talking about a film.

How did they react to the ending?

A They found it frightening.

B It took them by surprise.

C They felt it was unclear.

4 You hear a couple talking about their hotel.

What are they slightly dissatisfied with?

A the type of breakfast

B the view from the room

C the lack of entertainment

5 You hear two friends talking about a football match.

How do they feel?

A concerned about the future

B astonished at the result

C upset at their team's performance

6 You hear a voicemail message.

What problem does the boy have?

A He's had all his money stolen.

B He needs a lift to the shop.

C He needs to borrow some money.

7 You hear two people talking about a new colleague.

What does the man say about her?

A She often misses deadlines.

B She sometimes loses her temper.

C She seems distracted.

8 You hear an actor talking about her work.

What does she find most difficult about it?

A doing publicity interviews

B wearing heavy make-up

C remembering her words

Writing Part 2: article

You see this notice in an international magazine.

> **What makes you feel really happy?**
> Going on holiday? Being successful? Playing music? Seeing friends and family?
> Write us an article telling us what makes **you** happy and why.
> The best articles will be published in our magazine next month.

Write your **article** (140–190 words).

 💡 *Exam tip*

Make the article lively and interesting for people to read. Talk about your own feelings and experience.

29 Looking back

The past, time

1.1 **What do the photos show?**

_____

1.2 ▶39 **Listen to a teacher talking to his class about the photos. Write the information.**

A Location: _____France_____ Age: _____ Purpose: _____

B Location: _____ Age: _____ Purpose: _____

1.3 **Read what this student has written. Underline phrases you could use in your own writing. Then write a similar paragraph about a famous construction in your own country.**

One of the oldest things you can see in Egypt is the Great Pyramid of Giza. It was built about 4,500 years ago as a tomb for a king called Khufu. It's absolutely enormous, and for centuries it was the tallest man-made structure in the world. It's very famous because it is the only one of the seven ancient 'Wonders of the World' that has remained intact. There are lots of ancient sites all around it, and archaeologists have discovered temples and many other buildings there.

2.1 **Read this text and choose the correct words.**

> **The early history of Brittany (France)**
>
> We have archaeological **(1)** _evidence_ / _facts_ that people were living in Brittany, in north-western France, about 12,000 years ago. This period is known as prehistory, and there are no written **(2)** _catalogues_ / _records_ which go back this far, although the stone circles and monuments that the people built are still standing today in places like Carnac. The **(3)** _population_ / _community_ must have been very small in these prehistoric times. Historians have no precise **(4)** _scores_ / _figures_, but there were certainly far fewer **(5)** _residents_ / _inhabitants_ than there are today. They belonged to different Celtic **(6)** _tribes_ / _teams_ and they are the **(7)** _ancestors_ / _relatives_ of modern French people. They survived by **(8)** _hunting_ / _chasing_ animals and gathering berries and fruit in the wild.
>
> About 4,000 years ago, people in Brittany began to **(9)** _keep_ / _settle_ down rather than constantly moving around, and farming techniques improved. People began to grow crops and keep animals to provide meat, wool and milk. They also made **(10)** _tools_ / _gadgets_ out of iron, and this period is known as the Iron Age. The people of this time had quite sophisticated **(11)** _beliefs_ / _opinions_ and a strong tradition of telling **(12)** _histories_ / _stories_ orally, but they left no trace of a written language behind.

> **ERROR WARNING**
>
> **History** means all the events that happened in the past:
> _She's studying for a degree in ancient history because she's fascinated by it._
>
> A **story** is a description of real or imagined events, often told to entertain people:
> _The story is about three boys who explore an old castle._
>
> **Story** is also used to mean a news report:
> _The main story on the news today is about the election._

2.2 **WORD BUILDING** Complete the tables.

Noun	history	prehistory	archaeology	evidence	politics	presidency
Noun (person)	historian		_____		_____	_____
Adjective	historical historic	_____	_____	_____	_____	_____

Verb	populate	civilise	invade	reside	believe	survive
Noun	_____	_____	_____	_____	_____	_____
Noun (person)		_____	_____	_____	_____	_____

ERROR WARNING

Historic means important (or likely to be important): *a historic building, a historic event/day*
Historical means connected with the study or representation of things in the past: *a historical novel, historical documents*

3.1 Complete the sentences using the correct form of these verbs. Some of them can be used more than once.

> last   pass   spend   take

1 Several years have __passed__ since I saw my friend Jenna.
2 Driving lessons usually _____ for about an hour.
3 I _____ last weekend camping with friends.
4 If I travel during the rush hour, it _____ me an hour to get to the city centre.
5 Food _____ longer if you keep it in the fridge.
6 I _____ three hours writing the report for today's meeting.

4.1 Match each of the expressions in bold with its meaning.

1 The party started at eight, and we arrived **on time**.
2 We've lived here **for some time**.
3 I'm just getting off the bus so I'll be there **in no time**.
4 Ellie doesn't live near me now but I still see her **from time to time**.

A sometimes but not often
B very soon
C not early or late
D for quite a long period

Now do the same with these expressions.

5 I **have no time for** Lisa – she's so rude and negative!
6 I try to **make time for** sport at least three times a week.
7 I **killed time** playing on the computer until you got here.
8 **Take your time** deciding which course you want to study.

E to do something while waiting
F to do something without hurrying
G to have no respect for someone
H to leave enough time to do something

V Vocabulary note

We use **last** to say how long something goes on for:
The film lasts for an hour.

If you **spend** time doing something, you do it from the beginning to the end of the time:
He spent all day planning the trip.

The verb **pass** refers to time going by:
Time passes quickly when you're enjoying yourself.

If something **takes** time, you need that amount of time to do it:
It may take us several weeks to get back.

Exam practice

Reading and Use of English Part 1

For questions **1–8** read the text below and decide which answer (**A**, **B**, **C** or **D**) best fits each space. There is an example at the beginning (**0**).

 Exam tip

Look at the words before and after the gap, choose your word and then read the whole sentence.

The first people of Britain

The time from the arrival of the first modern humans to the beginning of recorded history was a (**0**) __C__ of about 100 centuries, or 400 generations. We know little about what (**1**) _____ then because these ancient people left no written records. What we know about them comes from the (**2**) _____ that archaeologists have found at different (**3**) _____ .

Throughout prehistoric times there were many different (**4**) _____ living in the British islands. These groups were often in (**5**) _____ with their neighbours and frequently attacked each other. However, they also had contact with people in other parts of Europe and (**6**) _____ with them regularly.

The first written accounts of Britain (**7**) _____ from the time when Julius Caesar and his army invaded over 2,000 years ago. Interestingly, the Romans did not increase the number of people in Britain by any great extent. To a population of three million, Caesar's army and administration (**8**) _____ only about 150,000.

0	**A**	duration	**B**	length	**C**	period	**D**	stretch
1	**A**	went on	**B**	passed out	**C**	went through	**D**	passed by
2	**A**	claim	**B**	proof	**C**	evidence	**D**	sign
3	**A**	sites	**B**	positions	**C**	settings	**D**	grounds
4	**A**	families	**B**	descendants	**C**	tribes	**D**	classes
5	**A**	contest	**B**	fight	**C**	battle	**D**	conflict
6	**A**	traded	**B**	dealt	**C**	exchanged	**D**	bargained
7	**A**	belong	**B**	exist	**C**	begin	**D**	date
8	**A**	grew	**B**	added	**C**	developed	**D**	raised

Writing Part 2: review

You see this notice on an international travel website.

 Exam tip

Give your review a title (the name of the museum) and use positive adjectives and phrases when you make recommendations.

> **Reviews wanted: museums across the world**
>
> We're doing a series on museums in different countries. Have you visited a museum that you found really fascinating? Describe it, and say why you found it so interesting. Recommend some exhibits that you think other visitors would enjoy, and explain why.
>
> The best reviews will be published on our website.

Write your **review** (140–190 words).

30 Everyone's different
Personality

1.1 ▶40 Listen to three people speaking about women they admire. Match them with the photos.

1.2 ▶40 Listen again and write down the adjectives used to describe each woman.

1 cheerful, _____

2 _____

3 _____

A
Angelina Jolie

B
Jessica Ennis-Hill

C
Michelle Obama

1.3 Write two sentences about a famous person you admire, using some of the adjectives above.

1.4 Read the descriptions that two students have written about a friend. Choose the best word for each gap.

I used to love playing with Sam when we were kids because he's very **(1)** __C__ so he was really good at making up exciting games to play. But he didn't enjoy being in large groups because he was very **(2)** _____ and he didn't like other children playing with us. He's become a bit more **(3)** _____ since then and as a result he's got more friends now. But we had an argument the other day because I made a joke about his clothes. He's much too **(4)** _____ so it's really easy to upset him. I have to be careful what I say.

I met Emma quite recently. The best thing about her is that she's great fun to be with as she's always **(5)** _____ and she never seems to be in a bad mood. She's always got something to say – in fact, she's the most **(6)** _____ person I've ever met. She never gets anxious but in some ways she's far too **(7)** _____ about everything. For example, she nearly always arrives late when we meet up. I don't mind that, though. The only thing I dislike about her is that she can be **(8)** _____ to other people – she sometimes makes fun of them, which isn't nice.

1	A easy-going	B thoughtful	C imaginative
2	A shy	B selfish	C hopeless
3	A stubborn	B outgoing	C bossy
4	A sensitive	B sensible	C sympathetic
5	A caring	B cheerful	C demanding
6	A talkative	B generous	C considerate
7	A competitive	B lively	C relaxed
8	A impatient	B unreliable	C unkind

ERROR WARNING

Sensitive = being easily upset:
Tim is sensitive – he cries at a sad story.

Sensible = showing good judgement:
Sam is sensible – he always makes wise decisions.

Sympathetic = understanding other people's problems:
She was sympathetic when I explained why I was late.

1.5 Using some of these expressions from 1.4, write two positive and two negative sentences about someone you know.

He's very/really …   He's so …   He's a bit …   He's much/far too …   She's never/always …
The only thing I dislike about her is that she …   The best thing about her is that she …   She can be …

2.1 Match the adjectives in A with their opposites in B.

amusing – serious

A	amusing adventurous generous gentle hard-working modest polite relaxed self-confident
B	aggressive arrogant cautious lazy mean rude serious shy tense

2.2 Choose the correct adjective from 2.1 for each sentence.

1   After Steve won the prize, he became rather _____arrogant_____ and expected everyone to look up to him.

2   People who are _____ with their money rarely leave a tip.

3   It's _____ to walk into someone's office without knocking.

4   She could be a really good musician but she's too _____ to practise.

5   The day before my driving test I couldn't concentrate on anything because I felt too _____ .

6   Animals are only _____ towards people if they are frightened or hungry.

2.3 Look back at all the personality adjectives. Choose some that describe you and make a list.

3.1   WORD BUILDING   We can add a prefix to some adjectives to make an opposite. The most common prefix is *un-*. Others are *dis-*, *in-*, *ir-* and *im-*. Write the correct prefix above each group of adjectives.

1 _____	2 _____	3 _____	4 _____	5 _____
polite	popular	considerate	honest	relevant
patient	kind	convenient	satisfied	responsible
possible	imaginative	expensive		regular

> **V** *Vocabulary note*
>
> These prefixes can be added to some nouns (e.g. *unhappiness, disapproval, impatience*).
>
> The prefixes *un-* and *dis-* can also be added to some verbs (e.g. *unlock, dislike*).

3.2   With some nouns, we can add *-ful* to make adjectives meaning 'having' and *-less* to make adjectives meaning 'lacking'. Complete the sentences by adding *-ful* or *-less* to these nouns.

care   colour   grace   harm   pain   power   thank

1   We were really _____thankful_____ that we'd reserved seats as the hall was full.

2   That's the second wallet you've lost. Why are you so _____ ?

3   The president is the most _____ person in the country.

4   My foot is still _____ from when I hurt it last week.

5   You needn't be afraid of that snake. It's quite _____ .

6   I love watching Mary dance because she's so _____ .

7   Water is a _____ liquid.

Exam practice

Reading and Use of English Part 5

You are going to read an extract from a novel. For questions **1–6**, choose the answer (**A**, **B**, **C** or **D**) which you think fits best according to the text.

Jenny half opened her eyes to stare at the glowing numbers of the clock radio on the bedside table. As it was still dark, she assumed that it was fairly early, but squinting at the clock she realised that
line 3   it was nearly time for her to get up. She was irritated that the winter darkness had *beguiled her* into thinking she still had a few hours in bed.

As she turned over, she heard a noise from the other bedroom. The sound bore no relation to the images in the dreams she was leaving behind as she slowly woke up. Still half asleep, she realised it was the creak of a cupboard door. This was followed by footsteps padding around the room next to hers and then another creak. It was her father opening and closing his cupboard doors as he prepared for the day. He was always the first one up in the morning. She imagined that he would already have his tracksuit on and was picking up his trainers, about to put them on. The squeak of
line 11   the bed as he sat down confirmed *that*.

Her father was predictable, she thought to herself fondly. The night before he had announced that he was going for his usual run by the lake, as he did every morning, no matter what the weather or what other people might want him to do instead. Jenny really admired the fact that he would stick to his plans, whatever obstacles were in his way. He'd do a few exercises to warm up on the terrace outside the house, and then he'd jog down the winding, tree-lined lane to the woods, where he would pick up speed before coming to the lake. He'd run twice around the lake, which at this time would inevitably be covered in mist, before coming home and having two boiled eggs for breakfast. But first of all, before even leaving the house, he'd have to find the woolly hat he always wore and fill his water bottle. This procedure would take a few minutes as he always threw his hat and bottle down on a chair in the kitchen when he came back, but he never remembered this the next morning and would therefore spend several grumpy minutes looking for them before he set off on his morning ritual.

Jenny heard her father go downstairs and waited for a few moments while she knew he would be filling his water bottle and fetching the back door key from a large hook. She then got out of bed, throwing on an old jumper that hung on the back of the door, in order to fend off the cold that enveloped the big old house at this time of year. She walked over to the window, and just at that moment, as she had anticipated, her father came out onto the terrace, stamping his feet to warm them up, his water bottle in his hand. How reassuring this was, in a world which sometimes seemed so confusing!

Jenny's father did his stretching exercises and, after a few minutes, he set off at a jogging speed down the line of leafless birch trees. As usual at this time of year, his movements were the only sign of life on the country lane as he headed off towards the woods and ultimately the lake. Then Jenny noticed something different. It was the figure of a man, his grey jacket camouflaged by the trunks of
line 34   the birch trees. Once her father had passed, the man *melted* out from behind the trees and started to follow him.

Exam practice

1 What is meant by 'beguiled her' in line 3?

  A tempted her to wake up

  B deceived her into a wrong conclusion

  C attracted her immediate attention

  D distracted her from the clock

2 What is suggested in the second paragraph about the noise Jenny heard?

  A She could identify from it what was happening.

  B She was unsure at first where it came from.

  C She was annoyed because it had disturbed her sleep.

  D She wondered if it meant she might still be dreaming.

3 What does 'that' refer to in line 11?

  A the fact that her father had already got up

  B the part of the house her father was in

  C what her father was going to do next

  D where her father had sat down

4 How did Jenny feel about her father's behaviour?

  A She respected the fact that he always did what he intended.

  B She found it irritating that he forgot where he had put things.

  C She didn't understand why things never went wrong for him.

  D She thought it might be good for him to vary his routine.

5 Jenny went to the window in order to

  A make sure her father had everything he needed.

  B see if the weather was suitable for her father to go running.

  C check that nothing unusual was happening outside.

  D confirm that her father was keeping to his usual habits.

6 The word 'melted' in line 34 is used to emphasise the fact that the person in the trees

  A didn't realise they had been seen.

  B had been waiting there a long time.

  C had to hurry to keep up with Jenny's father.

  D didn't want to make any sudden movements.

Exam tip

Read each paragraph carefully before you answer the question as it may test more than one or two sentences.

Writing Part 2: article

You see this announcement on an international website.

> **Articles wanted**
>
> ### What qualities do you look for in your friends?
>
> Do they have to be reliable and honest, amusing and good company, or something completely different? Write and tell us what you look for in your friends in general, and describe one of your closest friends. The best articles will be posted on the website.

Write your **article** (140–190 words).

31 Get active

Sport

1.1 Copy the table in your notebook and write these activities in the correct column.

running volleyball skating cycling judo squash jogging yoga rugby
aerobics walking swimming badminton athletics climbing skateboarding
skiing diving hockey snorkelling football table tennis baseball gymnastics
sailing snowboarding hiking martial arts surfing ice hockey

go	play	do
running	volleyball	judo

1.2 Complete the sentences below with words from boxes A and B. Some words are used more than once.

A a course   a court   a pitch   a track   **B** a bat   clubs   a racket   a stick

1 Golf is played with _____clubs_____ on _____ .
2 You play squash on _____ with _____ .
3 You play hockey on _____ using _____ .
4 Tennis is played on _____ and you need _____ .
5 Cricket is played with _____ on _____ .

One word in the boxes is not used in sentences 1–5. What is it, and which sport is it associated with?

1.3 Answer these questions about people who play sports.

1 Someone who goes running is a *runner*. Which of the other sports in 1.1 add *-er*?
   skater, _____

2 Someone who plays volleyball is a *volleyball player*. Which of the other sports add *player*?
   _____

3 What is the word for someone who does these each of these sports?
   cycling: _____   gymnastics: _____   athletics: _____

2.1 ▶41 Listen to three people talking about different sports/activities. Which sports do they describe?

Speaker 1: _____   Speaker 2: _____   Speaker 3: _____

2.2 ▶41 Listen again and write the adjectives used to describe each sport.

Speaker 1: _____   Speaker 2: _____   Speaker 3: _____

2.3 Write four sentences about a sport you play. Say how you feel about it, what you do and what equipment you use.

3.1 Complete these sentences with the correct form of *win* or *beat*.

1 They ___*beat*___ the favourites in the second round and went on to _____ the semi-final.

2 After years of training, Alison finally _____ her great rival in the final and _____ the trophy.

3 Peter _____ a gold medal in the 10,000 metres, _____ the world record by two seconds.

4 Fitzpatrick went on to _____ the race, _____ his rival by a tenth of a second.

5 There is no one who can _____ them now – they're bound to _____ the cup.

> **V** **Vocabulary note**
>
> We use **win** for competitions and prizes:
> *win a race, a semi-final, a cup, a medal, a trophy*
>
> We use **beat** for people and records:
> *beat another team, an opponent, a rival, a record, a time*
>
> We use **beat** (someone) **at** a game or sport:
> *My brother always beats me at chess.*

4.1 The verb *run* can be used in different ways. To show the meaning in each of these sentences, replace *run* with one of the verbs below in the correct form.

> flow   ~~manage~~   go   do   work

1 My cousin has been <u>running</u> a small restaurant for several years now.   ___*managing*___

2 Tears of laughter <u>ran</u> down her face as she watched the film.   _____

3 The washing machine is <u>running</u> much better since the electrician came.   _____

4 The mechanics <u>ran</u> a final check on the car before the Grand Prix started.   _____

5 There's a bus to the beach which <u>runs</u> several times a day in the summer.   _____

4.2 **PHRASAL VERBS** Write the correct noun and choose the correct phrasal verb in each of these sentences.

> children   families   friends   petrol   problem   ~~teachers~~

1 If you criticise the ___*teachers*___ at your college, you *run them down* / *run over them*.

2 You often find that dark hair *runs in* / *runs on* certain _____ .

3 When you meet some _____ unexpectedly in the street, you *run into* / *run over* them.

4 When _____ are very naughty, their parents sometimes *run up against* / *run out of* patience.

5 If you're facing a difficult _____ , you've *run up against* / *run through* it.

6 Most cars these days *run on* / *run into* unleaded _____ .

Exam practice

Reading and Use of English Part 4

For questions **1–6**, complete the second sentence so that it has a similar meaning to the first sentence, using the word given. **Do not change the word given.** You must use between **two** and **five** words, including the word given. There is an example at the beginning **(0)**.

---

0 Jane Ashdown won the final, pushing Olga Nemitov back to second place.

BEATEN

Olga Nemitov _____ *was beaten into* _____ second place in the final by Jane Ashdown.

1 Jill's boss explained all the details of the contract to her, but it took a long time.

RUN

It took Jill's boss a long time _____ all the details of the contract with her.

2 France managed to win the trophy at the end of a very tough match.

SUCCEEDED

France _____ the trophy at the end of a very tough match.

3 The local garage fixed my car and now it is working well.

RUNNING

My car has _____ was fixed by the local garage.

4 The builders faced many problems when they started laying the foundations.

RAN

The builders _____ of problems when they started laying the foundations.

5 I first took up sailing seven years ago.

WENT

I _____ time seven years ago.

6 I think Susie has inherited her musical ability from her parents and grandparents.

RUNS

I think being musical _____ family.

💡 **Exam tip**

You must always use the word in the same form as it is given.

Writing Part 2: email

You have received this email from your Canadian friend Michael.

> **From:** Michael
> **Subject:** sport
> I'm hoping you'll help me with a project I'm doing on sport. Could you write and tell me which sport is most popular in your country and why? And what about you – do you prefer playing sport or watching it? Write soon – thanks a lot!
> Michael

Write your **email** (140–190 words).

32 My world

Friends, family and relationships

1.1 ▶42 Listen to four people talking about a friendship. How well do they know the person they are talking about? Write A (very well), B (quite well) or C (not well at all).

Speaker 1: _____ Speaker 2: _____

Speaker 3: _____ Speaker 4: _____

1.2 ▶42 Use these verbs to complete the extracts from the recording. Then listen again to check.

> enjoy   fell   ~~fell~~   get   get   have   keep   lost   make   make   spoken   told

Speaker 1: I **(1)** _____fell_____ out with Mike over money.

We haven't **(2)** _____ to each other for three months.

I should **(3)** _____ in touch with him to **(4)** _____ up.

We **(5)** _____ each other everything.

Speaker 2: I **(6)** _____ madly in love with her.

We **(7)** _____ on really well together.

I'd really like to **(8)** _____ to know her.

Speaker 3: We **(9)** _____ touch for a while.

We **(10)** _____ each other's company.

We **(11)** _____ in touch now.

Speaker 4: I don't **(12)** _____ friends easily.

We **(13)** _____ things in common.

> **V** *Vocabulary note*
>
> We say **get engaged/married** to someone, but **get divorced from** someone.
>
> We also say **go out with** someone and **propose to** someone.

1.3 Read what Speaker 1 and Speaker 3 said. Which adjectives do they use with *friend(s)*?

1 We were very _____ friends.

2 He was my _____ friend.

3 Our fathers were _____ friends.

4 Jasmine and I became _____ friends.

2.1 Here is part of an email. Choose the correct words.

As you know, my family moved two months ago. During the summer holidays, my **(1)** *parents* / *relatives* were both busy at work and I didn't know anyone. So I joined a dance class to get to **(2)** *know* / *meet* some people. I very quickly **(3)** *got* / *made* some new friends, although I soon found out that I would never **(4)** *get* / *become* a brilliant dancer! One girl is a **(5)** *neighbour* / *colleague* who lives in the flat next door to ours and we have lots of things **(6)** *in* / *on* common. We see **(7)** *the* / *each* other nearly every day. We get **(8)** *on* / *with* well together and we almost never fall **(9)** *down* / *out*! So the move is working out well for me so far.

2.2 **Which of the people in the box below are relations? Underline them.**

> classmates colleagues <u>cousins</u> partner nephew widow flatmates couple acquaintance
> neighbours aunt stepfather sister-in-law boyfriend grandparents fiancé(e) penfriend

2.3 ▶43 **Listen to a teenage girl talking about her family and friends and mark the statements T (true) or F (false). Correct the sentences that are false.**

1   She gets on very well with her stepsister. _____

2   She thinks family are more important than friends. _____

3   She and her friends have different interests. _____

4   She rarely has disagreements with her friends. _____

5   She met her friend Meena at primary school. _____

3.1 **Read this biography and choose the correct words. Then put A–F in the correct order.**

BIOGRAPHY: David Davies (1818–1890)

David Davies made an incredible journey during his **(1)** *lifetime* / *generation*.

A   He then changed direction and became involved in building railways and then bought more land. His **(2)** *outlook* / *destiny* was decided when he found coal underneath.

B   In fact, he left school at 11 to work on the land. His father died when he was 20 years old and, as the **(3)** *eldest* / *older* of nine children, he was expected to **(4)** *support* / *provide* the family.

C   He later became a well-known politician but he never lost touch with his **(5)** *roots* / *ancestors*. He was popular, inspiring **(6)** *obligation* / *loyalty* among his friends, family and workers, paying for schools and chapels in his local **(7)** *household* / *community*.

D   He worked hard to do so and he managed to buy several farms in the area where he had been **(8)** *brought* / *grown up*.

E   He became the richest man in Wales even though he didn't come from a wealthy **(9)** *condition* / *background*.

F   It was from the mines which he set up there that his family made their **(10)** *fortune* / *funds*.

After his death, his granddaughters spent some of the money they had **(11)** *inherited* / *granted* from him on paintings, which have since become very famous. When they died, they **(12)** *saved* / *donated* 260 of these paintings to their country and they are now in the museum for everyone to see.

4.1 **There are lots of expressions with the word *life*. Choose one expression to follow each sentence below.**

1   She's always enthusiastic and loves being busy.

2   There's no point worrying about things that might not happen.

3   You should go out more instead of studying every weekend.

4   I haven't seen you for ages.

5   I don't want my daughter to give up her job but it's her decision.

6   The only day it rained last week was the day we chose for our picnic.

A   That's life.

B   It's her life.

C   She's full of life.

D   Get a life!

E   How's life?

F   Life's too short.

Exam practice

Listening Part 3

44 You will hear five short extracts in which people are talking about a family party. For questions **1–5**, choose from the list (**A–H**) what problem each speaker mentions about the party. Use the letters only once. There are three extra letters which you do not need to use.

A The arrangements were unclear.

B There was no public transport to the venue.

C The party was less formal than expected.

D The quality of the food was poor.

E Someone fell ill during the party.

F There wasn't enough for the children to do.

G The venue was unsuitable for some people.

H There wasn't enough space.

Speaker 1	**1**
Speaker 2	**2**
Speaker 3	**3**
Speaker 4	**4**
Speaker 5	**5**

 Exam tip

Several speakers may mention something connected to a statement, e.g. something about children or food, but only one speaker will say something which exactly matches it.

Writing Part 1: essay

In your English class you have been talking about families. Now your English teacher has asked you to write an essay.

Write an essay (140–190 words) using **all** the notes and give reasons for your point of view.

'You have to be strict to be a good parent.'
Do you agree with this statement?

Notes
Write about:
1 whether it's good for children to have rules to follow
2 whether children need to learn from their own mistakes
3 _____ (your own idea)

Exam tip

Remember to write about both the points in the notes and an idea of your own. There should be a clear conclusion at the end of your essay.

33 Moving around

Travel

1.1 The words in the box are from the text below. Is the text about a journey by train, car, plane, bus or underground?

board   control   crew   gate   headset   pass   ~~passport~~   security   terminal   visa

Now read the text and complete it with the words in the box.

First of all, don't forget to check that your **(1)** _passport_ is up to date and to find out whether you need a **(2)** _____ for the country you are visiting. Also, if you are travelling from a large airport, make sure you go to the right **(3)** _____ as there is sometimes more than one. When you arrive at the check-in desk, your bags will be weighed and you will be given a boarding **(4)** _____ with your seat number, if you haven't already checked in online. You then proceed to the departure lounge after going through passport **(5)** _____ and undergoing a **(6)** _____ check. Look at the departure **(7)** _____ in the lounge so you know which **(8)** _____ number you must go to when it's time to board. The cabin **(9)** _____ will direct you to your seat on the plane, and you have to fasten your seat belt before take-off. You will be served refreshments and most companies provide an entertainment system with a **(10)** _____ .

1.2 ▶45 Listen to four descriptions of journeys. What form of transport is each person describing?

1 _____   2 _____   3 _____   4 _____

1.3 ▶45 Listen again and underline the words below as you hear them. Then look at the words you didn't hear. What form of transport are they associated with?

carriages   commute   double-deckers   escalators   fares   landing   meter   pass   platform   rank
runway   rush hour   season ticket   seats   single-deckers   sliding doors   stop   tip   wing

2.1 Use these words to complete the sentences below.

accommodation   carpark   cash   coin   equipment   hotel
~~luggage~~   parking   suitcase   tent   transport   vehicle

1 There's no need to take a lot of ___luggage___ – you should be able to pack all your clothes into one _____ .

2 There's plenty of _____ available in Paris and we found a really nice _____ near a metro station.

3 You need to take quite a lot of _____ on a camping holiday, like a _____ and a sleeping bag.

4 You don't need to have a lot of _____ with you when you travel, but make sure you've got a _____ for the trolley at the airport.

5 I realised that _____ was impossible on the street, so I drove into a _____ as soon as I saw one.

6 I found that public _____ in Barcelona was excellent, so I never needed a _____ to get around.

2.2 Check your answers for 2.1 and then decide whether the words in the box are countable or uncountable. Mark them C or U in the box.

2.3 Complete the sentences with *travel*, *journey* or *trip*.

1 In August, I'm going on a ____trip____ to Mexico City with my brother.

2 They set off on the difficult _____ before dawn, and they didn't arrive until after dark.

3 We went on a three-hour boat _____ round the island.

4 He's away on a business _____ all next week, but I'll give him the message when he returns.

5 I know rail _____ takes longer than going by plane, but I really enjoy it.

6 I'm really looking forward to my _____ to New Zealand. I'll have lots to talk about when I get back.

7 My parents have always said that _____ makes you more independent.

8 How long is your _____ to college each morning?

> **V Vocabulary note**
>
> **Travel** can be a verb or a noun. When it is a noun, it is uncountable and describes the activity of travelling:
> *Air travel is becoming increasingly popular.*
>
> We use **journey** to describe going from one place to another. It is a countable noun.
> *The journey from home to work takes two hours.*
>
> We use **trip** to describe a short journey somewhere when you go for a short time and then come back. It is a countable noun.
> *My friend and I went on a weekend trip to Amsterdam.*
>
> We **go on** a trip or a journey. We also **make** a journey and **take** a trip.

3.1 ▶46 Listen to a woman and a boy talking about the kind of holidays they like. Write the answers they would give to the questions below.

Woman: 1 __B__ 2 _____ 3 _____ 4 _____ 5 _____ 6 _____

Boy: 1 _____ 2 _____ 3 _____ 4 _____ 5 _____ 6 _____

1 How do you usually travel when you go on holiday?

   A by road   **B** by train   **C** by boat

2 Where do you usually go for a holiday?

   A to a quiet spot near home   **B** to a resort in my own country   **C** somewhere abroad

3 What kind of holiday do you usually take?

   A an activity holiday   **B** a seaside holiday   **C** a sightseeing holiday

4 What do you like doing on holiday?

   A visiting museums and sites   **B** getting fit and doing exercise   **C** relaxing and having fun

5 Where do you stay on holiday?

   A in a hotel or guesthouse   **B** at a relative or friend's home   **C** at a campsite

6 What is the best thing about having a holiday?

   A getting to know new places   **B** getting away from routine   **C** getting together with family

3.2 How would you answer the questions in 3.1? Write a paragraph about what kind of holiday you usually take, which activities you enjoy doing and why.

Exam practice

Reading and Use of English Part 4

For questions **1–6**, complete the second sentence so that it has a similar meaning to the first sentence, using the word given. **Do not change the word given.** You must use between **two** and **five** words, including the word given. There is an example at the beginning (**0**).

0   The report contains a few details that need explaining.

   INFORMATION

   There _____*is some information in*_____ the report that needs explaining.

1   We travelled from Edinburgh to London by car.

   JOURNEY

   We _____ from Edinburgh to London by car.

2   My friend and I took a short break in Copenhagen last week.

   TRIP

   My friend and I went _____ Copenhagen last week.

3   Have you succeeded in booking a room in London yet?

   ACCOMMODATION

   Have you managed _____ in London yet?

4   I prefer flying to taking the train.

   TRAVEL

   I'd _____ train than fly.

5   For me, visiting new places is the best thing about a holiday.

   ON

   I personally think that the best thing to _____ to visit new places.

6   The flight I made to Australia was the longest I've ever been on.

   TAKEN

   I've never _____ the one I went on to Australia.

Writing Part 2: article

You see the following announcement in an international magazine.

> **Articles wanted**
>
> **The longest journey**
> What is the longest journey you have ever made?
> Write an article describing your journey, explaining how you felt about it and why you were making it.
> The best articles will be published next month.

Write your **article** (140–190 words).

34 Time off

Leisure time, hobbies and games

1.1 ▶47 **Listen to two people, Christa and James, talking about what they do in their free time. What do they prefer doing: going out or staying in?**

Speaker 1 (Christa): _____   Speaker 2 (James): _____

1.2 ▶47 **Listen again and mark what each person says they do: C for Christa and J for James.**

1	eat out with friends	__J__	7	watch sport on TV	_____	13	go to the beach	_____
2	go to a party	_____	8	paint and draw	_____	14	go surfing	_____
3	cook with friends	_____	9	collect old postcards	_____	15	go swimming	_____
4	have a takeaway	_____	10	go to junk shops	_____	16	watch DVDs	_____
5	play music	_____	11	go clubbing	_____	17	play online games	_____
6	cook for myself	_____	12	go to the cinema	_____	18	read a book	_____

Which of the phrases above could you use to describe your leisure time?

1.3 **Put the expressions in the correct place in the table below (some can go in more than one place). Then add any expressions from 1.2 to the table.**

a barbecue   cards   a club   a concert   a coffee   a drive   a film   friends round   games   a match
a~~ ~~party   a play   a quiet night in   a restaurant   shopping   the theatre   ~~TV~~   a walk

staying in	going out
have a party	go
watch TV	go to
play	go for

1.4 **Write two sentences about the things you prefer to do in your free time. Use some of the expressions from 1.2 and 1.3.**

When I have some free time, I prefer to ... , and I also enjoy ... and ...

I don't really like ... or ...

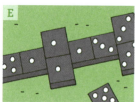

2.1 Match the pictures with the words for games and pastimes.

1 jigsaw __G__   2 crossword _____   3 computer game _____

4 dominoes _____   5 scrabble _____   6 backgammon _____

7 chess _____   8 sudoku _____

> **V** **Vocabulary note**
>
> We **play** games, e.g. chess. We **do** puzzles, e.g. a crossword. We **collect** objects, e.g. stamps.

2.2 Complete this paragraph about hobbies, using the correct form of *play*, *do* and *collect*.

Everyone in my family has a hobby. My brother (1) __plays__ chess; he only took it up recently and he is really good at it. My sister (2) _____ unusual shells and my parents (3) _____ the crossword in the newspaper every day. As for me, someone showed me how sudoku puzzles work and I've really taken to them, so I (4) _____ them all the time now. When we're all together, we often (5) _____ scrabble and we sometimes (6) _____ board games like snakes and ladders or backgammon too.

3.1 **PHRASAL VERBS** Match these phrasal verbs with an object and a meaning.

	Object	**Meaning**
take after	a few days	withdraw
take off	a business	accept
take out	someone you've just met	resemble
take over	money	fill up
take to	space	develop a liking for
take up	someone in your family	gain control of
take on	responsibility	spend time away from work

> **V** **Vocabulary note**
>
> **Take up** means to begin doing something as a hobby:
> *I took up chess last year.*
>
> **Take to** means to really enjoy doing something:
> *I've really taken to sudoku puzzles.*

3.2 Use the phrasal verbs with *take* to complete these sentences.

1 I __took to__ Gemma's flatmate, Kate, as soon as I met her.

2 I couldn't pay for my coursebooks by card, so I _____ some cash at lunchtime.

3 Peter _____ several days so that he could attend his sister's wedding.

4 Luke _____ his father – he looks and sounds just like him at times.

5 Amanda's decided to _____ some more teaching now the children are older.

6 GDC Electronics has finally _____ its rival, Telectrical.

7 The piano _____ a lot of space downstairs, but we all enjoy playing it.

Exam practice

Reading and Use of English Part 3

For questions **1–6**, read the text below. Use the word given in capitals at the end of some of the lines to form a word that fits in the gap **in the same line**. There is an example at the beginning (**0**).

The benefits of having a hobby

Hobbies can add (**0**) ___excitement___ to everyday life. Sometimes the daily routine   **EXCITE**

at work or school starts to drag, making you feel that everything is a bit

(**1**) _____ , and in these circumstances a hobby offers fun and escape   **POINT**

from your regular (**2**) _____ .   **COMMIT**

In fact, (**3**) _____ pastimes such as watching TV or listening to music,   **LIKE**

a hobby usually involves learning new skills. In (**4**) _____ , if there is a   **ADD**

social element to the hobby, you will have to interact with other people and so go

on to form new (**5**) _____ . It is also very positive to feel that you are   **FRIEND**

making progress with your own (**6**) _____ development, and as well as   **PERSON**

giving you the chance to learn new skills, a hobby will be a way of building on the

(**7**) _____ you already have. It's certainly the case that the more different   **STRONG**

activities you try as hobbies, the closer you'll get to being (**8**) _____   **TRUE**

fulfilled and the better you'll get to know yourself.

> *Exam tip*
>
> Think about what type of word is needed grammatically, e.g. an adjective, noun or verb.

Writing Part 2: email

You have received this email from your English-speaking friend Karen.

From:	Karen
Subject:	new hobby

Hi

I'm interested in taking up a new hobby, and I wondered if you could help. What hobbies are popular in your country? And could you tell me which hobby you would advise me to try, and why?

Thanks a lot,

Karen

Write your **email** (140–190 words).

35 Where you live

Cities and towns

1.1 Which of these phrases describe the place where you live?

> a port   a market town   a new town/city   a seaside town   a capital city
> an industrial town/city   a rural area   a historic town/city

1.2 Match each sentence with one of the cities in the photos.

1   In addition, its wide open spaces and the latest leisure facilities make it an ideal location for a family day out.   *B*

2   But now that cars have been banned from the narrow stone streets, a walk through the picturesque centre is even more pleasant.   _____

3   The city is in the heart of one of the country's fastest growing regions and is only about 50 years old.   _____

4   You'll certainly want to stop for a while in the beautiful old market square which is completely unspoiled.   _____

5   During that time it has grown into a modern city with up-to-date shopping centres and lively nightlife.   _____

6   The city has always been famous for its ancient churches and impressive medieval buildings.   _____

1.3 The sentences in 1.2 are from two tourist information brochures but they are mixed up. Put them in the correct order.

City A: Sentences ___6___ , _____ , _____   City B: Sentences _____ , _____ , _____

1.4 Underline any words or expressions in 1.2 which you could use to describe your home town or city or the town nearest to where you live. Which words below could you also use about your town or city?

> many attractions   delightful parks   huge temple   cosmopolitan atmosphere   ancient mosque
> famous art gallery   interesting museum   ruined castle   quiet and peaceful   full of life

2.1 ▶48 **Listen to a woman talking about living in a city. Which of the cities in the photos does she live in now, A or B?**

2.2 ▶48 **Listen again and mark these statements T (true) or F (false).**

1 She lives on the edge of the city.   _____T____

2 The part of the city where she lives is very crowded.   _____

3 She lives within cycling distance of the shopping mall.   _____

4 She takes the bus to the centre because it's hard to park there.   _____

5 She moved because she wanted to live somewhere more peaceful.   _____

6 The area where she used to live was well looked after.   _____

2.3 **Complete the sentences with words you heard in the recording. Then read the script to check your answers.**

1 A h_ousing_____ estate is a large group of houses or flats and an i_____ estate is where people work, often in a b_____ district.

2 A r_____ area is a part of a city or town where people live. People often live on the edge of a city which is sometimes called the o_____ or s_____ .

3 An office b_____ is another name for a building with many offices.

4 Modern towns usually have a shopping m_____ with a wide range of stores.

5 A car park on several levels is called a m_____-s_____ car park.

6 Areas or buildings that are in bad condition have been n_____ .

7 Bicycles and buses are sometimes separated from other traffic in a bus/cycle l_____ .

3.1 **Where do people do the things below (1–10)? Each answer is two words. Choose the second word from the box and write both words in the puzzle.**

| alley | ~~centre~~ | centre | centre | gallery | ground | hall | park | rank | rink | stadium |

1 go swimming and do other fitness activities

2 visit the doctor

3 leave their vehicle

4 look at paintings

5 listen to music

6 hire a cab

7 watch matches

8 go skating

9 compete in an indoor ball game

10 buy a variety of things

Crossword:
Row 1: L E I S U R E   C E N T R E
Row 2: H
Row 5: N
Row 7: O
Row 9: B
Row 10: P

3.2 **Find one word going down the puzzle and match it with the remaining word from the box above. What do people do there?**

Exam practice

Reading and Use of English Part 1

For questions **1–8**, read the text below and decide which answer (**A**, **B**, **C** or **D**) best fits each gap. There is an example at the beginning (**0**).

New York City

New York City has (**0**) _____ B _____ into the second largest city in North America. It has long been a major business, cultural and shopping centre, (**1**) _____ millions of visitors each year. Most tourists stay in the (**2**) _____ of the city, Manhattan, where you can see the sights on foot or take a tour bus. In (**3**) _____ , the main residential areas are on the (**4**) _____ of the city where, as in all large cities, some districts are quite in (**5**) _____ of repair.

During your visit you may want to take a boat trip to Ellis Island, where you can stop for a (**6**) _____ to read about the history of immigration. Many tourists also visit Queens, which has some interesting art galleries, and Brooklyn for cafés, shops and (**7**) _____ nightlife. Finally, you will certainly want to visit Central Park, a huge open (**8**) _____ which is ideal for relaxing on a hot summer day.

0	**A** become	(**B**) grown	**C** increased	**D** extended
1	**A** appealing	**B** advancing	**C** arriving	**D** attracting
2	**A** heart	**B** interior	**C** focus	**D** root
3	**A** response	**B** practice	**C** contrast	**D** reality
4	**A** suburbs	**B** surroundings	**C** borders	**D** outskirts
5	**A** demand	**B** wish	**C** need	**D** requirement
6	**A** period	**B** while	**C** duration	**D** piece
7	**A** vivid	**B** cheerful	**C** bright	**D** lively
8	**A** extension	**B** region	**C** space	**D** estate

Writing Part 2: article

You see this notice on an international travel website.

Articles wanted

My local town or city

We're looking for articles about the town or city where you live.
Write us an article about the places of interest there, both old and new.
Say whether you think it is a good place to live, and explain why / why not.

The best articles will be posted on the website next month.

Write your **article** (140–190 words).

Shared tastes

Food and art

1.1 ▶49 Listen to three people. What kind of food is each person describing: Mexican, Italian or Chinese?

Speaker 1: _____   Speaker 2: _____   Speaker 3: _____

1.2 ▶49 Listen again and write down the words that gave you the correct answers.

1.3 The verbs in bold describe ways to prepare food. Choose the correct word to complete each sentence.

1 I **poured** myself a glass of _orange juice_ / _coffee_.

2 To make an omelette, **beat** the _potatoes_ / _eggs_ in a bowl.

3 **Chop** the _vegetables_ / _salad_ for the soup into small pieces.

4 You can't eat a(n) _banana_ / _apple_ without **peeling** it first!

5 **Grate** the _cheese_ / _meat_ before putting it on the pizza.

6 You'll need to **melt** the _butter_ / _cream_.

7 **Slice** the _lemon_ / _nuts_ very thinly.

8 **Stir** the _cereal_ / _sauce_ regularly while it cooks.

2.1 Read this text from a restaurant website. Mark the sentences below T (true) or F (false). Correct the sentences that are false.

◀ ▶ C ⌂ [   ]   ⊖ ⊜ ⊗

Hungry? seafood chicken noodles rice dishes salads desserts   **Thirsty?** fresh juices soft drinks tea coffee

We have listed some of our best-selling starters and main meals to help you decide what to order on your first visit. You will find an explanation of these dishes by clicking **here**.

Our restaurant serves a range of popular dishes from different parts of Asia. Our menu consists of starters, main meals, side dishes and desserts.

Your order is taken on a handheld computer and sent to the kitchen, where it is cooked immediately. We want to ensure the freshness of your food so your dish will be delivered to your table as soon as it is ready. This means different dishes may be delivered at different times to your table. Don't wait – just tuck in and share!

- We provide a number of dishes designed specifically for children.
- Come and check out the specials, which change each week.
- You can buy our cookbook and easily re-create some of our dishes at home by following the recipes.

1 Various dishes are described on the website.   _____T_____

2 The restaurant prepares unusual recipes from a variety of places.   _____

3 This is a self-service restaurant.   _____

4 Food is microwaved to ensure speed of service.   _____

5 This restaurant caters for family dining.   _____

6 Some of the meals served are straightforward to make at home.   _____

> **ERROR WARNING** ❗
>
> A **cooker** is what you cook on:
> _Don't touch the cooker – it's hot._
>
> The person who cooks is a **cook**:
> _My husband is a very good cook._

2.2 We use the word *taste* literally when we talk about food. But we also use it to express our preferences in other areas, like art, fashion or films. Match the two halves of these sentences.

1 The sauce smells lovely   A   as I thought it was really tasteless.

2 I've always loved   B   although portraits are more to my taste.

3 I enjoyed the meal last night   C   so I told her she had good taste in clothes!

4 I loved Joanna's new dress   D   but I'll taste it to see if it needs salt.

5 I didn't enjoy the film   E   because it's really tasteful.

6 I like abstract paintings   F   because everything I ate was really tasty.

7 I like the way the gallery is decorated   G   the taste of garlic.

2.3 Write these adjectives with their definitions below: *tasty, tasteful, tasteless*.

1 in bad taste _____   2 delicious _____   3 in good taste _____

3.1 Complete each paragraph with the words in the box above it.

prints   oil paintings   ~~drawings~~   water colours

1 If you want to do _____*drawings*_____ , you'll need a pencil, but to do _____ you'll need a brush and some water. Many of the famous pictures which are on public display, like the *Mona Lisa*, are _____ . Even if you can never buy these pictures, you can often get _____ of them so you can have a copy of your favourite picture on the wall.

sculptures   textiles   jewellery   pottery

2 We use the word _____ to describe objects made out of clay, like vases. Materials woven by hand or machine are known as _____ . Since ancient times, people have worn _____ such as necklaces and bracelets and made _____ of their gods and animals.

still life   abstract   portrait   landscape

3 A(n) _____ is a picture of a person, but a(n) _____ is a picture of objects that do not move, like fruit, flowers or bowls. A(n) _____ is a picture of the countryside, but a(n) _____ painting shows line, shape and colour and does not attempt to be realistic.

3.2 Choose the correct words in this text. Then underline any phrases you could use in your own writing.

I'm fairly artistic. I do some painting, mostly **(1)** *sketches / still lifes*, but my big interest is **(2)** *pottery / jewellery* and I make a lot of vases and bowls. I also go to art **(3)** *collections / exhibitions*, mostly small ones in the local area; I don't go to big **(4)** *galleries / studios* very much these days.

I don't like abstract paintings because they seem to be just shapes and lines. I prefer something more **(5)** *creative / conventional* in **(6)** *style / presentation*, and what I really like is **(7)** *countrysides / landscapes*, although I sometimes find portraits interesting too.

My favourite picture is 'Niagara Falls', by an artist called Albert Bierstadt. It is so **(8)** *picturesque / realistic* that when I look at it I can almost hear the waterfall and feel the water. The **(9)** *shades / colours* are fantastic and it's absolutely **(10)** *extensive / huge*, which is what makes it so **(11)** *effective / impressive*.

3.3 Write a paragraph about your own skills and taste in art. Use vocabulary from 3.1 and 3.2 to help you.

Exam practice

Listening Part 2

▶ 50   You will hear a talk by an art student about an Australian artist called Anna Roberts. For questions **1–10**, complete the sentences with a word or short phrase.

Anna has become well known for pictures of really **(1)** _____ places.

Anna often walks to these places, but sometimes she gets there by **(2)** _____ if she can.

In her paintings Anna always tries to show that **(3)** _____ is extremely beautiful.

Her paintings tend to be very realistic, particularly those of **(4)** _____ , which look like photos.

Anna has recently done some paintings of the **(5)** _____ , using yellow and orange.

Her paintings are said to be special because of the way the **(6)** _____ is shown.

Anna prefers painting on **(7)** _____ rather than on other surfaces.

Although she has worked with other types of paint, Anna prefers to use **(8)** _____ paint.

Anna's paintings are sold to **(9)** _____ as well as private collectors.

In addition to being a painter, Anna has written **(10)** _____ about painting.

Exam tip

The answers for the gaps will be exactly the same as the words you hear. You do not have to make any changes.

Writing Part 1: essay

In your English class you have been talking about eating habits now and in the past. Now your teacher has asked you to write an essay.

Write an essay (140–190 words) using **all** the notes and give reasons for your point of view.

Do you think people in your country eat better or worse than they did 50 years ago?

Notes
Write about:
1   what kind of food people eat
2   how much food people eat
3   _____ (your own idea)

37 Entertain me

Television, cinema and theatre

1.1 ▶51 **Listen to three people talking about their favourite TV programmes. What types of programmes are they? Choose from the words in the box.**

| chat show | comedy | costume drama | current affairs | documentary | reality TV show | soap opera |

Speaker 1: _____   Speaker 2: _____   Speaker 3: _____

1.2 **Match the types of programmes in 1.1 with these definitions.**

1 _____comedy_____ a programme which aims to be humorous

2 _____ a programme which consists of discussion and analysis of recent events

3 _____ programmes with episodes broadcast daily or several times a week, following the lives of a cast of characters

4 _____ a factual programme giving information about a certain subject

5 _____ a programme telling a story set some time ago in the past

6 _____ a programme or series in which people are filmed without a script in a particular situation to see how they behave

7 _____ an informal programme in which famous people are asked questions about themselves and their work

1.3 **Does your favourite TV programme fit into one of the categories in 1.1? Tick the expressions below that you could use to talk about it.**

It makes me laugh.   It's so entertaining.   The acting is brilliant.   The storylines are gripping.
It's really good drama.   I love the characters.   The plots are good.   It's quite compelling.

1.4 **Write a brief paragraph about your favourite TV programme. Use words/phrases from 1.1. and 1.3.**

2.1 **Complete the sentences with these verbs.**

| heard | listened to | looked at | read about | ~~saw~~ | saw | watched |

1 He turned round and suddenly _____saw_____ Abby standing in the doorway.

2 Sadie always _____ music while she was working.

3 Tim _____ the map to see where they were.

4 I _____ an advert in the newspaper yesterday for a course in jewellery-making.

5 We _____ the sound of a motorbike coming down the road. It was Mark.

6 Kate stood by the window and _____ her children playing in the snow.

7 I _____ Johnny Depp's new film in a magazine.

> ### V Vocabulary note
>
> We can **see** things without trying:
> *I saw Rob when I was in the supermarket.*
>
> When we **look at**, **watch** or **read about** something, we make an effort:
> *She looked at the clock to see what the time was.*
>
> We **watch** things for a period of time and they are usually moving or changing:
> *I spent Saturday afternoon watching Jake play football.*
>
> We **hear** things without trying but when we **listen to** something we make an effort:
> *We stopped playing when we heard the whistle.*
> *I like to listen to the radio on Sunday mornings.*

3.1 **Look at the words below. Write C if they are for the cinema/films, T if they are for the theatre/plays or B if they are for both.**

1	actor	B	8	director	_____	15	reviews	_____
2	audience	_____	9	interval	_____	16	scenery	_____
3	box office	_____	10	location	_____	17	screen	_____
4	cartoon	_____	11	musical	_____	18	soundtrack	_____
5	cast	_____	12	performance	_____	19	special effects	_____
6	costumes	_____	13	plot	_____	20	stage	_____
7	critic	_____	14	rehearsal	_____	21	subtitles	_____

3.2 **▶52** **Listen to two people talking about whether they prefer going to the cinema or the theatre. Which does each one prefer, and why?**

The girl prefers going to the _____ because _____ .

The man prefers going to the _____ because _____ .

3.3 **Which do you prefer, and why? Write a short paragraph.**

4.1 **▶53** **Listen to two people each talking about a film they have enjoyed. Underline the adjectives they use. Listen again if you need to.**

> brilliant   confusing   convincing   delightful   dramatic   dull   fascinating   gripping   imaginative
> irritating   lively   memorable   moving   outstanding   predictable   stunning   superb   tedious   uninspired

4.2 **All the adjectives in the box above can be used with the words *film*, *play* and *story*. Mark them P if they have a positive meaning and N if they have a negative meaning.**

4.3 **Choose the appropriate adjectives in this paragraph.**

Friends had recommended a new thriller called 'Green Line'. They said that the plot was absolutely
(**1**) *fascinating / predictable* and that lead actor Gene Bruno gave a really (**2**) *dull / brilliant* performance.
But I was bitterly disappointed when I went to see it. I found the plot totally (**3**) *imaginative / confusing*
and hard to follow. The directing was very (**4**) *uninspired / gripping* as well – probably because the story,
which was based on a case of mistaken identity, was horribly (**5**) *tedious / stunning*.

Exam practice

Reading and Use of English Part 7

You are going to read an article about four people describing their favourite type of media. For questions **1–10**, choose from the people (**A–D**). The people may be chosen more than once.

Which person

says that they ignored someone else's opinion?	**1**	
mentions how they started to develop a daily routine?	**2**	
is aware that their interest in a type of media is illogical?	**3**	
describes a type of media that has lasted although it wasn't expected to?	**4**	
describes a feeling of anticipation?	**5**	
appreciates being shown a lifestyle they will never have?	**6**	
does not share a common reaction that people have?	**7**	
mentions how much mental effort is required by a type of media?	**8**	
appreciates being able to find something to suit their mood?	**9**	
mentions the increasing popularity of a type of media?	**10**	

A   Eleanor

Radio is still alive, despite all the predictions. It has been around for so long that it is part of the scenery. However much TV opens the eyes, I still love to close mine and listen. And I'm not the only one, as listening figures are rising again. In fact, despite iPods and downloads and podcasts, 91% of us still listen to a radio station each week. For me this comes as no surprise. It's the only medium that still requires my imagination to work hard. We can't see the people talking; we have to picture them and, more importantly, to really listen to what they're saying rather than getting distracted by their haircut or clothes as you might do watching TV. And of course, the voices we hear age slower and change less than faces.

A   Theo

It may be unfashionable, but I love my daily newspaper. I know I could get the same things on my iPad or smartphone, but for me, nothing quite beats the feeling of sitting down with my newspaper every morning. It's like that moment when the orchestra starts to play, before the theatre curtain rises. You're not sure exactly what's going to happen, but you know you'll enjoy the experience. I didn't discover newspapers until I first began working in the city. While my bus journey lasted 45 minutes, the emotional journey of reading the newspaper took me much further. By the time I arrived, I would feel interested, informed and ready to face the day. While I often look at online news for the latest updates, it is simply not the same as turning the pages of a newspaper.

C Alessandro

TV is my favourite, much more than newspapers, radio, or even the internet. An evening on my sofa with the TV guide in front of me – I love it. There's so much to choose from! Sometimes if I'm tired or fed up, I'll watch a silly comedy but if I've had a boring day, I'll look for something more exciting or maybe informative. A lot of people say they feel guilty when they're watching television. That's because it's easily available and requires a minimum amount of effort, whereas for other forms of entertainment you might have to go out or dress up or talk to other people. I have to say I don't feel this way – for me it's pure pleasure.

D Katarina

Although my parents never actually banned my sister and me from buying glossy magazines, they didn't approve of them either. They thought them silly and irrelevant, but from the first moment I flipped through a fashion magazine, I was hooked. It's strange really, as I don't particularly care about fashion. Yet each month I read articles about beauty treatments and look at dresses that cost more than my monthly rent. I am very aware that I am an outsider, looking in at a life I don't live. But from the very beginning, these glimpses into other lives have been a large part of why I love glossy magazines: they provided different perspectives, different ways to exist in the world. Of course, they aren't perfect. They are the end product of several thriving industries: advertising, entertainment, big business. I've stopped purchasing many of them because they became just too distant from my lifestyle, but I could never give them up entirely.

Exam tip

Underline the answer to each question in the text and check that the words in the text mean exactly the same as the question.

Writing Part 2: review

You see this notice on an international website.

TV reviews wanted

Is there a TV series in your country that has been popular for a long time?

Write us a review describing the series. Explain why it is popular, whether it is suitable for different age groups and whether you think viewers in other countries would enjoy it too.

The best reviews will be posted on the website next month.

Write your **review** (140–190 words).

1.1 Look at these groups of words about houses. Which is the odd one out in each group? Why?

1 cellar   basement   <u>loft</u>   _____This is under the roof; the others are below the house._____

2 lounge   mansion   staircase   _____

3 flowerbed   hedge   fence   _____

4 shutters   curtains   carpet   _____

5 cement   wardrobe   wood   _____

6 shed   lobby   garage   _____

1.2 Look at the pictures of houses and label them with these words.

> bricks   chimney   fence   ~~garage~~   gate   hedge   shutters   terrace

1.3 ▶54 Listen to a girl talking about her home. Which picture is she describing? _____

1.4 ▶54 Listen again. Then, in your notebook, list the ways in which the house described is similar to yours, and the ways in which it is different.

1.5 Use your notes from 1.4 to write a paragraph describing your house/flat.

> **V** *Vocabulary note*
>
> In Britain, the word **flat** is used. In the US, **apartment** is always used, and this word has become common in British English too.

2.1 Read this extract from a novel quickly and answer the questions below. Don't worry about any words you do not understand.

As we neared Black Oak, we passed the Clench farm, home of Foy and Leverl Clench and their eight children, all of whom, I was certain, were still in the fields. No one worked harder than the Clenches. Even the children seemed to enjoy picking cotton and doing the most **routine chores** around the farm. The hedges around the front yard were **perfectly manicured** into shape. The fences were straight and needed no repair. The garden was huge and its legendary **yield** fed the family all year.

And their house was painted.

Our house had been built before the First War, back when indoor bathrooms and electricity were unheard of. Its exterior was built from clapboards made of **oak**, probably cut from trees on the land which we now farmed. With time and weather the boards had faded to a pale brown colour, pretty much the same colour as the other farmhouses around Black Oak. According to my father and grandparents, paint was unnecessary. The boards were kept clean and in good repair, and besides, paint cost money.

My mother **vowed** to herself that she would not raise her children on a farm. She would one day have a house in a town or in a city, a house with indoor plumbing and flowers around the porch, and with paint on the boards, maybe even bricks.

'Paint' was a **sensitive word** around our farm.

1   What was the main difference between the Clenches' house and the writer's?

2   Where would the writer's mother have preferred to live? Why?

2.2 When you don't understand a word you should try to guess its meaning. Look at these words in the text above and try to answer the questions without a dictionary.

1   **Routine chores** are

   A   everyday tasks.   **B**   repetitive games.
   C   time-consuming jobs.

2   The words **perfectly manicured** refer to the hedges and mean

   A   well watered.   **B**   heavily fertilised.
   C   carefully cut.

3   The legendary **yield** of the garden refers to

   A   the flowers grown there.
   B   the vegetables it produced.
   C   the animals that lived there.

4   **Oak** is a kind of

   A   brick.   **B**   cement.   **C**   wood.

5   **Vowed** means

   A   encouraged.   **B**   promised.   **C**   dared.

6   'Paint' was a **sensitive word** around the farm because the writer's mother

   A   had a row with the rest of the family about it.
   B   desperately wanted to live in a painted house.
   C   was jealous of the neighbours' farm.

3.1 Who do you call to deal with problems around the house? Match each expert with a problem (1–5).

builder   decorator   electrician   ~~plumber~~   service agent

1   The tap in the kitchen is dripping and the pipe under the kitchen sink is leaking. _____plumber_____

2   You'd like some new lighting installed. _____

3   Your dishwasher has broken down while it's still under guarantee. _____

4   You'd like a new patio made outside your house. _____

5   You'd like your living room painted and you don't have time to do it yourself. _____

Exam practice

Reading and Use of English Part 3

For questions **1–6**, read the text below. Use the word given in capitals at the end of some of the lines to form a word that fits in the gap **in the same line**. There is an example at the beginning (**0**).

What makes a house a home?

From an (**0**) _evolutionary_ point of view, creating a home is all about the very **EVOLUTION**

basic need to have somewhere warm and safe where you can raise a family. These

days, however, our domestic (**1**) _____ are where we can truly find a way **SURROUND**

to express ourselves. Turning a house into a home is less about the building itself and

where it is than the (**2**) _____ connection and sense of comfort we're able **EMOTION**

to establish there.

According to experts, making a house a feel-good space is about (**3**) _____ **SURE**

that it reflects both our lifestyle and our (**4**) _____ , whether that means a **PERSON**

shared student house or an absolutely (**5**) _____ apartment. Some people, **LUXURY**

for example, are very (**6**) _____ to visuals, so feel disorientated when things **SENSE**

are out of place. For others, having a peaceful spot to sit and read will be the main

(**7**) _____ . Yet whatever home means to us individually, we all have high **REQUIRE**

(**8**) _____ of it, because many of our most significant memories are **EXPECT**

created there.

Writing Part 1: essay

In your English class you have been talking about the advantages and disadvantages of living in a house or an apartment. Now your teacher has asked you to write an essay.

Write an essay (140–190 words) using **all** the notes and give reasons for your point of view.

Is it better to live in a house or an apartment? Why?

Notes
Write about:
1   where you want to live
2   what facilities you need
3   _____ (your own idea)

39 Green planet

Science, the environment

1.1 These are things that scientists do as part of their work. For 1–3, match each verb with a noun or phrase. Check your answers, then tick the things you have done while studying science.

1	work	data into a computer	2	collect	exciting discoveries	3	make	conferences
	make	as part of a team		make	data		attend	statistics
	enter	observations		do	experiments		interpret	predictions

1.2 Write the words for scientists with the things they study (1–7).

> astronomer   biologist   chemist   ecologist   ~~geologist~~   mathematician   physicist

1 rocks: _geologist_   2 substances: _____   3 stars: _____   4 the environment: _____

5 living things: _____   6 matter and energy: _____   7 numbers and shapes: _____

1.3   **WORD BUILDING**   Complete the table.

Person (noun)	astronomer	biologist	chemist	ecologist	geologist	mathematician	physicist
Subject (noun)	astronomy						
Adjective	astronomical						

1.4 Read the texts about two famous scientists. Answer the questions below with N (Newton), L (Lovelock) or B (both).

Isaac Newton (1642–1727) had a profound impact on astronomy, physics and mathematics. He was raised by his grandparents and it was thanks to an uncle that he went to university to study mathematics. He made the first modern telescope and developed a branch of mathematics known as calculus. He is also famous for developing the scientific laws of motion and the law of gravity, which formed the basis of all models of the cosmos.

James Lovelock (b. 1919) first graduated as a chemist, and then obtained degrees in medicine and biophysics. He produced a range of technical instruments, many of which are now used by NASA in space exploration. He is most famous for the Gaia Theory, which considers planet Earth as a living being, capable of changing and restoring itself. He brought his concern about climate change to the attention of both the public and the scientific world.

Which scientist ...

1 obtained a degree in chemistry? ___L___   4 developed theories of global importance? _____

2 invented a scientific instrument? _____   5 had a keen interest in green issues? _____

3 worried about the future of the Earth? _____   6 showed a talent for mathematics? _____

2.1 **There are currently many problems with the environment. Match the two halves of the sentences.**

1 Global warming means that the weather   A pollute the air in most cities.

2 Heavy traffic and exhaust fumes   B is taken to rubbish dumps.

3 The emissions produced by factories   C have caused serious flooding.

4 The chemicals used on crops in the countryside   D create acid rain which destroys crops.

5 Heavy rain and rising water levels in rivers   E is becoming more extreme.

6 Most households produce large amounts of waste which   F are dangerous to birds and other wildlife.

2.2 **Underline the problems in 2.1 which exist in your area/country, and then write a short paragraph about them.**

3.1 **▶55** **Listen to a student talking about how he tries to live in a green way. Mark the sentences T (true) or F (false). Correct the false sentences.**

1 He recycles as much of his rubbish as he can.   _____

2 He switches off electrical equipment to avoid wasting power.   _____

3 He never sleeps with the air-conditioning on.   _____

4 He puts an extra sweater on instead of turning up the heating.   _____

5 He buys organic food which is produced in his local area.   _____

6 He mostly walks or uses public transport rather than driving.   _____

3.2 **Write a short paragraph about yourself, explaining how green you are.**

4.1 **Read this text from a town council leaflet and choose the correct words.**

It is now widely accepted that pollution (**1**) *injures / hurts / harms* humans, the environment and buildings. Some pollution spreads across local and national (**2**) *barriers / boundaries / limits* and lasts for many generations. For example, if the crops in our fields are sprayed carelessly, the chemicals have an immediate effect on local wildlife and can ultimately (**3**) *turn out / end up / put down* in our food.

Burning fossil fuels such as oil, gas and coal also (**4**) *causes / gives / begins* pollution, in particular carbon dioxide, which contributes to global (**5**) *heating / warming / melting*. In our region eight out of the ten hottest years on (**6**) *account / record / report* have occurred during the last decade. We should therefore (**7**) *develop / stimulate / assist* the use of renewable energy resources such as wind and solar energy, because these do not (**8**) *bring / create / invent* carbon dioxide.

However, the biggest single cause of pollution in our city is traffic. Poorly maintained, older vehicles and bad driving techniques (**9**) *increase / make / do* the problem worse, and this pollution has been directly (**10**) *combined / associated / linked* to the rising number of asthma sufferers in our region. We should be aiming to gradually (**11**) *keep out / take in / cut down* vehicle use in the city and educate the public on the importance of purchasing environmentally friendly vehicles and maintaining them to a high (**12**) *grade / mark / standard*.

Exam practice

Listening Part 4

▶ 56　You will hear an interview with an Australian sheep farmer called Gina Ellis, who is talking about her work and plans for the future. For questions **1–7**, choose the best answer (**A**, **B** or **C**).

1　What does Gina say about sheep farming in Australia?

　　A　It is a growing source of employment.

　　B　It takes place all over the country.

　　C　It is restricted to cooler areas.

2　What is the main challenge facing farmers who produce wool?

　　A　competition from artificial materials

　　B　falling production levels

　　C　increasingly dry weather

3　Gina says that in the future wool will have most potential in

　　A　manufacturing carpets.

　　B　insulating buildings.

　　C　making clothes.

4　What alternative form of energy is Gina investigating?

　　A　solar power

　　B　water power

　　C　wind power

5　What made Gina become interested in a new source of energy?

　　A　She wanted to help other farmers in her area.

　　B　It fitted in with her green view of life.

　　C　She hoped to make money from it.

6　What does Gina say about the advice she has received in England?

　　A　It has encouraged her to lead a more eco-friendly lifestyle.

　　B　It has taught her to analyse financial issues.

　　C　It has convinced her that she has to give up farming.

7　How does Gina feel about her project?

　　A　She's worried about high costs.

　　B　She's aware that her plans need adapting.

　　C　She's confident that she can succeed.

 Exam tip

The questions come in the order you hear the information.

Writing Part 2: letter

You have received a letter from your English-speaking friend Alice.

My college is aiming to become as environmentally friendly as possible, starting with recycling and a new heating system. The students have been asked to make suggestions too, so I'm looking for ideas. Is your college green? Do you do anything to help the environment which might be useful at our college too?

Thanks,

Alice

Write your **letter** (140–190 words).

 Exam tip

Remember, you can express any opinion you like. You could say that your college is very green, and explain in what ways. But you could also say that your college isn't green at all and explain why.

Read all about it

Books and writing

  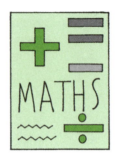  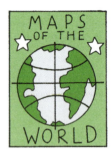

1.1 Write these publications in the correct category.

> ~~atlas~~   biography   brochure   catalogue   cookery book   detective story   fantasy
> ghost story   guidebook   romance   science fiction novel   textbook   thriller

Reference: atlas,

Fiction:

Publicity:

1.2 Quickly read this extract from a book. Don't worry about words you do not understand. What kind of book do you think it is from? Choose from the list in 1.1.

> I peered into the barn. A man was crouching in the corner, alive but groaning. As I crept towards him, I heard a shriek from behind me and a dark figure darted across the path with another one following. I dashed out of the barn, yelling at them to stop. Suddenly, several torches were shining in my eyes and I stumbled and fell, whimpering in pain as I twisted my ankle.

1.3 Find three verbs and a noun which describe sounds. Underline them. Find four verbs which describe ways of moving. Circle them. If there are words you don't understand, guess what they mean. Read the extract again and guess the meaning of the words you have marked. Then check in a dictionary.

1.4 Here are some more words often used in fiction. Which is the odd one out in each group? Why?

1	notice	glimpse	breathe
2	nod	gaze	peer
3	spot	blink	view
4	tremble	witness	stare
5	observe	sigh	glance

2.1 **Read this review and choose the correct words. Then underline any expressions you could use in a review about a book you like.**

My **(1)** *favourite / best* thriller is by the **(2)** *novelist / journalist* Sophie Hannah and it is **(3)** *called / named* 'Point of Rescue'. It was the first psychological thriller I read and I will always **(4)** *remember / remind* it for that reason. It's a great example of totally believable **(5)** *non-fiction / fiction*, and it has a cunning and unpredictable plot. The story is so well written you feel as though you are in the same room as the **(6)** *characters / personalities* and the **(7)** *relationships / relatives* between them are brilliantly developed. If you don't want to buy it, you may be able to **(8)** *borrow / lend* it from a **(9)** *library / bookshop* if you **(10)** *request / ask* it. Sophie Hannah puts together a tightly written tale which is a thoroughly **(11)** *entertaining / entertained* read. It's a book you won't be able to put down until you have finished the last **(12)** *chapter / verse*.

3.1 **▶57** **Listen to a girl talking about her favourite crime novels and answer the questions below.**

1 Why does she enjoy reading crime novels? _____

2 What is special about the novels of her favourite writer? _____

3.2 **▶57** **Listen again and complete these sentences with the words the girl uses.**

1 Well, I'm _____ crime novels.

2 I read a lot of them, _____ I'm on a long flight.

3 It _____ when I read those stories, so it's like doing a crossword.

4 I feel that all the scientific detail is a _____ for me.

5 I _____ read something by Lee Child.

6 His stories _____ .

7 His hero is a _____ .

3.3 **Write a short paragraph about your own reading and taste in books.**

4.1 **WORD BUILDING** **Complete the table.**

Crime	burglary	robbery	theft		murder
Criminal	burglar				
Verb			steal	shoplift	

> **ERROR WARNING** ❶
>
> A person **steals something** (e.g. a car or some money), but **robs someone or a place** (e.g. a wealthy person or a bank).
> **Steal** is often used in the passive: *My bike was stolen yesterday.*

4.2 **Complete these sentences with words from the table in 4.1. Put the verbs in the correct tense.**

1 Most stores will prosecute people who ___shoplift___ .

2 Five men in masks _____ a bank in the main street.

3 The cashier _____ £100 from the till in the supermarket.

4 The gang admitted they had committed four recent bank _____ .

5 The _____ admitted killing two people and the judge sentenced him to life imprisonment.

6 When I got back from holiday I found that the radio had been _____ from my car.

Exam practice

Reading and Use of English Part 5

You are going to read an extract from a newspaper article about writing fiction. For questions **1–6**, choose the answer (**A**, **B**, **C** or **D**) which you think fits best according to the text.

How to write fiction: Andrew Miller on creating characters

First, a note of caution. To slice up fiction into categories such as 'character', 'plot', 'voice' or 'point of view' is to risk presenting it in a way that neither writer nor reader normally experiences it. The suggestion might seem to be that the writing of a story or a novel is a strongly divided or layered activity, something orderly, dry and technical. But stories come with character tangled with plot, plot with setting, setting with bits of language embedded and so on. But laying that aside, there are a few remarks that might be usefully attempted under the heading of 'character'.

First off, let it be loudly asserted that characters, strong characters, are at the heart of all great literature and always will be. Plot, even in detective fiction, is a very secondary matter. Not many readers could outline the plot of the Sherlock Holmes story *The Sign of the Four* but many people have no difficulty bringing Sherlock Holmes and Dr Watson to mind. A writer who does not create convincing characters will fail. A writer who creates thrilling, troubling, insistent characters need not worry too much about any other aspect of writing.

Luckily, the raw material is close to hand. For every writer, it is his own being that constitutes the focus of his research. Year after year, he sits on a kind of umpire's chair watching the antics of his body, listening to the bubbling of his thoughts, sifting the material of his dreams. And when he wants more – other bodies, other thoughts – he simply looks up at those around him. Think, for a moment, of your own family. Almost everybody has one. You might never need to go beyond them. You could store them all in a kind of mental aquarium, sketching them into stories all your writing life. Change their names, of course, their hair colour; move them from that little town in the south you grew up in to a little town in the north you once drove through and wondered about …

But a writer is not confined to such a tactic. It may even be that such a tactic is not particularly common. In my own work I have very rarely set out to present a character who is knowingly based on someone familiar to me, someone whose name I might find in my address book. The great majority of my characters – and I would guess this is true for most writers of fiction – are 'inventions'. They emerge, quickly or slowly, shyly or boisterously, in the writing. They are members of that shifting population of men, women and children (not to mention cats, horses, etc.) who inhabit our inner worlds. Where they come from, whether they are curious versions of ourselves, figures out of the collective unconscious, reconfigurings of those we did indeed once know but have now forgotten, or a mix of all such, no one, to my knowledge, has ever convincingly answered.

There is, of course, another great reservoir of characters: those ready-made for us in books. A painter who wants to paint a tree needs to do two things: look at trees and look at paintings of trees. The first task shows what trees are like, the second shows the possibilities of the medium. Likewise, as a writer, it is by reading that you learn how, in language, a character can be presented – through dialogue, through action, through physical attributes, interior monologue, etc. – a process that continues until you have absorbed these methods, and they have become a reflex so embedded in your apprehending of the world that you will never notice anything about anybody without secretly assessing its potential for fiction writing.

line 5

line 18
line 19

Exam practice

1   In line 5, 'that' refers to the fact that

   A   it is difficult to separate the characters of a story out from other aspects.
   B   stories and their characters often fail to represent what happens in the real world.
   C   successful novels need to contain several different elements apart from characters.
   D   it is important that writers of novels take time to plan their characters carefully.

2   What is said about the role of characters in the second paragraph?

   A   They need to be carefully integrated into a novel's plot.
   B   They are less important in detective stories than other fiction.
   C   They can ensure the success of a novel if they fulfil certain criteria.
   D   They must be appealing so readers want to learn more about them.

3   The expression 'mental aquarium' in line 18 is used to give the idea of

   A   being methodical when researching for a particular novel.
   B   ideas from events and people being kept in mind for use in novels.
   C   the best suggestions for stories being made by other people.
   D   making sure the ideas for different stories are separated.

4   Why does the writer mention 'that little town in the south' in line 19?

   A   to demonstrate that many authors come from ordinary backgrounds
   B   to suggest that reality can be used with details changed
   C   to show that the smallest details are the most useful to an author
   D   to emphasise the importance of setting a novel in a real place

5   What does the writer say in the fourth paragraph about the characters in his own books?

   A   He is unclear about where their origins lie.
   B   He mixes aspects of people he knows to make one character.
   C   He likes to have planned them before he begins writing.
   D   He makes sure they are different from characters in books he has read.

6   The writer compares a novelist to a painter because they both

   A   have a natural talent for the work they produce.
   B   base their work on what happens in real life.
   C   need a lot of time to think about a new project.
   D   learn by looking at the methods used by others in their field.

Writing Part 2: review

You see this advertisement in an English-language magazine.

Book reviews wanted

Send us a review of an interesting book you've read recently. It can be any kind of book, fiction or non-fiction. Briefly explain the story or tell us what the book is about. Say what made the book interesting for you and whether you would recommend it to other people.

Write your **review** (140–190 words).

 A

 B

 C

 D

1.1 **Read Jasmine and Karim's messages. Which of the pictures above did they each put on the website?**

> ☐ **Jasmine:** My favourite outfit for parties is a knee-length silk dress. It's sleeveless and has a V-neck. It's light blue and I've got a necklace and some earrings to match. I wear it with some silver sandals with high heels. I love the colour and the material and it makes me feel good.
>
> ☐ **Karim:** I always wear my favourite pair of dark blue jeans when I go to somewhere special. They've got straight legs and they fit really well. I like to wear a plain white t-shirt with them. When I go out I usually wear my leather jacket – it's old now but it's very comfortable.

1.2 **Underline all the vocabulary about clothing in the messages above. Then write a short paragraph for the website about your favourite outfit.**

2.1 ▶ **58** **Listen to four customers in a clothes shop. Why don't they buy what they try on? Match each customer with a reason.**

Customer 1   A   It's a waste of money.

Customer 2   B   It doesn't fit.

Customer 3   C   It doesn't match another piece of clothing.

Customer 4   D   It doesn't suit him/her.

> **V** **Vocabulary note**
>
> Note these phrasal verbs with **wear**:
> *Joe's passion for football has **worn off** – he's into hockey now.* (= to gradually disappear)
> *These shoes are **worn out**.* (= too old and damaged from being used so much)
> *I have to work long hours – it **wears me out**.* (= to make someone tired)

2.2 **The sentences in each pair below have the same meaning. Complete them with the verbs in the box.**

dress	dressed	~~got~~	got	had	~~put~~
took	wear	wearing	wore		

1   a   I ___got___ dressed in a hurry.

    b   I ___put___ my clothes on quickly.

2   a   I have to _____ smartly for work.

    b   I have to _____ smart clothes for work.

3   a   The dancers were all _____ in black.

    b   The dancers were all _____ black.

4   a   He _____ undressed in the bathroom.

    b   He _____ off his clothes in the bathroom.

5   a   She _____ her new shoes on yesterday.

    b   She _____ her new shoes yesterday.

3.1 **Which of these items can you find in your room? Tick them.**

air conditioning   armchair   bookcase or shelves   carpet   heating   chest of drawers
computer   cushions   desk   duvet   lamp   mirror   pictures or posters   wardrobe

Other things not in the list: _____

3.2 **Read these comments that three teenagers have made about their rooms. Answer the questions below.**

A   My favourite room in the house is my bedroom. I sleep there, read there, do homework and relax
there. It's like a safe haven. It's a nice, dimly-lit place where I can listen to the rain outside, or sit and
look out of the window and daydream. I light candles occasionally or sit silently with my favourite
books. It's very restful so I can escape the stresses of daily life. No one tries to bug me or ask
anything of me when I'm in there. I wouldn't alter it, even if I could design my own room.

B   My bedroom is where I do my homework because it's so calm and quiet. I can concentrate and
get my work done. It's where I take naps and play my guitar, which relaxes me. I sleep well there
because I know my family are around me. But at the same time I can talk to my friends on my
phone when I'm stressed about something and know my family aren't listening. I am surrounded by
all the things I like, such as my posters. When it gets really messy, I spend a whole day tidying it up.

C   My favourite place is my room. I feel very comfortable and it has all of my favourite things. I always
do my homework and hang out there with my mates. I think it's good to have your own room. I have
my computer and TV within easy reach and can watch whatever I want without having to argue with
anyone. I also like my room because the stuff in it is an expression of me as an individual. I'm always
adding things and throwing out things I'm tired of.

Which of the teenagers

1   invites friends to their room? _____

2   sees their room as somewhere they can
get away from their worries? _____

3   thinks their room is a reflection of their
personality? _____

4   appreciates not having to compromise? _____

5   says they aren't easily distracted in their room? _____

6   says they like their room just as it is? _____

4.1 **Write a brief description of your room, describing the things in it, how you feel about it and why it is
important to you.**

Exam practice

You are going to read an article about the way teenagers sleep. Six sentences have been removed from the article. Choose from the sentences **A–G** the one which fits each gap (**1–6**). There is one extra sentence which you do not need to use.

Understanding teenagers' sleeping habits

As we enter adolescence our sleeping patterns change drastically. It is a phase of our lives when we seem to be able to go into the deepest sleep and not move for hours on end.

As any parent knows, rousing a sleeping adolescent can be, to put it mildly, difficult. Grumpy and uncommunicative until later in the day, it can be just as much of a struggle to get a teen to go to bed at night, what with homework, instant messaging, email and general late-night wakefulness. **1** [ ] So should we be concerned about this antisocial rite of passage? Or is there something more to an adolescent's sleep habits?

Relax. There is good news. Landmark studies into the adolescent brain have revealed that a teen's biorhythms are in fact just what nature intended. **2** [ ] As one adolescent health care specialist comments, most parents will be familiar with the situation where 'the kid who used to jump out of bed now has to be dragged out just to get on school on time'.

Importantly, it's not just a teen's shoe size that's getting bigger. **3** [ ] While it has been well documented that 95% of brain development takes place by the age of five years, research indicates that there is a second wave of brain growth, which continues into the teen years and even into the 20s.

During this time, new brain cells and neural connections or 'wires', which connect the right and left sides of the brain and are critical to intelligence, self-awareness and performance, grow like branches on a tree during the latter stages of sleep. **4** [ ] In other words, if you want to function really well, the best thing to do it is to get a good night's sleep. Experts say that the average amount of sleep needed by teens is 9.5 hours.

However, the reality of a typical teen life – early morning sports practice, homework and perhaps a part-time job after school – means that most are lucky to get 7.5 hours. **5** [ ] Yet since there is a good deal of variation in the amount of sleep individuals need for optimum performance, how do you tell if a teen is getting enough sleep to live up to his or her learning potential?

Dr Roger Tonkin, an adolescent health care specialist, suggests that while some teens seem to be able to cope with chronic sleep deprivation, others become irritable and apathetic. The treatment? Let him or her sleep whenever they can, including the weekends. 'If a teen wants to sleep until noon on Saturday,' advises Dr Tonkin, 'let him.' **6** [ ] If you study something on Tuesday and are short of sleep until Saturday, it's too late. You've got to get that sleep the same night.

Exam practice

A His or her brain is also developing rapidly at this stage.

B But according to the report, this doesn't mean that it is normal for teenagers not to get enough sleep.

C The result is that, at the weekend, the door to their bedroom remains shut until noon – or even later – while everyone else in the family, up for hours, goes about their business.

D Cut these short and performance is likely to suffer the next day.

E However, catching up on sleep at the weekend, while perfectly normal for most teens, may not help learning.

F According to new research, daytime sleepiness and late-night alertness are the result of a change in the sleep/wake cycle as growth hormones start to work.

G This mismatch is important because lack of sleep can affect mood and make it difficult for a teen to perform or even react appropriately.

Writing Part 2: story

(Note that writing a story is an option only in the *First for Schools* Writing paper.)

Your English teacher has asked you to write a story for the college magazine. Your story must begin with this sentence:

As soon as she walked into her room, Susanna knew that something was wrong.

Your story must include:
- a necklace
- a misunderstanding

Write your **story** (140–190 words).

 Exam tip

Remember to plan your story and divide it into paragraphs. Make sure you include the two points. Check carefully and correct any mistakes when you have finished.

42 School days

School and education

1.1 Look at these groups of words. Which word in each group is the odd one out? Why?

1 primary   secondary   state
   streamed   comprehensive   private

2 canteen   laboratory   library
   classroom   gym   playing fields

3 teachers   lecturers   principal
   head   teaching assistant

4 classes   housework   curriculum
   timetable   uniform   subjects

1.2 ▶59 Listen to a girl talking about her school. Tick the words in 1.1 that she uses.

1.3 ▶59 Listen again and write down:

1 what the girl likes about her school: _____

2 what she dislikes about her school: _____

1.4 Choose the correct words in this email to a penfriend.

Hi Paco

You asked me about the education system in my country. I'm still at **(1)** _school_ / _the school_ because it's **(2)** _essential_ / _compulsory_ here up to the **(3)** _age_ / _year_ of 16. We go to a kindergarten or nursery school first and then, when we're four or five years of **(4)** _old_ / _age_, we **(5)** _start_ / _join_ primary school, where we spend seven years.

I now **(6)** _go_ / _attend_ a state secondary school, which has about 1,000 **(7)** _pupils_ / _undergraduates_. We have six lessons a day and each subject is **(8)** _taught_ / _learnt_ by a different teacher. We have a lot of homework and projects, and if we **(9)** _lose_ / _miss_ an important deadline, we have to stay **(10)** _following_ / _after_ school to finish the work and hand it in. We have to wear a uniform until we're 15 but after that we're **(11)** _let_ / _allowed_ to wear our own clothes.

When we're 16 we **(12)** _take_ / _pass_ some exams. Then we can either **(13)** _leave_ / _depart_ school and go to a different college or stay on for two more years. During those years we **(14)** _learn_ / _study_ just three or four subjects. There are also **(15)** _opportunities_ / _occasions_ to do vocational courses like sport or mechanics at a college of further education. I haven't decided what to do yet.

All the best,

David

1.5 Rewrite the email in your notebook so that it is true for your country.

2.1 Look at this list of school subjects and cross out any that are not taught at your school. Add any extra subjects taught that are not on the list.

English   art   business studies   drama   computing   geography   history   literature   maths
music   psychology   science   physical education

_____

2.2 Tick the subjects you like best. Write a short paragraph giving reasons why you enjoy a particular subject. Use some of the phrases in the box below to help you give reasons.

The teacher is fantastic.   I like to use my imagination.   It's an interesting subject.
I'm better with numbers than words.   I'd like to study it at university.   I'm good at it.
I enjoy doing practical things.   I find it very stimulating.   I enjoy working in groups.

2.3 Look at the photos and answer the questions.

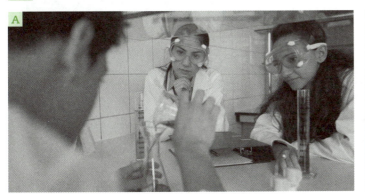

1   Which subjects do you think are being taught? A: _____   B: _____

2   What differences are there between the two lessons?
    Lesson A is very practical, _____

3   Which method of learning do you prefer? Why? _____

3.1 Complete the text below with the correct form of these verbs. Use each verb only once.

~~do~~   fail   give   pass   take   retake   revise   study

I'm 16 now, and I'm **(1)** _____doing_____ some important exams in a few weeks' time. They're called GCSEs, and my teachers have entered me for nine subjects, which is what most pupils at my school do. I'm going to go through all my notes to **(2)** _____ thoroughly for these exams, because I don't want to have to **(3)** _____ any of them next year. I've always thought it's better to **(4)** _____ all exams the first time you **(5)** _____ them. I'm certainly hoping I won't **(6)** _____ my maths exam. I've never been very good at maths, and I want to **(7)** _____ it up at the end of the year and spend more time **(8)** _____ history, geography and two foreign languages. I'm much better at those!

Exam practice

Reading and Use of English Part 2

For questions **1–8**, read the text below and think of the word which best fits each gap. Use only **one** word in each gap. There is an example at the beginning (**0**).

A different approach to education in Tamil Nadu, India

Kaumaram Sushila International Residential School is a school (**0**) _____ *with* _____ a difference. Every academic year, it makes a point of informing parents (**1**) _____ children are seeking admission that it gives more importance to organic farming and productive work (**2**) _____ to formal marks-based education. This is (**3**) _____ of those rare schools where children can ride horses as well as do some mountaineering and keep ducks, goats and bees. It is pointed (**4**) _____ to parents that if they are only keen on their children getting top marks in exams, the school may (**5**) _____ be suitable for them.

A small portion of the playground has (**6**) _____ turned into an area for growing vegetables, with students aged 4–8 being taught the importance of consuming healthy food. Organic farmers also come and talk to pupils about (**7**) _____ important it is to preserve the local environment. Finally, all children are encouraged to take responsibility (**8**) _____ the animals and crops in their care, and to understand the complex relationships of the natural world.

Writing Part 2: story

(Note that writing a story is an option only in the *First for Schools* Writing paper.)

Your English teacher has asked you to write a story for the school website. Your story must begin with this sentence:

Richard could not believe what he saw when he looked out of the classroom window.

Your story must include:
- a flood
- a rescue

Write your **story** (140–190 words).

The world of work

1.1 ▶60 **Listen to the two people in the photos talking about themselves. Which speaker does which job?**

Speaker 1 is a _____ .

Speaker 2 is a _____ .

1.2 ▶60 **Listen again and write down the words which helped you to answer. Can you think of any more personal qualities that are useful for each job?**

2.1 **Below are some adverts for job vacancies. Which job is each one advertising? Choose from this list.**

accountant   architect   builder   cleaner   mechanic   nursery assistant   receptionist   sales manager

---

A _____

You need to be efficient, well-organised and self-motivated and be able to work without supervision. You should also have good communication skills to deal with our customers.

Salary is dependent on qualifications and experience. Training will be given. If you would like a permanent job in a local hotel, call **0987 864829** for an application form.

B _____

Temporary job available in a local store for a reliable and flexible person.

Previous experience preferred but not essential as training can be given. You will be required to do shift work when the shop is closed (early mornings and evenings) and some overtime. Excellent wages for an honest hard-working person. Please contact James Havard to obtain an application form and a job description.

C _____

Enthusiastic person required to join our team.

We are looking for a caring, creative person. A full training programme will be given to the successful candidate so no previous experience with young children is necessary. Good rate of pay and possible promotion in the future.

Further details and an application form are available from office@mpr.co.uk.

2.2 **Answer these questions and write the words from the adverts which give you the answers.**

1 Which job is not forever? _____ _B, temporary_ _____

2 Which job is for a long time or forever? _____

3 Which job suggests you may get a higher position? _____

4 Which job has hours which change? _____

5 Which job needs you to get on well with members of the public? _____

6 Which job may involve working extra hours? _____

2.3 Each advert in 2.1 mentions how the person will be paid. Write *salary*, *rate of pay* and *wages* in the definitions below.

1 _____ a fixed amount of money agreed every year, usually paid into a bank account every month

2 _____ a fixed amount of money usually paid every week, often for work which does not require a lot of qualifications

3 _____ the amount of money someone will be paid per hour

2.4 Complete the letter of application, using the correct form of the words in brackets.

Dear Sir/Madam

I **(1)** _____recently_____ (*recent*) saw your advertisement on the website and I am interested in the **(2)** _____ (*vacant*) for assistant manager in your hotel restaurant. I attach an **(3)** _____ (*apply*) form.

I have worked in the **(4)** _____ (*cater*) industry for several years and I am **(5)** _____ (*passion*) about good food. I have several **(6)** _____ (*profession*) qualifications and enjoy working with people. I am also **(7)** _____ (*rely*), efficient and hard-working.

I have just finished a **(8)** _____ (*train*) course at the local college in administration, because I am very **(9)** _____ (*enthusiasm*) about having a career in the hotel business. I can provide you with excellent **(10)** _____ (*refer*) from my previous employers.

Yours faithfully

Anya Piekarski

3.1 ▶61 Listen to some people talking about work. Write ✓ for people who have a job and ✗ for people who don't have a job.

1 __✗__ 2 _____ 3 _____ 4 _____ 5 _____ 6 _____ 7 _____ 8 _____

3.2 ▶61 Listen again and answer these questions.

1 Two people decided to leave their jobs. What do they say? _____

_____

2 One person had to leave their job. What does he/she say? _____

3.3 Complete these sentences from the recording with *work*, *job* or *career*. Listen again if you need to.

1 I'm trying to change _____career_____ and I'm looking for _____ as a teacher.

2 I've just applied for a _____ at the theatre.

3 I had a long _____ in the police force.

4 I do four long days, which is very hard _____ .

5 The journey takes an hour each way so I don't have time to do much after _____ .

6 I gave up my _____ as a chef a year ago and I'm still out of _____ .

7 I'm going to get some unpaid _____ experience soon in an agency.

8 I was promoted last week so that's very good for my _____ .

> **ERROR WARNING** ❗
>
> **Occupation** is formal and is usually only used on forms:
> *I enjoy my job.* (**not** ~~I enjoy my occupation.~~)

Exam practice

Reading and Use of English Part 3

For questions **1–8**, read the text below. Use the word given in capitals at the end of some of the lines to form a word that fits in the gap **in the same line**. There is an example at the beginning (**0**).

Feelings run high in the workplace

In the workplace, jealousy can of course have a wide (**0**) _____*variety*_____ of	**VARY**
causes. It is a (**1**) _____ emotion and it can make people behave in	**WORRY**
totally (**2**) _____ ways. It could be that you are bitterly disappointed that	**PREDICT**
you didn't get the (**3**) _____ that you wanted in your department and as	**PROMOTE**
a result you can't bear to watch someone else succeed instead. The appropriate	
(**4**) _____ is to congratulate them warmly and not to reveal your	**RESPOND**
jealous feelings.	
In a different situation, jealousy may have its origins in the close personal nature	
of a particular (**5**) _____ , such as when a friend of yours succeeds in	**RELATION**
getting a job that you both applied for. You simply have to accept that the world	
of work is always (**6**) _____ . You should try not to show your	**COMPETE**
(**7**) _____ as this can make you look really small-minded, and will be	**ANNOY**
(**8**) _____ embarrassing for the other person, who should not be blamed	**ORDINARY**
for their success.	

Writing Part 2: letter of application

(Note that writing a letter of application is not one of the options in the *First for Schools* Writing paper.)

> ### Make a difference this summer!
>
> Enjoy travel?   Enthusiastic and energetic?   Work well in a team?
>
> We are looking for volunteers to spend 6 weeks abroad working on various building projects in different countries. Food and accommodation will be paid, but not flights.
> Write to Mrs Okawa, Volunteers International, explaining why you would be suitable as a volunteer.

Write your **letter** of application
(140–190 words).

 Exam tip

Remember to begin a letter of application with *Dear Mr ...* or *Dear Mrs ...* or *Ms ...* and end it with *Yours sincerely*.

Include any relevant information about your experience, qualifications and personal qualities.

University life

University courses; expressing opinions

1.1 Read this text from a university website. Who is it aimed at?

The university is on one campus which covers an area of 200 acres. There are five faculties – Humanities, Science and technology, Social sciences, Law and Medicine – and these are divided into departments like geography, art history, etc. You will have already looked at our website, but when you arrive, you can pick up a prospectus and book which tour you want to go on, according to your subject of interest.

Your tour will begin with a talk by one of the lecturers, who will tell you more about the courses. All our courses consist of a mixture of formal lectures, seminars in groups of up to twenty students, and at least two tutorials per term where groups of two or three students have the opportunity to discuss things in more detail with their own tutors. Most degree courses require students to write a dissertation of at least 6,000 words in their last year.

The tours will show you the halls of residence where students live, the students' union where lots of social events take place, and other useful facilities like the supermarket and launderette.

Our undergraduate courses all begin in October and most of our students are school leavers – just four per cent are mature students of 21 and over. At present the university year consists of three terms but we are changing to semesters (two a year) in three years' time. We will have different vacations as a result: slightly longer in spring and shorter in summer.

We have separate open days for graduates who want to go on to do a postgraduate course.

1.2 Complete these sentences with words from the text.

1 The buildings of a university and the land that surrounds them are called a ___campus___ .

2 The university is organised by subject into different _____ and a group of these form a _____ .

3 Information about the university can be found in a booklet called a _____ or on the website.

4 Students attend _____ , _____ and _____ where they are taught about their subject.

5 Students are taught by _____ and _____ .

6 A long piece of written work is called a _____ .

7 Students live in _____ and attend social events arranged by the _____ .

8 Students who are at least 21 are referred to as _____ students.

9 The university year is divided into _____ or _____ . The breaks are called _____ .

10 Students who are studying for a first degree are called _____ . When they finish they are called _____ . A student who continues to study after a first degree is called a _____ .

2.1 ▶62 **Listen to two students describing their courses at university and answer the questions below.**

1   What subject is each student studying?   Student 1: _____   Student 2: _____

architecture   English literature   biology   law   psychology   history   economics   chemistry   medicine

2   How does each student say they learn?

lecture   seminar   tutorial   essay   assignment   experiment   dissertation   presentation

Student 1: _____

Student 2: _____

3   What does each student think is good about their course?

Student 1: _____

Student 2: _____

> **V** *Vocabulary note*
>
> An **essay** is a short piece of writing about a particular subject. A **dissertation** is a much longer piece of work, often a requirement of a degree course. A **thesis** is usually written for a higher degree over an extended length of time and involves personal research.

2.2 ▶62 **Listen again and fill in the phrases the students use to express opinions.**

1   I _____ about the course I'm doing now.

2   They _____ students having to plan their own time.

3   But _____ , you've got to spend lots of time reading and thinking things through.

4   I _____ the timetable.

5   I _____ the lectures are very good.

6   I _____ it's a very good way of learning.

7   Now I _____ the system really works.

8   I _____ having the lectures each morning.

9   I _____ concentrating on the experiments for now.

2.3 **Look at your answers in 2.2. Mark the phrases P if they are used only for positive opinions, N for negative opinions, and B for both positive and negative opinions.**

3.1 **There are lots of idioms and expressions using the verb *think*. Match the two halves of these sentences.**

1   If I were you, I'd think through the implications

2   You've really got to think it over carefully

3   I'm sure you weren't thinking straight

4   If you think back to this time last year,

5   Personally, I wouldn't think twice

A   when you said you'd finish everything by Monday.

B   about applying for a better job with a higher salary.

C   you'll realise how much progress you've made.

D   of accepting a job involving a lot of travel.

E   as no one is going to make the decision for you.

Exam practice

Reading and Use of English Part 7

You are going to read an article about the use of technology in university lectures. For questions **1–10**, choose from the sections **A–D**. The sections may be chosen more than once.

Which section mentions

the view that students have always tended to lose attention in university lectures?	**1**
the idea that expecting students to provide their own technology may lead to a form of discrimination?	**2**
the increase in the number of students learning in other ways apart from listening to lectures?	**3**
technical problems reducing the amount of teaching which takes place?	**4**
the advantages for students of using technology they are accustomed to?	**5**
a lack of progress in adapting study materials to make best use of students' technology?	**6**
the disadvantage of students having access during lectures to material unconnected to their studies?	**7**
the economic advantage for universities if students use their own devices?	**8**
university studies requiring the kind of concentration which is hard to find nowadays?	**9**
universities being unable to impose restrictions on what students look at during lectures?	**10**

Students bring their own technology to lectures

A A trend known as Bring Your Own Device (BYOD) has swept across countless universities and institutions. The idea is that technology can allow students to access online learning tools and interactive resources: students will no longer sit passively in the lecture hall, but instead will be engaging with complementary material online. While supplying (and routinely upgrading) enough technology so that all students can access virtual learning environments is too costly, building a network that allows them to use online resources via their personal devices is less of a financial burden. The practice also allows students to use technology that they're familiar with, according to Jason Lodge, lecturer in higher education in learning futures at Griffith University in Brisbane. 'BYOD eliminates quite a bit of the cognitive load associated with learning. For example, any activity requires multiple levels of understanding in order for students to engage effectively. By using devices they are already familiar with, they have more resources available to understand what they are being asked to do and what the actual content of the task is.'

B Lodge admits that the BYOD trend does have a number of problems. His biggest concern? It encourages students to use technology during teaching time: 'The major downside of BYOD is the potential for distraction. Students' own devices are likely to include all the applications they use on a regular basis. This cannot be controlled like it can be with computers provided by the institution.' Tim Cappelli, a senior project manager at Manchester Medical School, disagrees. He explained: '93% of our students said they use their iPads for accessing social networks. I'm surprised it's not higher. Are they doing this in lectures? Probably. But is this any different from me reading a novel at the back of the lecture theatre, or doodling on my notepad, when I was a student?' However, of course the difference is that iPads offer a multitude of distractions far exceeding those of a novel or a biro.

C You don't have to look far to find studies warning that constant access to technology can damage an individual's concentration. A study by Professor Larry Rosen, California State University, found that people could only focus on a given task for six minutes before utilising some form of technology. This of course is particularly problematic at universities, where deep, analytical thinking is highly valued. The other aspect which can waste time is the issue of compatibility. Students utilise a multitude of laptops, mobiles and tablets, all of which may have different operating systems. Consequently, lectures and seminars can be dominated by struggles to make everything work properly. Not only does this take up valuable time to sort out, but most professors lack the specialised knowledge to resolve these issues.

D While technology is undoubtedly changing the way students learn, there's still some way to go before students' mobiles and tablets are seamlessly interwoven into the classroom environment, says Lodge. 'The emphasis of BYOD thus far has been more on infrastructure, i.e. making sure there is sufficient wireless bandwidth, rather than incorporating students' own devices into the learning activities they do. Teaching practice is notoriously slow to change in a university setting. To my knowledge, designing effective courses, subjects and activities that incorporate the students' devices happens very seldom at the moment.' Professor Steven Furnell, head of Plymouth University's school of computing and mathematics, points out another possible obstacle to universal access. Relying on students to buy their own devices could 'result in a situation of the "haves" and "have nots" amongst the student population'.

Writing Part 2: report

(Note that writing a report is not one of the options in the *First for Schools* Writing paper.)

> Your English teacher has asked you to write a report on a study course or training course you have attended. In your report you should:
>
> - give a brief description of the course
> - explain what you learnt from it
> - say whether you think any improvements are needed

Write your **report** (140–190 words).

 Exam tip

Give your report a title (for this question it could be the name of the course). Then give each section of the report a heading, one for each point you have to write about.

Answer key

Grammar section

Unit 1

A: Context listening

2 1 in her room / at home
   2 in a shopping centre/mall / outside a shop
   3 She's phoning to ask Lisa if she wants her to buy a bag.

3 2 She buys new clothes.
   3 She's looking for a new skirt / one of those new skirts.
   4 She's wearing a pair of old jeans.
   5 She's cleaning her room.
   6 She looks for a blue bag.
   7 She's looking at a navy blue bag (the one that Lisa wants).
   8 She wants Millie to buy the bag.

4 1 the present simple 2 the present continuous
   3 sentences 2 and 6 4 sentences 1, 3, 4, 5 and 7
   5 No. It is in the present simple but is not a regular action.

C: Grammar exercises

1 2 a 3 a 4 a 5 b 6 b (➤ B1–4)

2 2 smells 3 like, don't fit 4 are you thinking
   5 is, is your sister being, has (➤ B1–4)

3 1 looks 2 have, means, don't understand 3 Do/Can you see,
   're (are) looking, Do you recognise, seem, 're (are) coming
   4 are you doing, are waiting, 're (are) getting, want, 's (is)
   being, don't know (➤ B1–4)

4 2 're enjoying 3 cost 4 're staying 5 're paying 6 don't like
   7 serve 8 never eat 9 don't feel 10 seem 11 're having
   12 're visiting 13 love 14 behave 15 smile 16 says
   17 is always showing (shows is correct but does not make
   clear that she is criticising) 18 come 19 realise
   20 are taking (➤ B1–3)

5 2 belong 3 am thinking 4 knows 5 is having
   6 needs (➤ B1–3)

Exam practice
Listening Part 4
1 B 2 C 3 A 4 B 5 A 6 B 7 C

Grammar focus task
2 hear 3 call 4 am working 5 work 6 think 7 is getting
8 I'm always telling 9 don't realise 10 means

Unit 2

A: Context listening

2 2 J 3 G 4 M 5 J

3 1 b We went to see a film. 2 the past simple
   3 a I used to collect all the autographs of film stars
      and singers.
      b I would go up to town on my own.
      c I used to scream at pop concerts.
   4 No. 5 Yes.

4 1 were travelling 2 were queuing 3 was buying, were walking
5 the past continuous

C: Grammar exercises

1 2 found 3 explained 4 was 5 knew 6 wrote 7 seemed
   8 ate 9 drank 10 got 11 learnt/learned 12 fed 13 gave
   14 went 15 spoke 16 met 17 read 18 had 19 spread
   20 came (➤ B1)

2 2 travelled, always kept 3 saw, was waiting, didn't see
   4 filled, gave 5 was working, met, looked 6 bought, was
   always crashing 7 missed, was charging 8 was hoping,
   didn't get (➤ B1–2)

3 2 changed 3 asked 4 would lock 5 used to feel 6 met
   7 was walking 8 heard 9 were breaking 10 were sitting
   11 realised 12 didn't want 13 isn't used 14 thought (➤ B1–4)

4 2 're/are used to 3 is used to 4 isn't used to / wasn't used to
   5 Are you getting used to / Have you got used to 6 got used
   to (➤ B4)

5 2 was looking, stopped 3 went, was having 4 went, stood
   5 was hoping, said (➤ B1–2)

6 2 ~~used to often~~ often used to 3 ~~used~~ use 4 ~~use~~ used 5 ~~used
   to teach~~ is used to teaching 6 ~~was used~~ used (➤ B3–4)

Exam practice
Reading and Use of English Part 1
1 A 2 C 3 A 4 D 5 D 6 B 7 D 8 C

Grammar focus task
2 began 3 came 4 went 5 heard 6 held 7 led 8 made
9 spent 10 stood 11 took 12 thought

Unit 3

A: Context listening

2 1 They live next door to each other. 2 Mike plays a
   saxophone and Lucy can't concentrate on her work.

3 2 I've been at the gym this afternoon.
   3 I still haven't finished it.
   4 I started it last week.
   5 I never enjoyed studying history at school.
   6 I've lived next door since June.
   7 I've lived here for two years.
   8 Nobody's ever complained before.

4 1 the past simple 2 the present perfect 3 sentences 2, 3,
   6, 7 and 8 (Note that in sentence 2 the time period 'this
   afternoon' is still continuing – he has only recently
   returned from the gym.) 4 sentences 1, 4 and 5

C: Grammar exercises

1 2 H 3 D 4 F 5 C 6 B 7 I 8 E 9 A 10 G (➤ B1)

2 2 slept 3 has grown 4 sent, hasn't replied 5 Did you learn
   6 bought, 've (have) used 7 have you had 8 has just arrived
   9 've (have) never seen 10 dreamt/dreamed 11 met
   12 did you get, haven't noticed (➤ B1)

3 2 worked 3 have you eaten 4 have been doing 5 did
   6 have been waiting (➤ B1–2)

4 2 arrived 3 felt/was 4 've (have) already made 5 took/drove
   6 went/swam 7 enjoyed / loved / liked 8 've (have) learnt/
   learned 9 haven't been/gone 10 've (have) had 11 went
   12 played (➤ B1)

5 2 We've been standing 3 have you been playing
   4 We've played 5 we haven't finished 6 you've been playing
   7 We've read 8 Have you tried 9 we've already started
   10 we've booked (➤ B2)

Exam practice
Reading and Use of English Part 7
1 A 2 C 3 B 4 D 5 C 6 D 7 C 8 A 9 D 10 B

Grammar focus task
1 anticipated 2 've enjoyed, didn't own, bought 3 walked, got
4 fell, hasn't happened 5 've worn 6 worked, was, 've been

Unit 4

A: Context listening
2 1 He's been painting his room.
   2 She's angry because there is paint on the carpet.

3 2 'd painted 3 ran out of 4 was 5 'd been 6 'd done
   7 'd finished 8 'd been driving 9 broke down

4 1 3 happened after 1 and 2. He uses the past perfect for
     1 and 2 and the past simple for 3.
   2 4 happened after 5, 6 and 7. He uses the past simple for
     4 and the past perfect for 5, 6 and 7.
   3 8 happened first. She uses the past perfect continuous
     for 8 and the past simple for 9.

C: Grammar exercises
1 2 'd (had) ordered 3 'd (had) planned 4 had left
   5 had you answered 6 hadn't started 7 Had you already
   booked 8 'd (had) posted, 'd (had) forgotten 9 Hadn't
   anyone told, had changed 10 had never done (➤ B1)

2 2 had you been eating 3 hadn't been expecting 4 had been
   living 5 hadn't been paying 6 had Anya's family been living
   7 had been watching 8 Had the other boys been teasing
   9 'd been going 10 'd been wearing (➤ B2)

3 2 hadn't been learning/studying 3 had been planning/
   organising 4 'd (had) been worrying 5 'd (had) been waiting
   6 'd (had) been sending 7 hadn't been playing 8 'd (had)
   been saving 9 'd (had) only been speaking/talking
   10 had they been looking/searching (➤ B2)

4 2 No 3 Yes – had been snowing 4 No 5 No 6 No
   7 Yes – had been arguing 8 No 9 Yes – hadn't been speaking
   10 No (➤ B1–2)

5 2 came, fainted, hadn't seen 3 had begun, arrived 4 had
   you been applying, got 5 didn't see, 'd (had) gone 6 'd (had)
   been driving, realised 7 went, stopped, looked 8 'd (had)
   washed, hung 9 discovered, 'd (had) believed 10 Had you
   ever done, built (➤ B1–2)

6 2 'd (had) been playing 3 'd (had) ever had 4 'd (had) been
   moving 5 'd (had) arranged 6 didn't answer 7 came
   8 banged 9 'd (had) been phoning 10 hadn't heard
   11 arrived 12 'd (had) forgotten (➤ B1–2)

Exam practice
Reading and Use of English Part 5
1 C 2 B 3 A 4 C 5 D 6 B

Grammar focus task
1 1 had remodelled 2 had become, had experimented
   3 had been playing, decided 4 was, had received
   5 had forced, found

2 *Sample answer*:
   We can't be sure. Perhaps they'd realised there was someone
   in the house. Perhaps they'd heard a police siren. Perhaps
   they'd seen a ghost!

Unit 5

A: Context listening
2 1 C 2 B 3 D 4 A Tom is a journalist.

3 2 arrives 3 starts 4 'm playing 5 'm flying 6 'm having
   7 won't be 8 'll get 9 'll have 10 will be 11 won't be
   12 will live

4 1 sentences 1, 2 and 3; the present simple
   2 sentences 7, 8 and 9; the *will* future
   3 sentences 4, 5 and 6; the present continuous
   4 sentences 10, 11 and 12; the *will* future

C: Grammar exercises
1 2 doesn't leave 3 stops 4 doesn't arrive 5 are staying
   6 are spending 7 doesn't go 8 are having 9 leaves
   10 arrives (➤ B1–2)

2 2 is leaving 3 'm (am) giving, are you giving, 'll (will) probably
   get 4 're (are) moving, 'll (will) come 5 'll (will) have 6 's (is)
   staying 7 'll have 8 Are you doing, is arriving, 'm (am) driving
   9 'll get (➤ B2–3)

3 2 'll (will) be sitting 3 'll (will) apply 4 'll (will) be speaking
   5 are having 6 starts 7 is coming 8 'll (will) lose (➤ B1–4)

4 2 is seeing 3 will be 4 'll (will) be 5 'll (will) be flying 6 'll
   (will) be skiing 7 're (are) going 8 will lend/give (➤ B1–4)

Exam practice
Listening Part 2
1 landscapes 2 agriculture 3 beaches 4 penguin 5 insects
6 sunset(s) 7 questionnaire 8 walking 9 notebook 10 tents

Grammar focus task
2 're staying 3 're going 4 'll have 5 'll be waiting
6 'll be working 7 'll get 8 'll see 9 won't get 10 're hiring

Unit 6

A: Context listening

2 1 He's come to interview the people on the island.
   2 It's very tough (especially because of the weather).

3 2 Because they're fed up with the cold, the wind, the mud
     and the rain.
   3 as soon as possible
   4 They'll have survived there longer than anyone else.
   5 for nearly six months
   6 as soon as they find a restaurant
   7 Simon – because the other people take his boat.

4 1 questions 2, 3, 6 and 7 2 question 1 3 questions 4 and 5

C: Grammar exercises

1 *Sample answers:*
   2 're (are) going to / about to arrest him.
   3 's (is) going to / about to score a goal.
   4 's (is) going to / about to sink.
   5 's (is) going to / about to crash.
   6 's (is) going to / about to kiss him. (▷ B1, B5)

2 2 Robots will have replaced most manual workers.
   3 We will have used all the oil resources on Earth.
   4 Doctors will have discovered a cure for the common cold.
   5 Scientists will have invented new sources of energy.
   6 Sea temperatures will have risen by several degrees. (▷ B4)

3 2 b 3 b 4 a 5 b (▷ B3)

4 2 The gardener will have been cutting hedges for four hours.
   3 The manager will have been interviewing new staff for five
     and a half hours.
   4 The waitress will have been serving customers in the dining
     room for three hours.
   5 The cleaner will have been vacuuming floors for seven
     hours. (▷ B4)

5 2 's (is) going to be 3 're (are) going to stay 4 finds out
   5 was going to wash / was about to wash 6 'm (am) going to
   look round 7 're (are) going to miss 8 gets 9 will have taken
   10 'll (will) have been working 11 'm (am) going to start /
   'm (am) about to start (▷ B1–5)

6 2 I will see see 3 take have taken 4 will come comes
   5 been leaving left 6 are going to finish finish / have finished
   7 will 'm/am going to (▷ B2, B4)

Exam practice
Reading and Use of English Part 7

1 C 2 D 3 A 4 B 5 D 6 B 7 D 8 B 9 C 10 A

Grammar focus task

2 's going to do 3 'll have produced 4 get 5 recognises
6 will have been making 7 try 8 need

Unit 7

A: Context listening

2 1 a fitness centre 2 a wildlife park 3 a cleaning service
   4 a games centre/shop

3 1 stronger, slimmer and more self-confident.
   2 the most magnificent lions, the funniest monkeys you've
     ever seen
   3 tired (trying to keep the house clean)
   4 the greatest variety of games ever

4 1 sensible, friendly, excellent
   2 wonderful, the best, amazing, special
   3 fresh, shining, (no) sticky, reasonable
   4 fantastic, the latest, stunning, the most thrilling

C: Grammar exercises

1 2 as/so spacious as 3 more expensive than 4 worse
   5 the smartest 6 the loveliest 7 the poorest 8 (the) most
   exhausted 9 the best 10 younger 11 as cheap as
   12 nearer (▷ B1–2)

2 2 depressed 3 amazing 4 annoying 5 bored 6 interesting
   7 disgusting 8 relaxed (▷ B3)

3 2 bored boring 3 as beautiful than as beautiful as *or* more
   beautiful than 4 easyer easier 5 more quicker quicker
   6 more safe safer 7 greenner greener 8 more worse worse
   (▷ B1–3)

4 2 a 3 b 4 b 5 b 6 a 7 b 8 a (▷ B1–5)

5 2 beautiful blue Chinese silk 3 magic gold 4 elegant long
   leather riding 5 tight yellow (▷ B5)

Exam practice
Reading and Use of English Part 1

1 B 2 B 3 C 4 A 5 C 6 B 7 D 8 A

Grammar focus task

1 *adjectives:* daily, different, good, long, main, old
   nouns used as adjectives: leisure, school, postgraduate

2 2 old 3 school 4 good 5 different 6 long 7 postgraduate
   8 main 9 leisure

Unit 8

A: Context listening

2 1 stadium 2 spectators 3 whistle 4 ball 5 ground 6 quickly
   7 goal 8 scored 9 loudly

3 2 in the city today, late 3 patiently in their seats 4 happily
   5 steadily 6 heavily on the ground 7 rarely 8 well
   9 Last week 10 often

4 *When:* today, late, last week
   Where: in their seats, on the ground
   How: happily, steadily, heavily, quickly, well
   How often: often
   The adverbs in Exercise 1 go in the *How* column.

C: Grammar exercises

1 2 gratefully 3 anxiously 4 easily 5 sincerely 6 fast 7 hard
8 terribly (▷ B1–2)

2 2 complete 3 well 4 hard, fluent 5 awful 6 efficiently
7 normal 8 badly 9 further (▷ B1–2)

3 2 Nowadays they rarely eat steak because it is so expensive. /
They rarely eat steak because it is so expensive nowadays. /
They rarely eat steak nowadays because it is so expensive.

3 My grandfather used to take us swimming in the lake in the
summer holidays. / In the summer holidays my grandfather
used to take us swimming in the lake.

4 There is usually a good film on TV on Sunday evenings. /
On Sunday evenings there is usually a good film on TV.

5 My mother insisted that good manners are always terribly
important. / My mother always insisted that good manners
are terribly important.

6 The party had hardly started when the sound system broke,
which meant we couldn't dance all evening. (▷ B2, B5)

4 2 earlier 3 always 4 very/rather 5 skilfully 6 rather/very
7 hardly 8 stiffly 9 now 10 warmly (▷ B1–5)

5 2 b 3 b 4 a 5 a 6 b (▷ B1–5)

6 2 easy easily 3 hardly hard 4 really very 5 very great/good/
really 6 attention very well carefully attention very carefully /
very careful attention 7 fluent fluently 8 good well (▷ B1–5)

Exam practice
Reading and Use of English Part 3

1 scientific 2 equipment 3 extremely 4 dangerously 5 safety
6 unusually 7 luckily 8 amazing

Grammar focus task

2 extremely, extreme 3 well, good 4 dangerously, dangerous
5 calmly, calm 6 hard, hard 7 unusually, unusual 8 luckily, lucky

Unit 9

A: Context listening

2 He's a bit worried because Mina didn't phone yesterday
or answer his texts this morning.

3 2 three 3 to phone yesterday 4 They miss her. 5 It's Mina's
mum's birthday. 6 at the station 7 seeing Mum's face

4 2 <u>Have</u> you <u>been checking</u> up on me? <u>haven't</u>
3 You <u>promised</u> to phone me yesterday, <u>didn't</u> you? <u>did</u>
4 You <u>know</u> your mother and I miss you when you're away
at college, <u>don't</u> you? <u>do</u>
5 And you<u>'ll</u> definitely <u>come</u> home for mum's birthday at
the weekend, <u>won't</u> you? <u>will</u>
6 You <u>can</u> meet me at the station, <u>can't</u> you? <u>can</u>
7 Your train <u>gets</u> in at six, <u>doesn't</u> it? <u>does</u>
8 Mum <u>doesn't know</u> I'm coming, <u>does</u> she? <u>doesn't</u>
9 <u>Let's</u> keep it a surprise, <u>shall</u> we? <u>let's</u>

C: Grammar exercises

1 2 have we 3 has she got 4 can't you walk 5 didn't you
6 does 7 can't 8 do you prefer 9 are 10 invited you (▷ B1–4)

2 2 costs it does it cost 3 you are are you
4 does annoy annoys 5 was were 6 did paint painted
7 you don't don't you 8 it lasts the cookery course does the
cookery course last (▷ B1, B3)

3 2 doesn't he 3 wouldn't you 4 haven't I 5 shall we 6 could it
7 didn't they 8 won't she 9 can we 10 don't you (▷ B4)

4 2 Where was he born? / Where is he going to live?
3 Who did he telephone?
4 When did he telephone her / his wife / Shirley?
5 How many children do they have / have they got?
6 Why is she/Shirley really pleased?
7 Who is looking forward to welcoming them back to
Farley? (▷ B3)

5 2 C 3 H 4 G 5 A 6 F 7 B 8 E (▷ B5)

Exam practice
Listening Part 1

1 B 2 C 3 B 4 A 5 C 6 B 7 A 8 A

Grammar focus task

2 was it 3 can't we 4 wouldn't they 5 haven't you 6 are you
7 will you 8 did you

Unit 10

A: Context listening

2 *Sample answers:*
1 She's a sales executive. 2 He works for a garage. / He's a
mechanic. / He drives a recovery truck. 3 He delivers pizzas. /
He's a pizza delivery man. 4 She's a taxi driver.

3 2 travel 3 her health 4 the ones who run out of petrol
5 insurance 6 Because he needs cash. 7 chemistry
8 the traffic 9 Because there's a lot of unemployment.

4 1 biscuits and sweets 2 at a garage 3 pizzas 4 traffic jams
5 a job with a reasonable salary 6 She's got three kids/
children.

5 The nouns in Exercise 3 are uncountable; the nouns in
Exercise 4 are countable.

C: Grammar exercises

1 2 A, C 3 F 4 H 5 D 6 E 7 B, I (▷ B1)

2 *Always countable:* experiment, hobby, journey
Always uncountable: accommodation, advice, homework,
information, leisure, luck, meat, scenery, traffic
Can be countable or uncountable: cheese, coffee, experience,
glass, time (▷ B1)

3 2 an 3 the 4 the 5 the 6 a 7 the 8 a 9 a 10 the 11 the
12 a 13 the 14 – 15 – (▷ B2)

4 1 Birmingham Airport 2 the Mediterranean, Naples, Corsica
3 the Sahara, the Andes, Paris 4 a ski instructor, Switzerland
5 a terrible journey, the internet, Computer User, Microsoft
(▷ B3)

5 We had *a* great trip to ~~the~~ France last weekend. We went to *the* little hotel that you recommended and it was very pleasant. ~~Foods~~ *The food* at the hotel ~~weren't~~ *wasn't* so good, as you warned us, but we strolled down to *the* city centre on Saturday evening and had *a* lovely meal there. In fact, we ate so much for ~~the~~ dinner that we didn't want ~~a~~ breakfast on Sunday! Thanks again for the advice. ~~The~~ Wikipedia gave us some good ~~informations~~ *information* about the town, but your local knowledge really helped. Now I must unpack and do the ~~washings~~ *washing*. Here is *a* photo of the hotel to remind you. (▷ B1–3)

6 2 – 3 shopping 4 in**formation** 5 furniture 6 – (▷ B1–2)

Exam practice
Reading and Use of English Part 4

1 takes (great) pleasure in buying / gets (great) pleasure from buying
2 gave me (some) advice about/on
3 will havebeen waiting (for)
4 but/although/though he hardly ever
5 the exact sum/amount of money
6 item of news was/news item was / item on the news was

Grammar focus task
2 B 3 U 4 C 5 B 6 U 7 C 8 U

Unit 11

A: Context listening
2 *Suggested answer*: He starts work early every morning and he has to stay until all the food is cooked and served in the evening.
3 2 hardly any 3 Because it's his day off. 4 He has two days off every week instead of one. 5 He offers to show Ahmed the kitchen.
4 2 C 3 A 4 G 5 I 6 J 7 B 8 F 9 H 10 D
5 needn't, must

C: Grammar exercises
1 2 doesn't have to / hasn't got to 3 mustn't 4 'll (will) have to 5 has to / has got to 6 didn't have to 7 must 8 Do you have to / Have you got to 9 mustn't 10 must / 'll (will) have to 11 had to 12 have to / 've got to 13 must 14 don't have to / haven't got to (▷ B1–2)
2 2 F 3 E 4 D 5 A 6 H 7 C 8 B (▷B2–3)
3 2 should have locked it 3 should have asked 4 shouldn't have lied 5 should have revised (▷ B2)
4 2 worn his latest designer clothes 3 stand in the queue 4 carry his luggage 5 walk from the car park 6 got angry with his driver (▷ B3)
5 2 needn't / don't need to / don't have to phone me before you come
   3 must / need to buy a good dictionary
   4 shouldn't have taken money from my purse without asking

5 didn't need to / didn't have to drive to the station to pick up my sister
6 should help me (to) do the washing-up
7 mustn't use their phones during classes
8 needn't have turned the music down
9 shouldn't make promises which she doesn't keep
10 don't have to / don't need to / needn't give the tour guide a tip (▷ B1–3)

Exam practice
Reading and Use of English Part 6
1 E 2 G 3 B 4 F 5 A 6 C

Grammar focus task
2 The first thing you must address is tiredness.
3 You should also take exercise regularly in the evenings.
4 It (The exercise) has to be vigorous.
5 Walking or tennis have to be kept up for at least an hour.
6 You should choose something you like doing.
7 You need to keep reminding yourself of the advantages.
8 You don't need to behave in the same way.

Unit 12

A: Context listening
2 1 She went to the beach last year (photo A).
   2 He would prefer the quiet mountain holiday (photo C).
3 2 myself, of mine 3 Neither 4 by myself 5 each other 6 somewhere 7 None

C: Grammar exercises
1 2 there is 3 It is 4 there are 5 There are 6 there are 7 It is 8 It is 9 there is 10 it is (▷ B5)
2 2 b 3 a 4 a 5 b (▷ B1–3)
3 2 each other 3 every 4 Each 5 everyone 6 Everyone 7 all the 8 each other 9 The whole 10 nobody (▷ B4, B6–8)
4 2 each 3 all 4 none 5 every 6 some 7 most 8 no (▷ B7–8)
5 2 Both John and Rob have an earring.
   3 Neither Pete nor John has a moustache.
   4 All of them have short hair / wear glasses.
   5 They all have short hair / wear glasses.
   6 None of them has/have a beard. (▷ B7, B9)
6 2 ~~mine~~ my own 3 ~~us~~ each other 4 ~~There~~ It 5 ~~feel myself~~ feel 6 ~~It~~ There (▷ B2–5)

Exam practice
Reading and Use of English Part 2
1 everyone/everybody 2 own 3 there 4 mine 5 else 6 mine/it 7 Neither 8 both

Grammar focus task
2 their own names 3 a close friend of mine 4 somebody else 5 neither of them appeared to mind 6 they both agreed

Unit 13

A: Context listening

2 **2** Can you lend me your new jacket?
  3 Can you give me a lift to town now?
  4 Will you get me some shampoo later?
  5 Can you collect me from the city centre at midnight tonight?

3 **2** ✗ **3** ✗ **4** ✗ **5** ✓

4 Would you please give me a lift? Could you collect me? She asks differently because she wants to be more polite.

C: Grammar exercises

1 **2** R **3** O **4** S **5** A **6** R **7** O **8** P **9** A **10** S
  2 c **3** j **4** e **5** f **6** i **7** d **8** g **9** h **10** a (▷ B1–5)

2 **2** send **3** can **4** spending **5** given **6** ought not **7** Could **8** should (▷ B1–5)

3 **2** May/Could **3** How/What about **4** could **5** Will/Can/Would/Could (*Would* and *Could* are more formal, less likely for a simple request to a family member.) **6** can/could/'ll (will) **7** Shall / Why don't **8** could/would/can (*Can* is less polite, so less suitable when speaking to a stranger.) **9** Can/May **10** Would you mind (▷ B1–4)

4 **2** Can I do **3** Could I see **4** I'm afraid **5** You can't have **6** Would you exchange **7** You shouldn't have done **8** You should ask **9** Shall I ask **10** You'd better not **11** You could give (▷ B1–5)

5 **2** Shall I help you clean your new flat?
  3 What about buying her some perfume?
  4 You ought not to put so much salt on your food.
  5 Could you order the book for me?
  6 Can I pay by credit card?
  7 You should charge it every night.
  8 Would you like me to help you clear up?
  9 Can you get me a tube of sun cream?
  10 Would you mind giving me a lift home? (▷ B1–5)

Exam practice
Listening Part 3

1 D **2** B **3** C **4** G **5** E

Grammar focus task

2 You could go hiking in Cape Breton.
3 You shouldn't do that course.
4 You'd better not cycle along those roads.
5 Why don't you take these tracks across the fields instead?
6 You shouldn't have done that.
7 You must wear your life jacket.

Unit 14

A: Context listening

2 The woman isn't his mother, but she could be his sister or his girlfriend – Clare and Fiona aren't sure.

3 **1** his mother
  2 The woman can't be his mother because she's much too young.
  3 to walk across together and pretend they're looking in the shop window
  4 Danni's autograph
  5 Because the young woman could be Danni's girlfriend.
  6 a photo of Danni
  7 She thinks they might get into a lot of trouble.

4 **2** must be **3** can't be **4** might notice **5** could be **6** can't be

5 **1** sentences 2, 3 and 6 **2** sentences 1, 4 and 5

C: Grammar exercises

1 **2** couldn't / wasn't able to **3** can **4** was able to **5** 'll (will) be able to **6** 've (have) never been able to **7** to be able to **8** could **9** couldn't / wasn't able to **10** can't **11** could/can (▷ B1–2)

2 **2** past **3** future **4** future **5** past **6** present **7** present **8** past **9** past **10** past
  A 5, 6, 10 **B** 2, 3, 4, 7, 8, 9 (▷ B2)

3 **2** should/must be swimming **3** should be **4** must have grown **5** must be **6** can't have forgotten (*shouldn't have forgotten* is also possible, but with a different meaning: see Unit 13.) (▷ B2–3)

4 **2** can't/couldn't have left **3** might not / may not have seen **4** might/may/could be **5** might not / may not come **6** should have lost, must have been (▷ B2–3)

5 *Sample answers:*
  2 can't have stolen, she was with the other cleaners after 6.00.
  3 may/might/could have stolen, she was alone there between 6.05 and 6.15 and nobody saw her leave.
  4 could/may/might have stolen, he was there until 7.15 and was alone after his phone call.
  5 must have stolen, he stayed after the gallery was shut and he bought an expensive car.
  6 couldn't have stolen, she was with the cleaners and they left together. (▷ B2)

Exam practice
Reading and Use of English Part 3

1 occasionally **2** confidently **3** socialise **4** deliveries **5** payments **6** impression **7** attractive **8** unlikely

Grammar focus task

2 might/may/could be **3** must be **4** can't have **5** must have moved **6** might/may/could have

Unit 15

A: Context listening

2 She's asking him about his position, his chances of winning the race and the conditions on board the yacht.

3 2 haven't seen 3 think I might 4 was 5 didn't sleep
6 's, 's shining 7 can 8 'll spend 9 must get

4 1 are you 2 think you're going 3 's the weather
4 Can you see

5 When one speaker uses a present tense, the other reports with a past tense. When they use a past tense or the present perfect, it is reported with the past perfect.

C: Grammar exercises

1 2 could easily find another one
3 was going to travel round Africa
4 had lived there as a child
5 might get a part-time job there
6 was packing his bag
7 was really excited
8 would be away for a year
9 might stay longer
10 could come/go too
Yes, it is possible here to report without changing the verbs because Luke's situation is still the same. (▷ B1–2)

2 2 F 3 A 4 E 5 H 6 B 7 G 8 D (▷ B3–B5)

3 2 how old I was 3 I was studying 4 I came from 5 whether/
if I had worked 6 I played 7 whether/if I would work
8 whether/if I could start 9 whether/if I needed
10 whether/if I would like (▷ B1 and 5)

4 2 did he feel he felt 3 replied me replied 4 did wanted wanted
5 did I want if/whether I wanted 6 for giving to give (him) / for
7 told had told 8 will would or if I will to (▷ B1, B3–5)

5 2 me (that) I could do well
3 if/whether I studied every evening
4 what time I went to bed
5 me (that) I wouldn't get good marks
6 that I spent too much time with my friends
7 (me) if/whether I had decided on a career yet (▷ B1, B3, B5)

6 Woman: The same thing happened to me yesterday.
Suzie: What did you do?
Woman: Someone lent me the fare and I'm going to give it back this afternoon on the bus, so I'm happy to do the same for you. You can give the money back to me tomorrow.
Suzie: Thank you very much. I'm very glad you're here. (▷ B1, B3–6)

Exam practice
Reading and Use of English Part 4

1 sun will shine / is going to shine 2 told me (that) he had
3 if she had booked 4 will we leave tomorrow 5 I can dress
myself 6 whether they/we were meeting David

Grammar focus task

Paul complained (to me) that he hadn't heard from Helen for a long time. (sentence 2)
The little boy insisted (that) he could dress himself without any help. (sentence 5)
The weatherman predicted (that) it would be sunny all day. (sentence 1)

Unit 16

A: Context listening

2 1 D 2 B 3 A 4 C

3 2 were being 3 had been 4 is 5 were being 6 was 7 is
8 was 9 had been 10 to be 11 has been 12 is

4 all of them

C: Grammar exercises

1 2 delayed 3 hadn't 4 had been 5 being 6 opened
7 by (▷ B1)

2 2 had been done 3 were made 4 to be left 5 is said
6 are being counted 7 had been sacked / was sacked
8 was thought, is agreed 9 will be awarded
10 to have been opened, was delivered (▷ B1, B3)

3 2 C, get it fixed 3 G, get it cleaned 4 A, 've (have) had it
coloured 5 D, have it redecorated 6 B, have them taken in
7 H, had it designed 8 F, 're (are) having it checked (▷ B2)

4 2 has been (completely) crushed 3 has been destroyed
4 was captured 5 was broadcast 6 was announced
7 had been liberated 8 were asked 9 have been arrested
10 are being taken 11 is claimed 12 will be put (▷ B1–2)

5 2 having being being / having been 3 was been was
4 was happened happened 5 cut my hair have my hair cut
6 fixing fixed (▷ B1–2)

Exam practice
Reading and Use of English Part 4

1 was given by the 2 have my computer repaired
3 it was reported that 4 was not / wasn't given to
5 was accused of cheating by 6 weren't / were not given
the right

Grammar focus task

1 a sentence 2 b sentence 3

2 a It identifies the type of person who must do the repair.
b It identifies the source of the reports.

Unit 17

A: Context listening

2 She is asking Double X to find the man in the photo.

3 1 It's out of focus. 2 Because she doesn't have a better one.
3 a woman 4 Look at it with your eyes half closed.
5 Double X 6 *Sample answer:* Perhaps Double X's former
girlfriend sent it, because she was angry with him and
wanted to cause trouble.

4 1 'll be 2 had, 'd give 3 'd told, wouldn't have needed
4 would give, knew 5 is, look

5 1 present simple 2 present simple 3 past simple
4 past perfect

C: Grammar exercises

1 2 E 3 A 4 I 5 H 6 B 7 C 8 G 9 D 10 F (➤ B1–4)

2 2 want 3 cared 4 won't be 5 wouldn't have told 6 weren't
7 would have been 8 falls 9 hadn't expected 10 'll (will)
discover (➤ B1–4)

3 2 wouldn't have sat opposite that man 3 If the service
hadn't been really/so slow 4 If she hadn't been bored
5 she wouldn't have applied for that job (➤ B4)

4 2 wouldn't have applied 3 were 4 would have taken
5 earned 6 come 7 'd/had stayed 8 go 9 gets (➤ B1–4)

Exam practice
Reading and Use of English Part 6

1 G 2 D 3 C 4 E 5 A 6 B

Grammar focus task

2 F 3 E 4 C 5 B 6 A 7 D

Unit 18

A: Context listening

2 a fruit cake

3 2 adding 3 beating 4 to add 5 using 6 to use 7 to add
8 to use 9 to check 10 adding 11 to ice 12 to have

4 Some of the verbs are the *to* infinitive and some are
the *-ing* form.

C: Grammar exercises

1 2 working 3 doing 4 to stay 5 working 6 to stop 7 singing
8 to tell 9 working 10 to ignore 11 going 12 to go (➤ B1, B3)

2 2 to take 3 coming 4 to have 5 come 6 jump 7 phoning
8 to hear 9 to eat 10 to become (➤ B1–4, B6, B8)

3 2 to get 3 making, to finish 4 to book 5 throwing
6 to inform 7 lending 8 to leave 9 wearing 10 to chat
11 to send 12 going 13 to write 14 watching (➤ B5)

4 3 ~~knowing~~ to know 4 ✓ 5 ~~getting~~ to get 6 ✓ 7 ~~to be~~ being
8 ~~to tell~~ telling 9 ✓ 10 ✓ 11 ✓ 12 ~~to take~~ taking (➤ B1, B3)

Exam practice
Reading and Use of English

1 A 2 D 3 D 4 C 5 B 6 C 7 A 8 C

Grammar focus task

Verb + *to* infinitive: attempt, decide, demand, expect,
hope, learn, want
Verb + *-ing*: consider, delay, imagine, suggest
Verb + *object* + *to* infinitive: expect, persuade, remind, want

Unit 19

A: Context listening

2 They're going to climb a mountain.

3 2 Provided 3 unless 4 in case 5 I'd rather 6 As long as
7 wish 8 It's time

4 The verbs are in the present tense.

C: Grammar exercises

1 2 They'll be here soon unless their plane is delayed.
3 Unless you're in a hurry, you could take the bus.
4 I won't be able to come to see you tomorrow unless my
brother can give me a lift.
5 Unless the factory increases its production, it will close
down.
6 Unless you write your address down for me, I'll forget it.
7 I won't stay in that hotel unless it's got a good restaurant.
8 Unless I hear from you, I'll meet you at six. (➤ B1)

2 2 if 3 if 4 in case 5 in case 6 if 7 in case 8 in case (➤ B2)

3 2 provided that 3 in case 4 as long as 5 in case 6 unless
(➤ B1–3)

4 *Sample answers:*
3 I'd brought my phone
4 I could speak the language
5 I'd bought a phrase book
6 I wasn't/weren't hot and thirsty / I had something to drink
7 I hadn't come here alone / I'd come here with someone else
8 someone would help me
9 I hadn't come here
10 I was/were back in my hotel (➤ B4)

5 2 use 3 are 4 finishes 5 didn't bring 6 would learn
7 behaves 8 don't know 9 can't 10 changes
11 hadn't been 12 'll (will) miss (➤ B1–5)

Exam practice
Reading and Use of English Part 4

1 unless you press

2 in case the coach left

3 provided (that) you give

4 started cooking (now) or else

5 if you keep (on)playing

6 would (really) rather not eat

Grammar focus task

2 D (*In good time* means early.) 3 S 4 D (The sentences above
are about making sure the food will be ready.) 5 D (This
sentence suggests that the neighbours may not complain about
the drumming, whereas in the sentences above it is certain that
they will complain.) 6 S

Unit 20

A: Context listening

1 *Suggested answers:* **A** a pop star **B** a bank robbery **C** traffic jams on a motorway **D** something about the US President

2 1 D 2 A 3 C 4 B

3 2 at the weekend 3 as it was flying across the Mediterranean 4 by the weekend 5 beyond the beginning of the motorway 6 until this afternoon 7 by the door of the bank 8 during the night

4 1 at, by, until, during 2 at, in, across, beyond, by

C: Grammar exercises

1 2 at 3 above 4 through 5 between 6 in (▷ B1–2)

2 2 at 3 during 4 for 5 till 6 at 7 by 8 in 9 by 10 in 11 over (▷ B1–2)

3 2 in 3 in 4 for 5 At 6 by 7 on 8 at 9 in 10 between 11 among 12 for (▷ B1–2)

4 2 on 3 across 4 beyond 5 at 6 in 7 Until 8 in 9 along 10 on 11 through 12 among (▷ B1–2)

5 2 ~~in~~ at 3 ~~in~~ on 4 ~~on~~ at 5 ~~during~~ for 6 ~~by~~ until/till 7 ~~during~~ for 8 ~~until~~ by 9 ~~for~~ during 10 ~~at~~ on (▷ B1–2)

Exam practice
Reading and Use of English Part 2

1 into 2 as 3 addition 4 At 5 what 6 it 7 each 8 on

Grammar focus task

1 between 2 at 3 in 4 at 5 among 6 across

Unit 21

A: Context listening

1 *Suggested answers:*
   A A man is on a ladder and he is breaking a window. Fire is coming from the door.
   B A man is taking a toolbox out of a car. Fire is coming from an upstairs window.
   C A man is looking out of an upstairs window. Smoke is coming from downstairs.

2 Picture B fits best. Picture A is wrong because the fire was upstairs and Andy broke in downstairs; also he didn't put his handkerchief over his face until he was inside the house. Picture C also shows the fire downstairs; and there is someone upstairs, but Andy didn't go upstairs and there was no one else in the house.

3 2 at 3 on 4 on 5 by 6 by 7 with 8 in 9 in 10 for 11 for 12 with

4 by

C: Grammar exercises

1 2 Laura on winning the tournament 3 about trains to Scotland 4 the young man from coming in / entering the club 5 Mike for not phoning her 6 about the book (▷ B1)

2 2 of 3 with 4 in 5 on 6 of (▷ B1–3)

3 **A** 2 by 3 by 4 in 5 in 6 of 7 at 8 about 9 in 10 to
   B 1 in 2 out of 3 at 4 at 5 in 6 out of 7 in 8 by 9 in (▷ B1–3)

4 2 ~~with~~ to 3 ~~in~~ on 4 ~~about~~ of 5 ~~of~~ about 6 ~~with~~ for 7 ~~on~~ in 8 ~~with~~ on (▷ B1–3)

Exam practice
Reading and Use of English

1 spoken 2 graduation 3 political 4 tendency 5 protection 6 Naturally 7 supposing 8 unaffordable

Grammar focus task

2 for 3 with 4 in 5 by 6 for

Unit 22

A: Context listening

1 1 They lived in the 17th century. 2 Yes, they were.

2 **A** Edmund **B** Margaret **C** Henry and William **D** William and Jane

3 2 that hangs next to Margaret's portrait
   3 who's holding the book
   4 which lost
   5 when their youngest son was born

4 1 *Which* refers to *the one* (= the ship).
   2 *That* refers to *the picture*.
   3 *Who* refers to *the one* (= William).
   4 *Which* refers to *the side*.
   5 *When* refers to *the year*.

C: Grammar exercises

1 2 who 3 which 4 who 5 (which) 6 which 7 (which) 8 which 9 which 10 which (▷ B1–2, B5)

2 2 where, F 3 which, G 4 when, B 5 why, A 6 who, D 7 whose, H 8 which, E (▷ B1–3)

3 2 b 3 a 4 a 5 b 6 a 7 b (▷ B1–5)

4 2 My uncle's cottage, where we usually spend our holidays, has been damaged by floods.
   3 The chemistry exam, which we had been worrying about, was actually quite easy.
   4 My brother, whose classmates had been teasing him, got into a fight near the school.
   5 There are dreadful traffic jams during the summer, when everyone goes on holiday.
   6 My parents, who don't often go to the cinema, enjoyed that film very much. (▷ B2–4)

5 2 neither of which 3 none of whom 4 one of which 5 most of which (▷ B5)

Exam practice
Reading and Use of English Part 4
1 in which we had lunch / (which/that) we had lunch in
2 who works for an airline
3 is the reason (why)
4 book (which/that) I lent him
5 the concert (which/that) I went
6 the boy whose mother is

Grammar focus task
1 all of them
2 Sentence 2 is non-defining; all the others are defining.
3 We can tell by the punctuation. The clause in sentence 2 is enclosed by commas and if we remove this clause, the sentence still makes sense. In the other sentences the relative clause is necessary in order to identify the thing/person we are talking about.

Unit 23

A: Context listening
2 Josie does judo and Adam plays volleyball.
3 2 good enough 3 since 4 tall enough 5 so quick 6 enough exercise 7 too much time 8 too many practice games 9 in order to 10 well enough 11 as, so much revision
4 It goes after an adjective or adverb but before a noun (*good* and *tall* are adjectives, *well* is an adverb and *exercise* is a noun).

C: Grammar exercises
1 2 in order to 3 As 4 so 5 enough, so, too 6 so that (≽ B1–3)
2 2 S 3 D (In 3a we understand that his father doesn't allow him to have a motorbike, but in 3b he may have one although he's unusually young.) 4 S 5 S 6 D (In 6a we understand that she's confused by too much advice, but in 6b she's had as much advice as she needs, no more, no less.) 7 S 8 S (≽ B1–3)
3 2 G 3 D 4 E 5 F (B is also possible, though less likely.) 6 C (G is also possible, though less likely.) 7 B 8 A (≽ B3)
4 2 since 3 so 4 as 5 Therefore 6 such 7 Because (≽ B1–3)
5 2 fit enough to 3 enough room/space for 4 old enough to 5 too expensive for me to 6 too well for me to 7 too far (away) (for us) to 8 too windy for the ferry to (≽ B3)

Exam practice
Reading and Use of English Part 1
1 B 2 B 3 A 4 D 5 A 6 C 7 C 8 D

Grammar focus task
1 that 2 enough, to 3 Therefore 4 too 5 in order to

Unit 24

A: Context listening
1 B (A is wrong because Gemma didn't sign a contract and hasn't made any more films. C is wrong because she was not a film actor before she got the part. D is wrong because she was already at theatre school – it was only in films that she had no experience.)
2 2 in spite of having 3 after visiting 4 before accepting 5 while making 6 working 7 but I'm 8 despite being
3 the *-ing* form

C: Grammar exercises
1 2 C 3 D 4 H 5 F 6 I 7 A 8 B 9 E (≽ B1–2 and 4–6)
2 2 D (In 1a Sam showed the map to the farmer and asked the way, but in 1b the farmer asked Sam the way and Sam showed him his map.) 3 S 4 D (In 4a Chloe's father promised her a car after she'd failed the exam, but in 4b he promised it before she took the exam.) 5 S 6 D (In 6a the mountain guide warned us, but in 6b the guide received the warning from someone else.) (≽ B1–4)
3 2 Waving to her fans, the singer got into her car.
3 Grumbling about the amount of homework he had, Simon took out his grammar book.
4 Designed by a famous architect, the school buildings won several prizes.
5 Being a sensible girl, Wendy didn't panic when she cut her hand.
6 Hearing cries for help, Paul dived into the water.
7 Recorded only last week, this song has already been downloaded a million times. (≽ B4)
4 2 While 3 before 4 even though 5 even if 6 though 7 Since (≽ B1–4, B6)
5 2 b 3 b 4 a 5 a (≽ B1, B5)

Exam practice
Reading and Use of English Part 2
1 even 2 from 3 fact 4 which/that 5 apart 6 but 7 to 8 Despite

Grammar focus task
1 B 2 A 3 D 4 E 5 C

Vocabulary section

Unit 25

1.1 **A** India   **B** Brazil

1.2 Photo A

  2 pine   **3** streams   **4** vegetation   **5** slopes
  6 orchards   **7** tracks   **8** valleys   **9** bank
  10 springs

1.3 **2** trunks   **3** sunlight   **4** plants   **5** leaves   **6** soil
  7 roots   **8** branches   **9** insects   **10** butterflies

1.4 **2** wide   **3** straight   **4** muddy   **5** cultivated
  6 mountainous   **7** steep

2.1 **2** A   **3** B   **4** B   **5** A   **6** B   **7** A   **8** B
  9 A   **10** A   **11** B   **12** A

2.2 Join 1 and 3, 10 and 12 with *and*.
  Join 2 and 5, 6 and 8, 7 and 9 with *but*.
  (See Web page for the full texts.)

2.3 It's in the Arctic. (The speaker is talking about Greenland.)

3.1 **2** frozen   **3** misty   **4** tropical   **5** warmth   **6** global

Exam practice
Reading and Use of English Part 6
1 C   2 G   3 B   4 F   5 A   6 D

Writing Part 2: email
See Web page for model answer.

Unit 26

1.1 Meal A is high in salt, fat, protein, carbohydrate, sugar and
  calories and low in vitamins and fibre.
  Meal B is high in vitamins, protein and fibre and low in salt,
  fat and sugar.

1.2 eating lean meat   needing carbohydrate for energy
  not putting on weight   doing regular training
  getting enough sleep   handling stress

1.3 **2** False   **3** True   **4** False   **5** True   **6** False
  7 True   **8** False

1.5 **2** cut down on   **3** putting on   **4** live on
  5 get round to   **6** taking up   **7** going for
  8 coming down with

2.1 **2** C   **3** E   **4** A   **5** B   **6** D

2.2 **2** stitches   **3** antihistamines   **4** prescription
  5 plaster   **6** vaccination   **7** scales   **8** symptoms

3.1 **2** made up for, A   **3** made for, B   **4** make out, E
  5 made (them) into, C

Exam practice
Reading and Use of English Part 1
1 a   2 Although/Though/While   3 too   4 it   5 into
6 any   7 when/whenever/if   8 as

Writing Part 1: essay
See Web page for model answer.

Unit 27

1.1 **1** composer. A composer writes music; the others
  perform it.
  2 chapter. This word relates to books; the others relate
  to music.

1.2 **2** Yes   **3** Yes (the cello and violin)   **4** Yes
  5 Yes (but only occasionally)

1.3 **2** have always counted it among
  3 got to quite a high standard
  4 sang solo
  5 sometimes make a special trip
  6 always got something playing, my headphones on

2.1 rock: 3   pop: 2   classical: 4   world music: 1

2.2 **2** harmonies   **3** album   **4** composers
  5 tracks   **6** cover version   **7** distinctive style
  8 fans   **9** old favourites   **10** lyrics

3.1 **1** rock 'n' roll   **2** jazz   **3** country and western
  4 folk

4.1 **2** whistle   **3** tap   **4** sneeze   **5** snore   **6** bang
  7 splash   **8** smash

4.2 **2** B   **3** G   **4** H   **5** D   **6** A   **7** E   **8** C

Exam practice
Reading and Use of English Part 2
1 much   2 each/every   3 in   4 what   5 not
6 who   7 as   8 why

Writing Part 1: essay
See Web page for model answer.

Unit 28

1.1 **1** A coach from the national team came to
  choose the three best players.
  2 Nick tripped and broke his leg.
  3 his brother

1.2 *positive:* confident, excited, proud, relaxed
  negative: ashamed, disappointed, embarrassed,
  guilty, jealous, upset

1.3 **1** excited, confident, proud
  2 disappointed, upset, jealous

1.4 ashamed, embarrassed, guilty

2.1, 2.2

amazed	annoyed	depressed
surprised astonished	angry <u>furious</u>	fed up miserable
frightened	**pleased**	**worried**
scared afraid <u>terrified</u>	glad <u>delighted</u>	anxious concerned

3.1 *Sample answers:*
Paul: happy, keen, excited, thrilled, eager, enthusiastic
Don: nervous, scared, frightened, anxious, worried, apprehensive

4.1 **2** disappointing **3** surprised **4** excited
5 worried **6** terrifying **7** relaxing

4.2 *Noun:* embarrassment, pleasure, excitement
Verb: amaze, embarrass, please, annoy
Adjective: amazing, amazed, annoying, annoyed
Noun: anger, jealousy
Adjective: depressing, depressed, proud, anxious, miserable

Exam practice
Listening Part 1
1 C **2** B **3** C **4** A **5** A **6** B **7** C **8** A

Writing Part 2: article
See Web page for model answer.

Unit 29

1.1 **A** (prehistoric) paintings of animals in a cave
B a long wall and a tower (Great Wall of China)

1.2 **A** *Age:* 17,000 years *Purpose:* to show the importance of animals to people's survival
B *Location:* China *Age:* 2,000 years *Purpose:* to protect the border / prevent invasion

2.1 **2** records **3** population **4** figures **5** inhabitants
6 tribes **7** ancestors **8** hunting **9** settle **10** tools
11 beliefs **12** stories

2.2 *prehistory:* prehistoric *archaeology:* archaeologist, archaeological
evidence: evident *politics:* politician, political
presidency: president, presidential
populate: population *civilise:* civilisation, civilian
invade: invasion, invader *reside:* residence, resident
believe: belief, believer *survive:* survival, survivor

3.1 **2** last **3** spent **4** takes **5** lasts **6** spent

4.1 **2** D **3** B **4** A **5** G **6** H **7** E **8** F

Exam practice
Reading and Use of English Part 1
1 A **2** C **3** A **4** C **5** D **6** A **7** D **8** B

Writing Part 2: review
See Web page for model answer.

Unit 30

1.1 **1** B **2** C **3** A

1.2 **1** energetic, relaxed, determined, ambitious, outstanding
2 fashionable, fit, self-confident, charming, sympathetic, dedicated
3 versatile, talented, graceful, courageous, devoted

1.4 **2** A **3** B **4** A **5** B **6** A **7** C **8** C

2.1 adventurous – cautious generous – mean gentle –

aggressive hard-working – lazy modest – arrogant
polite – rude relaxed – tense self-confident – shy

2.2 **2** mean **3** rude **4** lazy **5** tense **6** aggressive

3.1 **1** im- **2** un- **3** in- **4** dis- **5** ir-
im- is added to some adjectives beginning with *p*
ir- is added to some adjectives beginning with *r*

3.2 **2** careless **3** powerful **4** painful
5 harmless **6** graceful **7** colourless

Exam practice
Reading and Use of English Part 5
1 B **2** A **3** C **4** A **5** D **6** D

Writing Part 2: article
See Web page for model answer.

Unit 31

1.1 *go:* skating, cycling, jogging, walking, swimming, climbing, skateboarding, skiing, diving, snorkelling, sailing, snowboarding, hiking, surfing
play: squash, rugby, badminton, hockey, football, table tennis, baseball, ice hockey
do: yoga, aerobics, athletics, gymnastics, martial arts

1.2 **1** a course **2** a court, a racket **3** a pitch, a stick
4 a court, a racket **5** a bat, a pitch
The word not used is *a track*. It is associated with athletics/running.

1.3 **1** jogger, walker, swimmer, climber, skateboarder, skier, diver, snorkeller, footballer, snowboarder, hiker, surfer
2 volleyball, squash, rugby, badminton, hockey, football, table tennis, baseball, ice hockey
3 cyclist, gymnast, athlete
(Note: There is no word in English for someone who does judo, yoga or aerobics.)

2.1 Speaker 1: yoga Speaker 2: squash Speaker 3: hockey

2.2 Speaker 1: great, varied, relaxing Speaker 2: demanding, exciting, challenging Speaker 3: satisfying

3.1 **1** win **2** beat, won **3** won, beating **4** win, beating **5** beat, win

4.1 **2** flowed **3** working **4** did **5** goes

4.2 **2** runs in, families (*run on* something means to work or function by means of it: *Most motor boats run on diesel.*)
3 friends, run into (*run over* someone/something means to hit and drive over: *I dropped my hat on the road and a car ran over it.*)
4 children, run out of (*run up against* something means to face an obstacle: *The council ran up against a lot of opposition when they decided to cut down the tree.*)
5 problem, run up against (*run through* means to read or practise something quickly from beginning to end: *Before the meeting I ran through what I was going to say.*)
6 run on, petrol (*run into* also means to hit accidentally: *I lost control of my bike and ran into a tree.*)

Exam practice

Reading and Use of English Part 4

1 to run through/over **2** succeeded in winning **3** been running well since it **4** ran up against / ran into a lot / lots **5** went sailing for the first **6** runs in Susie's

Writing Part 2: email

See Web page for model answer.

Unit 32

1.1 Speaker 1: A   Speaker 2: C   Speaker 3: A   Speaker 4: B

1.2 **2** spoken **3** get **4** make **5** told **6** fell
7 got **8** get **9** lost **10** enjoy **11** keep
12 make **13** have

1.3 **1** close **2** best **3** old **4** good

2.1 **2** know **3** made **4** become **5** neighbour
6 in **7** each **8** on **9** out

2.2 nephew, widow, aunt, stepfather, sister-in-law, grandparents

2.3 **1** F She and her stepsister often fall out.   **2** T
3 F They share a lot of interests.   **4** T
5 F They met when Meena moved in next door.

3.1 **2** destiny **3** eldest **4** support **5** roots
6 loyalty **7** community **8** brought
9 background **10** fortune **11** inherited
12 donated
Correct order: E, B, D, A, F, C

4.1 **2** F **3** D **4** E **5** B **6** A

Exam practice
Listening Part 3

1 H **2** A **3** G **4** F **5** C

Writing Part 1: essay

See Web page for model answer.

Unit 33

1.1 by plane
2 visa **3** terminal **4** pass **5** control **6** security
7 board **8** gate **9** crew **10** headset

1.2 **1** train **2** bus **3** underground **4** taxi

1.3 Words not used: landing, runway, wing. They are associated with planes.

2.1 **1** suitcase **2** accommodation, hotel
3 equipment, tent **4** cash, coin **5** parking, car park
6 transport, vehicle

2.2 *Countable:* hotel, vehicle, suitcase, tent, car park, coin
Uncountable: equipment, transport, luggage, cash, accommodation, parking

2.3 **2** journey **3** trip **4** trip **5** travel **6** trip
7 travel **8** journey

3.1 *Woman:* **2** C **3** C **4** A **5** A **6** B
Boy: **1** A **2** B **3** B **4** C **5** C **6** C

Exam practice

Reading and Use of English Part 4

1 made the journey / went on a journey
2 on a short trip to
3 to book (some/any) accommodation
4 rather travel by
5 do on (a) holiday is
6 taken a longer flight than

Writing Part 2: article

See Web page for model answer.

Unit 34

1.1 Speaker1: staying in   Speaker 2: going out

1.2 **2** C **3** J **4** J **5** C **6** C **7** J **8** C
9 C **10** C **11** J **12** J **13** J **14** J
15 J **16** C **17** J **18** J

1.3 *have:* a barbecue, a coffee, friends round, a quiet night in (1.3); a takeaway (1.2)
watch: a film, a match, a play (1.3); sport on TV, DVDs (1.2)
play: cards, games, a match (1.3); music, online games (1.2)
go: shopping (1.3); clubbing, surfing, swimming (1.2)
go to: a barbecue, a club, a concert, a film, a match, a play, a restaurant, the theatre (1.3); a party, junk shops, the cinema, the beach (1.2)
go for: a coffee, a drive, a walk (1.3)

2.1 **2** F **3** C **4** E **5** D **6** B **7** A **8** H

2.2 **2** collects **3** do **4** do **5** play **6** play

3.1 take off a few days: spend time away from work
take out money: withdraw
take over a business: gain control of
take to someone you've just met: develop a liking for
take up space: fill up
take on responsibility: accept

3.2 **2** took out **3** took off **4** takes after **5** take on
6 taken over **7** takes up

Exam practice
Reading and Use of English Part 3

1 pointless **2** commitments **3** unlike **4** addition
5 friendships **6** personal **7** strengths **8** truly

Writing Part 2: email

See Web page for model answer.

Unit 35

1.2 **2** A **3** B **4** A **5** B **6** A

1.3 City A: Sentences 6, 2, 4   City B: Sentences 3, 5, 1

2.1 B

2.2 **2** F **3** T **4** F **5** T **6** F

2.3 **1** industrial, business **2** residential, outskirts, suburbs
3 block **4** mall **5** multi-storey **6** neglected **7** lane

3.1 **2** health centre **3** car park **4** art gallery **5** concert hall **6** taxi rank **7** football stadium **8** ice rink **9** bowling alley **10** shopping centre

3.2 recreation ground. People play games there.

Exam practice
Reading and Use of English Part 1
1 D **2** A **3** C **4** D **5** C **6** B **7** D **8** C

Writing Part 2: article
See Web page for model answer.

Unit 36

1.1 **1** Chinese **2** Mexican **3** Italian

1.2 **1** prawns, ginger, spices, soy sauce, stir fries, rice, noodles
2 hot spicy food, chilli, corn, tortillas, beans
3 herbs, tomatoes, pasta, olives

1.3 **2** eggs **3** vegetables **4** banana
5 cheese **6** butter **7** lemon **8** sauce

2.1 **2** F The restaurant serves well-known (popular) dishes, not unusual ones. **3** F Dishes are delivered to your table by waiters. **4** F The food is served as soon as it has been cooked. **5** T **6** T

2.2 **2** G **3** F **4** C **5** A **6** B **7** E

2.3 **1** tasteless **2** tasty **3** tasteful

3.1 **1** water colours, oil paintings, prints
2 pottery, textiles, jewellery, sculptures
3 portrait, still life, landscape, abstract

3.2 **2** pottery **3** exhibitions **4** galleries **5** conventional
6 style **7** landscapes **8** realistic **9** colours
10 huge **11** impressive

Exam practice
Listening Part 3
1 remote **2** plane **3** nature **4** beaches **5** desert
6 light **7** board **8** oil **9** companies
10 (magazine) articles

Writing Part 1: essay
See Web page for model answer.

Unit 37

1.1 Speaker 1: reality TV   Speaker 2: comedy   Speaker 3: costume drama

1.2 **2** current affairs **3** soap opera **4** documentary
5 costume drama **6** reality TV show **7** chat show

2.1 **2** listened to **3** looked at **4** saw
5 heard **6** watched **7** read about

3.1 **2** B **3** B **4** C **5** B **6** B **7** B **8** B **9** B
10 C **11** B **12** B **13** B **14** B **15** B **16** T
17 C **18** C **19** B **20** T **21** C

3.2 The girl prefers going to the theatre because there's more atmosphere and every performance is special.
The man prefers going to the cinema because of the darkness in the cinema, the film music and the locations in the films.

4.1 Speaker 1: lively, moving, dramatic, superb
Speaker 2: delightful, memorable, convincing, outstanding

4.2 brilliant P   confusing N   convincing P   delightful P
dramatic P   dull N   fascinating P   gripping P
imaginative P   irritating N   lively P   memorable P
moving P   outstanding P   predictable N   stunning P
superb P   tedious N   uninspired N

4.3 **2** brilliant **3** confusing **4** uninspired **5** tedious

Exam practice
Reading and Use of English Part 7
1 D **2** B **3** D **4** A **5** B **6** D **7** C **8** A
9 C **10** A

Writing Part 2: review
See Web page for model answer.

Unit 38

1.1 **2** mansion. This is a huge house; the others are found inside a house.
3 flowerbed. This is in a garden; the others enclose a garden.
4 carpet. This is on the floor; the others are at a window.
5 wardrobe. This is a piece of furniture; the others are building materials.
6 lobby. This is the entrance area inside a public building; the others are structures outside a house.

1.2 **1** shutters **2** garage **3** gate **4** fence **5** terrace
6 chimney **7** bricks **8** hedge

1.3 A

2.1 **1** The Clenches' house was painted but the writer's house wasn't.
2 In a modern house in a city or town, because she wanted one with painted walls, an indoor bathroom, electricity and flowers round the porch.

2.2 **1** A **2** C **3** B **4** C **5** B **6** B

3.1 **2** electrician **3** service agent **4** builder **5** decorator

Exam practice
Reading and Use of English Part 3
1 surroundings **2** emotional **3** ensuring
4 personality/personalities **5** luxurious **6** sensitive
7 requirement **8** expectations

Writing Part 1: essay
See Web page for model answer.

Unit 39

1.1 1 make observations, enter data into a computer
2 collect data, make exciting discoveries, do experiments
3 make predictions, attend conferences, interpret statistics

1.2 2 chemist 3 astronomer 4 ecologist 5 biologist
6 physicist 7 mathematician

1.3 biology, biological; chemistry, chemical; ecology, ecological;
geology, geological; mathematics/maths; mathematical;
physics, physical

1.4 2 B 3 L 4 B 5 L 6 N

2.1 2 A 3 D 4 F 5 C 6 B

3.1 1 T 2 F It's easier to leave them on. 3 T 4 T
5 F He can't afford to buy it. 6 T

4.1 2 boundaries 3 end up 4 causes 5 warming
6 record 7 develop 8 create 9 make 10 linked
11 cut down 12 standard

Exam practice
Listening Part 1
1 B 2 C 3 B 4 C 5 C 6 A 7 C

Writing Part 2: letter
See Web page for model answer.

Unit 40

1.1 *Reference:* biography, cookery book, guidebook, textbook
Fiction: detective story, fantasy, ghost story, romance,
science fiction novel, thriller
Publicity: brochure, catalogue

1.2 thriller or detective story

1.3 *Sounds:* groaning, shriek, yelling, whimpering
Movements: crept, darted, dashed, stumbled

1.4 1 breathe 2 nod 3 blink 4 tremble 5 sigh
In each group the other two words are connected with
seeing.

2.1 2 novelist 3 called 4 remember 5 fiction
6 characters 7 relationships 8 borrow 9 library
10 request 11 entertaining 12 chapter

3.1 1 Because they make you think (like a crossword puzzle).
2 His stories move fast and he has a great hero.

3.2 1 mad about 2 especially when 3 makes me think
4 bit too much 5 'd rather 6 move really fast
7 real tough guy

4.1 **Crime:** shoplifting
Criminal: robber, thief, shoplifter, murderer
Verb: burgle, rob, murder

4.2 2 robbed 3 stole 4 robberies 5 murderer
6 stolen

Exam practice
Reading and Use of English Part 5
1 A 2 C 3 B 4 B 5 A 6 D

Writing Part 2: review
See Web page for model answer.

Unit 41

1.1 Jasmine: C Karim: A

2.1 1 C 2 B 3 D 4 A

2.2 2 a dress b wear 3 a dressed b wearing
4 a got b took 5 a had b wore

3.2 1 C 2 A 3 C 4 C 5 B 6 A

Exam practice
Reading and Use of English Part 6
1 C 2 F 3 A 4 D 5 G 6 E

Writing Part 2: story
See Web page for model answer.

Unit 42

1.1 1 streamed. Classes are streamed if the pupils are divided
into different groups according to ability; the other
words describe different types of school.
2 playing fields. These are outdoors; the other places are
indoors.
3 lecturers. They work at a university; the other people
work in a school.
4 housework. This is work done at home (e.g. cooking,
cleaning); the other words are related to school.

1.2 1 secondary, state, comprehensive 2 laboratory,
playing fields 3 teachers 4 timetable, uniform,
subjects

1.3 1 living nearby / being able to walk there, science lessons,
the varied timetable
2 having a lot of homework, uniform

1.4 2 compulsory 3 age 4 age 5 start 6 attend
7 pupils 8 taught 9 miss 10 after 11 allowed
12 take 13 leave 14 study 15 opportunities

2.3 1 A: [chemistry] B: [geography]
2 *Suggested answers:* In lesson A the students are
working in a group, but in lesson B the teacher is talking
to the whole class. In lesson A the students are wearing
special clothes and protective glasses.

3.1 2 revise 3 retake 4 pass 5 take 6 fail 7 give
8 studying

Exam practice
Reading and Use of English Part 2
1 whose 2 than 3 one 4 out 5 not 6 been
7 how 8 for

Writing Part 2: story
See Web page for model answer.

Unit 43

1.1 Speaker 1 is a hairdresser. Speaker 2 is a carpenter.

1.2 *Suggested answers:*
Hairdresser: cheerful, friendly, on my feet all day, salon
Carpenter: physically fit, good with my hands, creative, design cupboards or shelves

2.1 **A** receptionist **B** cleaner **C** nursery assistant

2.2 **2** A, permanent **3** C, possible promotion
4 B, shift work **5** A, good communication skills
6 B, overtime

2.3 **1** salary **2** wages **3** rate of pay

2.4 **2** vacancy **3** application **4** catering
5 passionate **6** professional **7** reliable
8 training **9** enthusiastic **10** references

3.1 **2** ✓ **3** ✗ **4** ✗ **5** ✓ **6** ✓ **7** ✗ **8** ✓

3.2 **1** Speaker 1: I resigned. Speaker 7: I gave up my job.
2 Speaker 3: I was made redundant.

3.3 **1** work **2** job **3** career **4** work **5** work
6 job, work **7** work **8** career

Exam practice
Reading and Use of English Part 3

1 worrying **2** unpredictable **3** promotion **4** response
5 relationship **6** competitive **7** annoyance
8 extraordinarily

Writing Part 2: letter of application
See Web page for model answer.

Unit 44

1.1 It is aimed at people who are thinking of coming to the university as undergraduates.

1.2 **2** departments, faculty **3** prospectus **4** lectures, seminars, tutorials **5** lecturers, tutors **6** dissertation
7 halls of residence, students' union **8** mature
9 terms, semesters, vacations **10** undergraduates, graduates, postgraduate

2.1 **1** Student 1: English literature Student 2: chemistry
2 Student 1: lectures, seminars, tutorials, essays, presentations Student 2: lectures, experiments
3 Student 1: studying on his own / reading and thinking things through, the timetable, the lectures, seminars and tutorials
Student 2: the system – morning lectures and afternoon laboratory experiments

2.2 **1** 'm really enthusiastic about **2** are totally against
3 in my view **4** approve of **5** personally think
6 believe **7** 'm convinced that **8** really appreciate
9 'm in favour of

2.3 **1** P **2** N **3** B **4** P **5** B **6** B **7** B **8** P **9** P

3.1 **1** D **2** E **3** A **4** C **5** B

Exam practice
Reading and Use of English Part 7

1 B **2** D **3** A **4** C **5** A **6** D **7** B **8** A
9 C **10** B

Writing Part 2: report
See Web page for model answer.